# With Lee in Virginia
## A Story Of The American Civil War

# G.A. Henty

# Contents

PREFACE. ............................................................................7
CHAPTER I. A VIRGINIAN PLANTATION. ..........................9
CHAPTER II. BUYING A SLAVE. ........................................23
CHAPTER III. AIDING A RUNAWAY. ................................38
CHAPTER IV. SAFELY BACK. ............................................53
CHAPTER V. SECESSION. ..................................................65
CHAPTER VI. BULL RUN. ..................................................77
CHAPTER VII. THE MERRIMAC AND THE MONITOR. .....94
CHAPTER VIII. McCLELLAN'S ADVANCE. ......................107
CHAPTER IX. A PRISONER. .............................................120
CHAPTER X. THE ESCAPE. ..............................................133
CHAPTER XI. FUGITIVES. ................................................147
CHAPTER XII. THE BUSHWHACKERS. ...........................161
CHAPTER XIII. LAID UP. ..................................................176
CHAPTER XIV. ACROSS THE BORDER. .........................190
CHAPTER XV. FREDERICKSBURG. ................................205
CHAPTER XVI. THE SEARCH FOR DINAH. ....................219
CHAPTER XVII. CHANCELLORSVILLE. .........................235
CHAPTER XVIII. A PERILOUS UNDERTAKING. .............253
CHAPTER XIX. FREE. .......................................................268
CHAPTER XX. THE END OF THE STRUGGLE. ................284

# WITH LEE IN VIRGINIA
## A STORY OF THE AMERICAN CIVIL WAR

### BY
## G.A. Henty

# PREFACE.

My Dear Lads:

The Great War between the Northern and Southern States of America possesses a peculiar interest for us, not only because it was a struggle between two sections of a people akin to us in race and language, but because of the heroic courage with which the weaker party, with ill-fed, ill-clad, ill-equipped regiments, for four years sustained the contest with an adversary not only possessed of immense numerical superiority, but having the command of the sea, and being able to draw its arms and munitions of war from all the manufactories of Europe. Authorities still differ as to the rights of the case. The Confederates firmly believed that the States having voluntarily united, retained the right of withdrawing from the Union when they considered it for their advantage to do so. The Northerners took the opposite point of view, and an appeal to arms became inevitable. During the first two years of the war the struggle was conducted without inflicting unnecessary hardship upon the general population. But later on the character of the war changed, and the Federal armies carried wide-spread destruction wherever they marched. Upon the other hand, the moment the struggle was over the conduct of the conquerors was marked by a clemency and generosity altogether unexampled in history, a complete amnesty being granted, and none, whether soldiers or civilians, being made to suffer for their share in the rebellion. The credit of this magnanimous conduct was to a great extent due to Generals Grant and Sherman, the former of whom took upon himself the responsibility of granting terms which, although they were finally ratified by his government, were at the time received with anger and indignation in the North. It was impossible, in the course of a single volume, to give even a sketch of the numerous and complicated operations of the war, and I have therefore confined myself to the central point of the great struggle--the attempts of the Northern armies to force their way to Richmond, the capital of Virginia and the heart of the Confederacy. Even in recounting the leading events in these campaigns, I have burdened my story with as few details as possible, it being my object now, as always, to amuse as well as to give instruction in the facts of history.

G. A. HENTY.

## CHAPTER I. A VIRGINIAN PLANTATION.

"I won't have it, Pearson; so it's no use your talking. If I had my way you shouldn't touch any of the field hands. And when I get my way--that won't be so very long--I will take good care you sha'n't. But you sha'n't hit Dan."

"He is not one of the regular house hands," was the reply; "and I shall appeal to Mrs. Wingfield as to whether I am to be interfered with in the discharge of my duties."

"You may appeal to my mother if you like, but I don't think that you will get much by it. I tell you you are a deal too fond of that whip, Pearson. It never was heard of on the estate during my father's time, and it sha'n't be again when it comes to be mine, I can tell you. Come along, Dan; I want you at the stables."

So saying, Vincent Wingfield turned on his heel, and followed by Dan, a negro lad of some eighteen years old, he walked off toward the house, leaving Jonas Pearson, the overseer of the Orangery estate, looking after him with an evil expression of face.

Vincent Wingfield was the son of an English officer, who, making a tour in the States, had fallen in love with and won the hand of Winifred Cornish, a rich Virginian heiress, and one of the belles of Richmond. After the marriage he had taken her home to visit his family in England; but she had not been there many weeks before the news arrived of the sudden death of her father. A month later she and her husband returned to Virginia, as her presence was required there in reference to business matters connected with the estate, of which she was now the mistress.

The Orangery, so called from a large conservatory built by Mrs. Wingfield's grandfather, was the family seat, and the broad lands around it were tilled by upward of two hundred slaves. There were in addition three other properties lying in different parts of the State. Here Vincent, with two sisters, one older and one younger than himself, had been born. When he was eight years old Major and Mrs.

Wingfield had gone over with their children to England, and had left Vincent there for four years at school, his holidays being spent at the house of his father's brother, a country gentleman in Sussex. Then he had been sent for unexpectedly; his father saying that his health was not good, and that he should like his son to be with him. A year later his father died.

Vincent was now nearly sixteen years old, and would upon coming of age assume the reins of power at the Orangery, of which his mother, however, would be the actual mistress as long as she lived. The four years Vincent had passed in the English school had done much to render the institution of slavery repugnant to him, and his father had had many serious talks with him during the last year of his life, and had shown him that there was a good deal to be said upon both sides of the subject.

"There are good plantations and bad plantations, Vincent; and there are many more good ones than bad ones. There are brutes to be found everywhere. There are bad masters in the Southern States just as there are bad landlords in every European country. But even from self-interest alone, a planter has greater reason for caring for the health and comfort of his slaves than an English farmer has in caring for the comfort of his laborers. Slaves are valuable property, and if they are overworked or badly cared for they decrease in value. Whereas if the laborer falls sick or is unable to do his work the farmer has simply to hire another hand. It is as much the interest of a planter to keep his slaves in good health and spirits as it is for a farmer to feed and attend to his horses properly.

"Of the two, I consider that the slave with a fairly kind master is to the full as happy as the ordinary English laborer. He certainly does not work so hard, if he is ill he is carefully attended to, he is well fed, he has no cares or anxieties whatever, and when old and past work he has no fear of the workhouse staring him in the face. At the same time I am quite ready to grant that there are horrible abuses possible under the laws connected with slavery.

"The selling of slaves, that is to say, the breaking up of families and selling them separately, is horrible and abominable. If an estate were sold together with all the slaves upon it, there would be no more hardship in the matter than there is when an estate changes hands in England, and the laborers upon it work for the new master instead of the old. Were I to liberate all the slaves on this estate to-morrow and to send them North, I do not think that they would be in any way benefited by the change. They would still have to work for their living as they do now, and being naturally indolent and shiftless would probably fare much worse. But against the selling of families separately and the use of the lash I set my face strongly.

"At the same time, my boy, whatever your sentiments may be on this subject, you must keep your mouth closed as to them. Owing to the attempts of Northern Abolitionists, who have come down here stirring up the slaves to discontent, it is not advisable, indeed it is absolutely dangerous, to speak against slavery in the Southern States. The institution is here, and we must make the best we can of it. People here are very sore at the foul slanders that have been published by Northern writers. There have been many atrocities perpetrated undoubtedly, by brutes who would have been brutes whenever they had been born; but to collect a series of such atrocities, to string them together into a story, and to hold them up, as Mrs. Beecher Stowe has, as a picture of slave-life in the Southern States, is as gross a libel as if any one were to make a collection of all the wife-beatings and assaults of drunken English ruffians, and to publish them as a picture of the average life of English people.

"Such libels as these have done more to embitter the two sections of America against each other than anything else. Therefore, Vincent, my advice to you is, be always kind to your slaves--not over-indulgent, because they are very like children and indulgence spoils them--but be at the same time firm and kind to them, and with other people avoid entering into any discussions or expressing any opinion with regard to slavery. You can do no good and you can do much harm. Take things as you find them and make the best of them. I trust that the time may come when slavery will be abolished; but I hope, for the sake of the slaves themselves, that when this is done it will be done gradually and thoughtfully, for otherwise it would inflict terrible hardship and suffering upon them as well as upon their masters."

There were many such conversations between father and son, for feeling on the subject ran very high in the Southern States, and the former felt that it was of the utmost importance to his son that he should avoid taking any strong line in the matter. Among the old families of Virginia there was indeed far less feeling on this subject than in some of the other States. Knowing the good feeling that almost universally existed between themselves and their slaves, the gentry of Virginia regarded with contempt the calumnies of which they were the subject. Secure in the affection of their slaves, an affection which was afterward abundantly proved during the course of the war, they scarcely saw the ugly side of the question. The worst masters were the smallest ones; the man who owned six slaves was far more apt to extort the utmost possible work from them than the planter who owned three or four hundred. And the worst masters of all were those who, having made a little money in trade or speculation in the towns, purchased a dozen slaves, a small piece of land, and tried to set up as gentry.

In Virginia the life of the large planters was almost a patriarchal one; the indoor slaves were treated with extreme indulgence, and were permitted a far higher degree of freedom of remark and familiarity than is the case with servants in an English household. They had been the nurses or companions of the owners when children, had grown up with them, and regarded themselves, and were regarded by them, as almost part of the family. There was, of course, less connection between the planters and their field hands; but these also had for the most part been born on the estate, had as children been taught to look up to their white masters and mistresses, and to receive many little kindnesses at their hands.

They had been cared for in sickness, and knew that they would be provided for in old age. Each had his little allotment, and could raise fruit, vegetables, and fowls for his own use or for sale in his leisure time. The fear of loss of employment or the pressure of want, ever present to English laborers, had never fallen upon them. The climate was a lovely one, and their work far less severe than that of men forced to toil in cold and wet, winter and summer. The institution of slavery assuredly was capable of terrible abuses, and was marked in many instances by abominable cruelty and oppression; but taken all in all, the negroes on a well-ordered estate, under kind masters, were probably a happier class of people than the laborers upon any estate in Europe.

Jonas Pearson had been overseer in the time of Major Wingfield, but his authority had at that time been comparatively small, for the major himself personally supervised the whole working of the estate, and was greatly liked by the slaves, whose chief affections were, however, naturally bestowed upon their mistress, who had from childhood been brought up in their midst. Major Wingfield had not liked his overseer, but he had never had any ground to justify him making a change.

Jonas, who was a Northern man, was always active and energetic; all Major Wingfield's orders were strictly and punctually carried out, and although he disliked the man, his employer acknowledged him to be an excellent servant.

After the major's death, Jonas Pearson had naturally obtained greatly increased power and authority. Mrs. Wingfield had great confidence in him, his accounts were always clear and precise, and although the profits of the estate were not quite so large as they had been in her husband's lifetime, this was always satisfactorily explained by a fall in prices, or by a part of the crops being affected by the weather. She flattered herself that she herself managed the estate, and at times rode over it, made suggestions, and issued orders, but this was only in fits and starts; and although Jonas came up two or three times a week to the house nominally to receive her orders, he managed her so adroitly that while she believed that everything was done by her directions, she in reality only followed out the suggestions which, in the first place, came from him.

She was aware, however, that there was less content and happiness on the estate than there had been in the old times. Complaints had reached her from time to time of overwork and harsh treatment. But upon inquiring into these matters, Jonas had always such plausible reasons to give that she was convinced he was in the right, and that the fault was among the slaves themselves, who tried to take advantage of the fact that they had no longer a master's eye upon them, and accordingly tried to shirk work, and to throw discredit upon the man who looked after the interests of their mistress; and so gradually Mrs. Wingfield left the management of affairs more and more in the hands of Jonas, and relied more implicitly upon him.

The overseer spared no pains to gain the good-will of Vincent. When the latter declared that the horse he rode had not sufficient life and spirit for him, Jonas had set inquiries on foot, and had selected for him a horse which, for speed and bottom, had no superior in the State. One of Mrs. Wingfield's acquaintances, however, upon hearing that she had purchased the animal, told her that it was notorious for its vicious temper, and she spoke angrily to Jonas on the subject in the presence of Vincent. The overseer excused himself by saying that he had certainly heard that the horse was high spirited and needed a good rider, and that he should not have thought of selecting it had he not known that Mr. Vincent was a first-class rider, and would not care to have a horse that any child could manage.

The praise was not undeserved. The gentlemen of Virginia were celebrated as good riders; and Major Wingfield, himself a cavalry man, had been anxious that Vincent should maintain the credit of his English blood, and had placed him on a pony as soon as he was able to sit on one. A pony had been kept for his use during his holidays at his uncle's in England, and upon his return Vincent had, except during the hours he spent with his father, almost lived on horseback, either riding about the estate, or paying visits to the houses of other planters.

For an hour or more every day he exercised his father's horses in a paddock near the house, the major being wheeled down in an easy-chair and superintending his riding. As these horses had little to do and were full of spirit, Vincent's powers were often taxed to the utmost, and he had many falls; but the soil was light, and he had learned the knack of falling easily, and from constant practice was able at the age of fourteen to stick on firmly even without a saddle, and was absolutely fearless as to any animal he mounted.

In the two years which had followed he had kept up his riding. Every morning after breakfast he rode to Richmond, six miles distant, put up his horse at some stable there, and spent three hours at school; the rest of the day was his own, and he would often ride off with some of his schoolfellows who had also come in from a distance, and not return home till late in the evening. Vincent took after his English father rather than his Virginian mother both in appearance and character, and was likely to become as tall and brawny a man as the former had been when he first won the love of the rich Virginian heiress.

He was full of life and energy, and in this respect offered a strong contrast to most of his schoolfellows of the same age. For although splendid riders and keen sportsmen, the planters of Virginia were in other respects inclined to indolence; the result partly of the climate, partly of their being waited upon from childhood by attendants ready to carry out every wish. He had his father's cheerful disposition and good temper, together with the decisive manner so frequently acquired by a service in the army, and at the same time he had something of the warmth and enthusiasm of the Virginian character.

Good rider as he was he was somewhat surprised at the horse the overseer had selected for him. It was certainly a splendid animal, with great bone and power; but there was no mistaking the expression of its turned-back eye, and the ears that lay almost flat on the head when any one approached him.

"It is a splendid animal, no doubt, Jonas," he said the first time he inspected it; "but he certainly looks as if he had a beast of a temper. I fear what was told my mother about him is no exaggeration; for Mr. Markham told me to-day, when I rode down there with his son, and said that we had bought Wildfire, that a friend of his had had him once, and only kept him for a week, for he was the most vicious brute he ever saw."

"I am sorry I have bought him now, sir," Jonas said. "Of course I should not have done so if I had heard these things before; but I was told he was one of the finest horses in the country, only a little tricky, and as his price was so reasonable I thought it a great bargain. But I see now I was wrong, and that it wouldn't be right for you to mount him; so I think we had best send him in on Saturday to the market and let it go for what it will fetch. You see, sir, if you had been three or four years older it would have been different; but naturally at your age you don't like to ride such a horse as that."

"I sha'n't give it up without a trial," Vincent said shortly. "It is about the finest horse I ever saw; and if it hadn't been for its temper, it would be cheap at five times the sum you gave for it. I have ridden a good many bad-tempered horses for my friends during the last year, and the worst of them couldn't get me off."

"Well, sir, of course you will do as you please," Jonas said; "but please to remember if any harm comes of it that I strongly advised you not to have anything to do with it, and I did my best to dissuade you from trying."

Vincent nodded carelessly, and then turned to the black groom.

"Jake, get out that cavalry saddle of my father's, with the high cantle and pommel, and the rolls for the knees. It's like an armchair, and if one can't stick on on that, one deserves to be thrown."

While the groom was putting on the saddle, Vincent stood patting the horse's head and talking to it, and then taking its rein led it down into the inclosure.

"No, I don't want the whip," he said, as Jake offered him one. "I have got the spurs, and likely enough the horse's temper may have been spoiled by knocking it about with a whip; but we will try what kindness will do with it first."

"Me no like his look, Massa Vincent; he debbil ob a hoss dat."

"I don't think he has a nice temper, Jake; but people learn to control their temper, and I don't see why horses shouldn't. At any rate we will have a try at it. He looks as if he appreciates being patted and spoken to already. Of course if you treat a horse like a savage he will become savage. Now, stand out of the way."

Gathering the reins together, and placing one hand upon the pommel, Vincent sprang into the saddle without touching the stirrups; then he sat for a minute or two patting the horse's neck. Wildfire, apparently disgusted at having allowed himself to be mounted so suddenly, lashed out viciously two or three times, and then refused to move. For half an hour Vincent tried the effect of patient coaxing, but in vain.

"Well, if you won't do it by fair means you must by foul," Vincent said at last, and sharply pricked him with his spurs.

Wildfire sprang into the air, and then began a desperate series of efforts to rid himself of his rider, rearing and kicking in such quick succession that he seemed half the time in the air. Finding after awhile that his efforts were unavailing, he subsided at last into sulky immovability. Again Vincent tried coaxing and patting, but as no success attended these efforts, he again applied the spur sharply. This time the horse responded by springing forward like an arrow from a bow, dashed at the top of his speed across the inclosure, cleared the high fence without an effort, and then set off across the country.

He had attempted to take the bit in his teeth, but with a sharp jerk as he drove the spurs in, Vincent had defeated his intention. He now did not attempt to check or guide him, but keeping a light hand on the reins let him go his own course. Vincent knew that so long as the horse was going full speed it could attempt no trick to unseat him, and he therefore sat easily in his saddle.

For six miles Wildfire continued his course, clearing every obstacle without abatement to his speed, and delighting his rider with his power and jumping qualities. Occasionally, only when the course he was taking would have led him to obstacles impossible for the best jumper to surmount, Vincent attempted to put the slightest pressure upon one rein or the other, so as to direct it to an easier point.

At the end of six miles the horse's speed began slightly to abate, and Vincent, abstaining from the use of his spurs, pressed it with his knees and spoke to it cheerfully urging it forward. He now from time to time bent forward and patted it, and for another six miles kept it going at a speed almost as great as that at which it had started Then he allowed it gradually to slacken its pace, until at last first the gallop and then the trot ceased, and it broke into a walk.

"You have had a fine gallop, old fellow," Vincent said, patting it; "and so have I. There's been nothing for you to lose your temper about, and the next road we come upon we will turn our face homeward. Half a dozen lessons like this, and then no doubt we shall be good friends."

The journey home was performed at a walk, Vincent talking the greater part of the time to the horse. It took a good deal more than six lessons before Wildfire would start without a preliminary struggle with his master, but in the end kindness and patience conquered. Vincent often visited the horse in the stables, and, taking with him an apple or some pieces of sugar, spent some time there talking to and petting it. He never carried a whip, and never used the spurs except in forcing it to make its first start.

Had the horse been naturally ill-tempered Vincent would probably have failed, but, as he happened afterward to learn, its first owner had been a hot-tempered and passionate young planter, who, instead of being patient with it, had beat it about the head, and so rendered it restive and bad-tempered. Had Vincent not laid aside his whip before mounting it for the first time, he probably would never have effected a cure. It was the fact that the animal had no longer a fear of his old enemy the whip as much as the general course of kindness and good treatment that had effected the change in his behavior.

It was just when Vincent had established a good under standing between himself and Wildfire that he had the altercation with the overseer, whom he found about to flog the young negro Dan. Pearson had sent the lad half an hour before on a message to some slaves at work at the other end of the estate, and had found him sitting on the ground watching a tree in which he had discovered a possum. That Dan deserved punishment was undoubted. He had at present no regular employment upon the estate. Jake, his father, was head of the stables, and Dan had made himself useful in odd jobs about the horses, and expected to become one of the regular stable hands. The overseer was of opinion that there were already more negroes in the stable than could find employment, and had urged upon Mrs. Wingfield that one of the hands there and the boy Dan should be sent out to the fields. She, however, refused.

"I know you are quite right, Jonas, in what you say. But there were always four hands in the stable in my father's time, and there always have been up to now; and though I know they have an easy time of it, I certainly should not like to send any of them out to the fields. As to Dan, we will think about it. When his father was about his age he used to lead my pony when I first took to riding, and when there is a vacancy Dan must come into the stable. I could not think of sending him out as a field hand, in the first place for his father's sake, but still more for that of Vincent. Dan used to be told off to see that he did not get into mischief when he was a little boy, and he has run messages and been his special boy since he came back. Vincent wanted to have him as his regular house servant; but it would have broken old Sam's heart if, after being my father's boy and my husband's, another had taken his place as Vincent's."

And so Dan had remained in the stable, but regarding Vincent as his special master, carrying notes for him to his friends, or doing any odd jobs he might require, and spending no small portion of his time in sleep. Thus he was an object of special dislike to the overseer; in the first place because he had not succeeded in having his way with regard to him, and in the second because he was a useless hand, and the overseer loved to get as much work as possible out of every one on the estate. The message had been a somewhat important one, as he wanted the slaves for some work that was urgently required; and he lost his temper, or he would not have done an act which would certainly bring him into collision with Vincent.

He was well aware that the lad did not really like him, and that his efforts to gain his good-will had failed, and he had foreseen that sooner or later there would be a struggle for power between them. However, he relied upon his influence with Mrs. Wingfield, and upon the fact that she was the life-owner of the Orangery, and believed that he would be able to maintain his position even when Vincent came of age. Vincent on his side objected altogether to the overseer's treatment of the hands, of which he heard a good deal from Dan, and had already remonstrated with his mother on the subject. He, however, gained nothing by this. Mrs. Wingfield had replied that he was too young to interfere in such matters, that his English ideas would not do in Virginia, and that naturally the slaves were set against the overseer; and that now Pearson had no longer a master to support him, he was obliged to be more severe than before to enforce obedience. At the same time it vexed her at heart that there should be any severity on the Orangery estate, where the best relations had always prevailed between the masters and slaves, and she had herself spoken to Jonas on the subject.

He had given her the same answer that she had given her son: "The slaves will work for a master, Mrs. Wingfield, in a way they will not for a stranger. They set themselves against me, and if I were not severe with them I should get no work at all out of them. Of course, if you wish it, they can do as they like; but in that case they must have another overseer. I cannot see a fine estate going to ruin. I believe myself some of these Abolition fellows have been getting among them and doing them mischief, and that there is a bad spirit growing up among them. I can assure you that I am as lenient with them as is possible to be. But if they won't work I must make them, so long as I stay here."

And so the overseer had had his way. She knew that the man was a good servant, and that the estate was kept in excellent order. After all, the severities of which she had heard complaints were by no means excessive; and it was not to be expected that a Northern overseer could rule entirely by kindness, as the owner of an estate could do. A change would be most inconvenient to her, and she would have difficulty in suiting herself so well another time. Besides, the man had been with her sixteen years, and was, as she believed, devoted to her interests. Therefore she turned a deaf ear to Vincent's remonstrances.

She had always been somewhat opposed to his being left in England at school, urging that he would learn ideas there that would clash with those of the people among whom his life was to be spent; and she still considered that her views had been justified by the result.

The overseer was the first to give his version of the story about Dan's conduct; for on going to the house Vincent found his sisters, Rosa and Annie, in the garden, having just returned from a two days' visit to some friends in Richmond, and stayed chatting with them and listening to their news for an hour, and in the meantime Jonas had gone in and seen Mrs. Wingfield and told his story.

"I think, Mrs. Wingfield," he said when he had finished, "that it will be better for me to leave you. It is quite evident that I can have no authority over the hands if your son is to interfere when I am about to punish a slave for an act of gross disobedience and neglect. I found that all the tobacco required turning, and now it will not be done this afternoon owing to my orders not being carried out, and the tobacco will not improbably be injured in quality. My position is difficult enough as it is; but if the slaves see that instead of being supported I am thwarted by your son, my authority is gone altogether. No overseer can carry on his work properly under such circumstances."

"I will see to the matter, Jonas," Mrs. Wingfield said decidedly. "Be assured that you have my entire support, and I will see that my son does not again interfere."

When, therefore, Vincent entered the house and began his complaint he found himself cut short.

"I have heard the story already, Vincent. Dan acted in gross disobedience, and thoroughly deserved the punishment Jonas was about to give him. The work of the estate cannot be carried on if such conduct is to be tolerated; and once for all, I will permit no interference on your part with Jonas. If you have any complaints to make, come to me and make them; but you are not yourself to interfere in any way with the overseer. As for Dan, I have directed Jonas that the next time he gives cause for complaint he is to go into the fields."

Vincent stood silent for a minute, then he said quietly:

"Very well, mother. Of course you can do as you like; but at any rate I will not keep my mouth shut when I see that fellow ill-treating the slaves. Such things were never done in my father's time, and I won't see them done now. You said the other day you would get me a nomination to West Point as soon as I was sixteen. I should be glad if you would do so. By the time I have gone through the school, you will perhaps see that I have been right about Jonas."

So saying, he turned and left the room and again joined his sisters in the drawing-room.

"I have just told mother that I will go to West Point, girls," he said. "Father said more than once that he thought it was the best education I could get in America."

"But I thought you had made up your mind that you would rather stop at home, Vincent?"

"So I had, and so I would have done, but mother and I differ in opinion. That fellow Jonas was going to flog Dan, and I stopped him this morning, and mother takes his part against me. You know, I don't like the way he goes on with the slaves. They are not half so merry and happy as they used to be, and I don't like it. We shall have one of them running away next, and that will be a nice thing on what used to be considered one of the happiest plantations in Virginia. I can't make mother out; I should have thought that she would have been the last person in the world to have allowed the slaves to be harshly treated."

"I am sure we don't like Jonas more than you do, Vincent; but you see mamma has to depend upon him so much. No, I don't think she can like it; but you can't have everything you like in a man, and I know she thinks he is a very good overseer. I suppose she could get another?"

Vincent said he thought that there could not be much difficulty about getting an overseer.

"There might be a difficulty in getting one she could rely on so thoroughly," Rosa said. "You see a great deal must be left to him. Jonas has been here a good many years now, and she has learned to trust him. It would be a long time before she had the same confidence in a stranger; and you may be sure that he would have his faults, though, perhaps, not the same as those of Jonas. I think you don't make allowance enough for mamma, Vincent. I quite agree with you as to Jonas, and I don't think mamma can like his harshness to the slaves any more than you do; but every one says what a difficulty it is to get a really trustworthy and capable overseer, and, of course, it is all the harder when there is no master to look after him."

"Well, in a few years I shall be able to look after an overseer," Vincent said.

"You might do so, of course, Vincent, if you liked; but unless you change a good deal, I don't think your supervision would amount to much. When you are not at school you are always on horseback and away, and we see little enough of you, and I do not think you are likely for a long time yet to give up most of your time to looking after the estate."

"Perhaps you are right," Vincent said, after thinking for a minute; "but I think I could settle down too, and give most of my time to the estate, if I was responsible for it. I dare say mother is in a difficulty over it, and I should not have spoken as I did; I will go in and tell her so."

Vincent found his mother sitting as he had left her. Although she had sided with Jonas, it was against her will; for it was grievous to her to hear complaints of the treatment of the slaves at the Orangery. Still, as Rosa had said, she felt every confidence in her overseer, and believed that he was an excellent servant. She was conscious that she herself knew nothing of business, and that she must therefore give her entire confidence to her manager. She greatly disliked the strictness of Jonas; but if, as he said, the slaves would not obey him without, he must do as he thought best.

"I think I spoke too hastily, mother," Vincent said as he entered; "and I am sure that you would not wish the slaves to be ill-treated more than I should. I dare say Jonas means for the best."

"I feel sure that he does, Vincent. A man in his position cannot make himself obeyed like a master. I wish it could be otherwise, and I will speak to him on the subject; but it will not do to interfere with him too much. A good overseer is not easy to get, and the slaves are always ready to take advantage of leniency. An easy master makes bad work, but an easy overseer would mean ruin to an estate. I am convinced that Jonas has our interests at heart, and I will tell him that I particularly wish that he will devise some other sort of punishment, such as depriving men who won't work of some of their privileges instead of using the lash."

"Thank you, mother. At any rate, he might be told that the lash is never to be used without first appealing to you."

"I will see about it, Vincent, and talk it over with him." And with that Vincent was satisfied.

## CHAPTER II. BUYING A SLAVE.

MRS. Wingfield did talk the matter over with the overseer, and things went on in consequence more smoothly. Vincent, however, adhered to his wish, and it was arranged that as soon as he could get a nomination he should go to West Point, which is to the American army what Sandhurst and Woolwich are to England. Before that could be done, however, a great political agitation sprang up. The slaves States were greatly excited over the prospect of a Republican president being chosen, for the Republicans were to a great extent identified with the abolition movement; and public feeling, which had for some time run high, became intensified as the time approached for the election of a new president, and threats that if the Democrats were beaten and a Republican elected the slave States would secede from the Union, were freely indulged in.

In Virginia, which was one of the most northern of the slave States, opinion was somewhat divided, there being a strong minority against any extreme measures being taken. Among Vincent's friends, however, who were for the most part the sons of planters, the Democratic feeling was very strongly in the ascendant, and their sympathies were wholly with the Southern States. That these had a right to secede was assumed by them as being unquestionable.

But in point of fact there was a great deal to be said on both sides. The States which first entered the Union in 1776 considered themselves to be separate and sovereign States, each possessing power and authority to manage its own affairs, and forming only a federation in order to construct a central power, and so to operate with more effect against the mother country. Two years later the constitution of the United States was framed, each State giving up a certain portion of its authority, reserving its own self-government and whatever rights were not specifically resigned.

No mention was made in the constitution of the right of a State to secede from the Union, and while those who insisted that each State had a right to secede if it chose to do so declared that this right was reserved, their opponents affirmed that such a case could never have been contemplated. Thus the question of absolute right had never been settled, and it became purely one of force.

Early in November, 1860, it became known that the election of Mr. Lincoln, the Republican candidate, was assured, and on the ninth of that month the representatives of South Carolina met at Charleston, and unanimously authorized the holding of a State convention to meet in the third week in December. The announcement caused great excitement, for it was considered certain that the convention would pass a vote of secession, and thus bring the debated question to an issue. Although opinion in Virginia was less unanimous than in the more southern States, it was generally thought that she would imitate the example of South Carolina.

On the day following the receipt of the news, Vincent, who had ridden over to the plantations of several of his friends to talk the matter over, was returning homeward, when he heard the sound of heavy blows with a whip and loud curses, and a moment later a shrill scream in a woman's voice rose in the air.

Vincent checked his horse mechanically with an exclamation of anger. He knew but too well what was going on beyond the screen of shrubs that grew on the other side of the fence bordering the road. For a moment he hesitated, and then muttering, "What's the use!" was about to touch the horse with the whip and gallop on, when the shriek again rose louder and more agonizing than before. With a cry of rage Vincent leaped from his horse, threw the reins over the top of the fence, climbed over it in a moment, and burst his way through the shrubbery.

Close by a negro was being held by four others, two having hold of each wrist and holding his arms extended to full length, while a white lad, some two years Vincent's senior, was showering blows with a heavy whip upon him. The slave's back was already covered with weals, and the blood was flowing from several places. A few yards distant a black girl, with a baby in her arms, was kneeling on the ground screaming for mercy for the slave. Just as Vincent burst through the bushes, the young fellow, irritated at her cries, turned round and delivered a tremendous blow with the whip on her bare shoulders.

This time no cry came from her lips, but the slave, who had stood immovable while the punishment was being inflicted upon himself, made a desperate effort to break from the men who held him. He was unsuccessful, but before the whip could again fall on the woman's shoulders, Vincent sprang forward, and seizing it, wrested it from the hands of the striker. With an oath of fury and surprise at this sudden interruption, the young fellow turned upon Vincent.

"You are a coward and a blackguard, Andrew Jackson!" Vincent exclaimed, white with auger. "You are a disgrace to Virginia, you ruffian!"

Without a word the young planter, mad with rage at this interference, rushed at Vincent; but the latter had learned the use of his fists at his English school, and riding exercises had strengthened his muscles, and as his opponent rushed at him, he met him with a blow from the shoulder which sent him staggering back with the blood streaming from his lips. He again rushed forward, and heavy blows were exchanged; then they closed and grappled. For a minute they swayed to and from but although much taller, the young planter was no stronger than Vincent, and at last they came to the ground with a crash, Vincent uppermost, Jackson's head as he fell coming with such force against a low stump that he lay insensible.

The contest had been so sudden and furious that none had attempted to interfere. Indeed the negroes were so astonished that they had not moved from the moment when Vincent made his appearance upon the scene. The lad rose to his feet.

"You had better carry him up to the house and throw some water on him," he said to the negroes, and then turned to go away. As he did so, the slave who had been flogged broke from the others, who had indeed loosened their hold, and ran up to Vincent, threw himself on his knees, and taking the lad's hand pressed it to his lips.

"I am afraid I haven't done you much good," Vincent said. "You will be none the better off for my interference; but I couldn't help it." So saying he made his way through the shrubbery, cleared the fence, mounted, and rode homeward.

"I have been a fool," he said to himself as he rode along. "It will be all the worse for that poor beggar afterward; still I could not help it. I wonder will there be any row about it. I don't much expect there will, the Jacksons don't stand well now, and this would not do them any good with the people round; besides I don't think Jackson would like to go into court to complain of being thrashed by a fellow a head shorter than himself. It's blackguards like him who give the Abolitionists a right to hold up the slave-owners as being tyrants and brutes."

The Jacksons were newcomers in Virginia. Six years before, the estate, of which the Cedars, as their place was called, formed a part, was put up for sale. It was a very large one, and having been divided into several portions to suit buyers, the Cedars had been purchased by Jackson, who, having been very successful as a storekeeper at Charleston, had decided upon giving up the business and leaving South Carolina, and settling down as a land-owner in some other State. His antecedents, however, were soon known at Richmond, and the old Virginian families turned a cold shoulder to the newcomer.

Had he been a man of pleasant manners, he would gradually have made his way; but he was evidently not a gentleman. The habits of trade stuck to him, and in a very short time there were rumors that the slaves, whom he had bought with the property, found him a harsh and cruel master. This in itself would have been sufficient to bring him disrepute in Virginia, where as a rule the slaves were treated with great kindness, and indeed considered their position to be infinitely superior to that of the poorer class of whites. Andrew Jackson had been for a few months at school with Vincent; he was unpopular there, and from the rumors current as to the treatment of the slaves on the estate, was known by the nickname of the "slave-driver."

Had Vincent been the son of a white trader, or a small cultivator, he knew well enough that his position would be a very serious one, and that he would have had to ride to the border of the State with all speed. He would have been denounced at once as an Abolitionist, and would have been accused of stirring up the slaves to rebellion against their masters; a crime of the most serious kind in the Southern States. But placed as he was, as the heir of a great estate worked by slaves, such a cry could hardly be raised against him. He might doubtless be filled and admonished for interfering between a master and his slave; but the sympathy of the better classes in Virginia would be entirely with him. Vincent, therefore, was but little concerned for himself; but he doubted greatly whether his interference had not done much more harm than good to the slave and his wife, for upon them Andrew Jackson would vent his fury. He rode direct to the stables instead of alighting as usual at the door. Dan, who had been sitting in the veranda waiting for him, ran down to the stables as he saw him coming.

"Give the horse to one of the others, Dan; I want to speak to you. Dan," he went on when he had walked with him a short distance from the stables, "I suppose you know some of the hands on Jackson's plantation."

Dan grinned, for although there was not supposed to be any communication between the slaves on the different estates, it was notorious that at night they were in the habit of slipping out of their huts and visiting each other.

"I know some ob dem, Massa Vincent. What you want ob dem? Berry bad master, Massa Jackson. Wust master hereabouts."

Vincent related what had happened, to Dan's intense delight.

"Now, Dan," he went on, "I am afraid that after my interference they will treat that poor fellow and his wife worse than before. I want you to find out for me what is going on at Jackson's. I do not know that I can do anything, however badly they treat them; but I have been thinking that if they ill-treat them very grossly, I will get together a party of fifteen or twenty of my friends and we will go in a body to Jackson's, and warn him that if he behaves with cruelty to his slaves, we will make it so hot for him that he will have to leave the state. I don't say that we could do anything; but as we should represent most of the large estates round here, I don't think old Jackson and his son would like being sent to Coventry. The feeling is very strong at present against ill-treatment of the slaves. If these troubles lead to war almost all of us will go into the army, and we do not like the thought of the possibility of troubles among the hands when the whites are all away."

"I will find out all about it for you to-night, sah. I don't suspect dat dey will do nuffin to-day. Andrew Jackson too sick after dat knock against de tump. He keep quiet a day or two."

"Well, Dan, you go over to-night and find out all about it. I expect I had better have left things alone, but now I have interfered I shall go on with it."

Mrs. Wingfield was much displeased when Vincent told her at dinner of his incident at Jackson's plantation and even his sisters were shocked at this interference between a master and his slave.

"You will get yourself into serious trouble with these fanciful notions of yours," Mrs. Wingfield said angrily. "You know as well as I do how easy it is to get up a cry against any one as an Abolitionist and how difficult to disprove the accusation; and just at present, when the passions of every man in the South are inflamed to the utmost, such an accusation will be most serious. In the present instance there does not seem that there is a shadow of excuse for your conduct. You simply heard cries of a slave being flogged. You deliberately leave the road and enter these people's plantation and interfere without, so far as I can see, the least reason for doing so. You did not inquire what the man's offense was; and he may for aught you know have half murdered his master. You simply see a slave being flogged and you assault his owner. If the Jacksons lay complaints against you it is quite probable that you may have to leave the state. What on earth can have influenced you to act in such a mad-brained way?"

"I did not interfere to prevent his flogging the slave, mother, but to prevent his flogging the slave's wife, which was pure wanton brutality. It is not a question of slavery one way or the other. Any one has a right to interfere to put a stop to brutality. If I saw a man brutally treating a horse or a dog I should certainly do so; and if it is right to interfere to save a dumb animal from brutal ill-treatment surely it must be justifiable to save a woman in the same case. I am not an Abolitionist. That is to say, I consider that slaves on a properly managed estate, like ours, for instance, are just as well off as are the laborers on an estate in Europe; but I should certainly like to see laws passed to protect them from ill-treatment. Why, in England there are laws against cruelty to animals; and a man who brutally flogged a dog or a horse would get a month's imprisonment with hard labor. I consider it a disgrace to us that a man may here ill-treat a human being worse than he might in England a dumb animal."

"You know, Vincent," his mother said more quietly, "that I object as much as you do to the ill-treatment of the slaves, and that the slaves here, as on all well-conducted plantations in Virginia, are well treated; but this is not a time for bringing in laws or carrying out reforms. It is bad enough to have scores of Northerners doing their best to stir up mischief between masters and slaves without a Southern gentleman mixing himself up in the matter. We have got to stand together as one people and to protect our State rights from interference."

"I am just as much in favor of State rights as any one else, mother; and if, as seems likely, the present quarrel is to be fought out, I hope I shall do my best for Virginia as well as other fellows of my own age. But just as I protest against any interference by the Northerners with our laws, I say that we ought to amend our laws so as not to give them the shadow of an excuse for interference. It is brutes like the Jacksons who have afforded the materials for libels like 'Uncle Tom's Cabin' upon us as a people; and I can't say that I am a bit sorry for having given that young Jackson what he deserved."

"Well, I hope there will be no trouble come of it," Mrs. Wingfield said. "I shouldn't think the Jacksons would like the exposure of their doings which would be caused by bringing the matter into court; but if they do, you may be quite sure that a jury in Richmond at the present time would find against you."

"I don't suppose that they will do anything, mother. But if they must, they must; and I don't suppose anything serious will come of it any way."

The next morning Vincent went down early to the stables. As he approached them Dan came out to meet him.

"Well, Dan, what's your news?"

"Berry great bobbery ober at Jackson's last night, Massa Vincent. Fust of all I crept round to de huts ob de field hands. Dey all know nuffin bout it; but one of dem he goes off and gets to hab a talk with a gal employed in de house who was in de habit of slipping out to see him. She say when de young un war carried in de old man go on furious; he bring suit against you, he hab you punished berry much--no saying what he not going to do. After a time de young un come round, he listen to what the old man say for some time; den he answer: 'No use going on like dat. Set all de county families against us if we have suit. As to dat infernal young villain, me pay him out some other way.' Den de old man say he cut de flesh off de bones ob dat nigger; but de young one say: 'Mustn't do dat. You sure to hear about it, and make great bobbery. Find some oder way to punish him.' Den dey talk together for some time, but girl not hear any more."

"Well, then, there will be no suit anyhow," Vincent said. "As to paying me out some other way, I will look after myself, Dan. I believe that fellow Jackson is capable of anything, and I will be on the lookout for him."

"Be sure you do, Massa Vincent. You ride about a great deal, dat fellow bery like take a shot at you from behind tree. Don't you go near dat plantation, or sure enuff trouble come."

"I will look out, Dan. There is one thing, I always ride fast; and it wants a very good shot to hit one at a gallop. I don't think they will try that; for if he missed, as he would be almost sure to do, it would be a good deal worse for him than this affair would have been had he brought it into court. You keep your ears open, Dan, and find out how they are thinking of punishing that poor fellow for my interference on his behalf."

After breakfast a negro arrived with a note for Mrs. Wingfield from Mr. Jackson, complaining of the unwarrantable and illegal interference by her son on behalf of a slave who was being very properly punished for gross misconduct; and of the personal assault upon his son. The writer said that he was most reluctant to take legal proceedings against a member of so highly respected a family, but that it was impossible that he could submit to such an outrage as this.

Although Mrs. Wingfield had expressed her disapproval of Vincent's conduct on the evening before, there was no trace of that feeling in her reply to this letter. She wrote in the third person, coldly acknowledging the receipt of Mr. Jackson's letter, and saying that she had heard from her son of his interference to put a stop to one of those brutal scenes which brought discredit upon the Southern States, and that she considered he had most rightly punished Mr. Jackson, jun., for his inhuman and revolting conduct; that she was perfectly aware the interference had been technically illegal, but that her son was fully prepared to defend his conduct if called upon to do so in the courts, and to pay any fine that might be inflicted for his suffering himself to be carried away by his righteous indignation. She ended by saying that as Mr. Jackson was a stranger in Virginia, he was perhaps not aware that the public sentiment of that State was altogether opposed to such acts of brutality as that of which his son had been guilty.

"What have you been doing to that fellow Andrew Jackson?" one of Vincent's friends, a young fellow two years older than himself, said to him a few days later. "There were a lot of us talking over things yesterday, in Richmond, and he came up and joined in. Something was said about Abolitionists, and he said that he should like to see every Abolitionist in the State strung up to a tree. He is always pretty violent, as you know; but on the present occasion he went further than usual, and then went on to say that the worst and most dangerous Abolitionists were not Northern men but Southerners, who were traitors to their State.

"He said: 'For example, there is that young Wingfield. He has been to England, and has come back with his heart filled with Abolitionist notions;' and that such opinions at the present time were a danger to the State.

"Two or three of us took the matter up, as you might guess, and told him he had better mind what he was saying or it would be the worse for him. Harry Furniss went so far as to tell him that he was a liar, and that if he didn't like that he would have satisfaction in the usual way. Master Jackson didn't like it, but muttered something and slunk off. What's the matter between you?"

"I should not have said anything about it," Vincent replied, "if Jackson had chosen to hold his tongue; but as he chooses to go about attacking me, there is no reason why I should keep the matter secret." And he then related what had taken place.

The young Virginian gave a low whistle.

"I don't say I blame you, Wingfield; but I tell you, you might have got yourself into an awful mess if the Jacksons had chosen to take it up. You know how hot the feeling is at present, and it is a serious matter at any time to interfere between a master and his slaves in the Southern States. Of course among us our feelings would be all against Jackson; but among the poorer class of whites, who have been tremendously excited by the speeches, both in the North and here, the cry of Abolitionist at the present moment is like a red rag to a bull. However, I understand now the fellow's enmity to you.

"None of us ever liked him when he was at school with us. He is an evil-tempered brute, and I am afraid you may have some trouble with him. If he goes about talking as he did to us, he would soon get up a feeling against you. Of course it would be nonsense to openly accuse a member of an old Virginian family of being an Abolitionist; but it would be easy enough to set a pack of the rough classes of the town against you, and you might get badly mauled if they caught you alone. The fellow is evidently a coward or he would have taken up what Furniss said; but a coward who is revengeful is a good deal more dangerous than an open foe. However, I will talk it over with some of the others, and we will see if we can't stop Andrew Jackson's mouth."

The result of this was that the next day half a dozen of Vincent's friends wrote a joint letter to Andrew Jackson, saying that they regarded his statements respecting Vincent as false and calumnious, and that if he repeated them they would jointly and severally hold him responsible; and that if, as a result of such accusations, any harm happened to Vincent, they should know where to look for the originator of the mischief, and punish him accordingly.

"You should be more careful, Andrew," his father said, as white with fury, he showed him his letter. "It was you who were preaching prudence the other day, and warning me against taking steps that would set all the whole country against us; and now, you see, you have been letting your tongue run, and have drawn this upon yourself. Keep quiet for the present, my son; all sorts of things may occur before long, and you will get your chance. Let this matter sleep for the present."

A day or two later when Vincent went down to the stables he saw that Dan had something to tell him, and soon found out that he wished to speak to him alone.

"What is your news, Dan?"

"I heard last night, Massa Vincent, that old man Jackson is going to sell Dinah; dat de wife ob de man dey flogged."

"They are going to sell her!" Vincent repeated indignantly. "What are they going to do that for?"

"To punish Tony, sah. Dar am no law against dar selling her. I hear dat dey are going to sell two oder boys, so dat it cannot be said dat dey do it on purpose to spite Tony. I reckon, sah, day calculate dat when dey sell his wife Tony get mad and run away, and den when dey catch him again day flog him pretty near to death. Folk always do dat with runaway slaves; no one can say nuffin agin dem for dat."

"It's an infamous shame that it should be lawful to separate man and wife," Vincent said. "However, we will see what we can do. You manage to pass the word to Tony to keep up his spirits, and not let them drive him to do anything rash. Tell him I will see that his wife does not get into bad hands. I suppose they will sell the baby too?"

"Yes, Massa Vincent. Natural the baby will go wid de modder."

Vincent watched the list of advertisements of slaves to be sold, and a day or two later saw a notice to the effect that Dinah Morris, age twenty-two, with a male baby at her breast, would be sold on the following Saturday. He mounted his horse and rode into Richmond. He had not liked to speak to his mother on the subject, for she had not told him of the letter she had written to Jackson; and he thought that she might disapprove of any interference in the matter, consequently he went down to Mr. Renfrew, the family solicitor.

"Mr. Renfrew," he said, "I want some money; can you lend it me?"

"You want money," the solicitor said in surprise. "What on earth do you want money for? and if you want it, why don't you ask your mother for it? How much do you want?"

"I don't know exactly. About eight hundred dollars, I should think; though it may be a thousand. I want to buy a slave."

"You want to buy a slave!" repeated Mr. Renfrew. "What on earth do you want to buy a slave for? You have more than you want now at the Orangery."

"It's a slave that man Jackson is going to sell next Saturday, on purpose to spite the poor creature's husband and drive him to desperation," and Vincent then repeated the whole story of the circumstances that had led up to the sale.

"It is all very abominable on the part of these Jacksons," Mr. Renfrew said, "but your interference was most imprudent, my young friend; and, as you see, it has done harm rather than good. If you are so quixotic as to become the champion of every ill-treated slave in the State, your work is pretty well cut out for you."

"I know that, sir," Vincent replied, smiling, "and I can assure you I did not intend to enter upon any such crusade; but, you see, I have wrongly or rightly mixed myself up in this, and I want to repair the mischief which, as you say, I have caused. The only way I can see is to buy this negress and her baby."

"But I do not see that you will carry out your object if you do, Vincent. She will be separated just as much from her husband if you buy her as if any one else does. He is at one plantation and she is at another, and were they ten miles apart or a hundred, they are equally separated."

"I quite see that, Mr. Renfrew; but, at least, she will be kindly treated, and his mind will be at rest on that score. Perhaps some day or other the Jacksons may put him up for sale, and then I can buy him, and they will be reunited. At any rate, the first step is to buy her. Can you let me have the money? My mother makes me a very good allowance."

"And I suppose you spend it," the lawyer interrupted.

"Well, yes, I generally spend it; but then, you see, when I come of age I come in for the outlying estates."

"And if you die before, or get shot, or any other accident befalls you," Mr. Renfrew said, "they go to your sisters. However, one must risk something for a client, so I will lend you the money. I had better put somebody up to bid for you, for after what has happened the Jacksons would probably not let her go if they knew that you were going to be the purchaser."

"Thank you very much," Vincent said warmly; "it will be a great weight off my mind," and with a light heart he rode back to the Orangery.

Vincent said nothing during the next two days to any of his friends as to the course the Jacksons were taking in selling Tony's wife; for he thought that if the news got about, some of his friends who had heard the circumstances might go down to the auction and make such a demonstration that Jackson would be obliged to withdraw Dinah from the sale, in which case he would no doubt dispose of her privately. On the Saturday he mounted his horse and rode into Richmond, telling Dan to meet him there. At the hour the sale was announced he went to the yard where it was to take place.

This was a somewhat quiet and secluded place; for although the sale of slaves was permitted by law in Virginia, at any rate these auctions were conducted quietly and with as little publicity as possible. For although the better classes still regarded slavery as a necessary institution, they were conscious that these sales, involving as they did the separation of families, were indefensible, and the more thoughtful would gladly have seen them abolished, and a law passed forbidding the sale of negroes save as part and parcel of the estate upon which they worked, an exception only being made in the case of gross misconduct. Many of the slave-owners, indeed, forbade all flogging upon their estates, and punished refractory slaves, in the first place, by the cutting off of the privileges they enjoyed in the way of holidays, and if this did not answer, threatened to sell them--a threat which was, in the vast majority of cases, quite sufficient to ensure good behavior; for the slaves were well aware of the difference between life in the well-managed establishments in Virginia and that in some of the other Southern States. Handing his horse to Dan, Vincent joined a knot of four or five of his acquaintances who had strolled in from mere curiosity.

There were some thirty or forty men in the yard, a few of whom had come in for the purpose of buying; but the great majority had only attended for the sake of passing an idle hour. Slaves had fallen in value; for although all in the South professed their confidence that the law would never attempt by force of arms to prevent their secession, it was felt that slave property would in future be more precarious, for the North would not improbably repeal the laws for the arrest of fugitive slaves, and consequently all runaways who succeeded in crossing the border would be lost to their masters.

Upon the other side of the yard Vincent saw Andrew Jackson talking to two or three men who were strangers to him, and who, he guessed, were buyers from some of the more southern States There were in all twelve lots to be disposed of. Of these two or three were hands who were no longer fit for field work, and who were bought at very low prices by men who owned but a few acres of land, and who could utilize them for odd jobs requiring but little strength. Then there was a stir of attention. Dinah Moore took her stand upon the platform, with her baby in her arms. The message which Dan had conveyed from Vincent to her husband had given her some hope, and though she looked scared and frightened as she clasped her babe to her breast, she was not filled with such utter despair as would otherwise have been the case.

The auctioneer stated the advantages of the lot in the same business-like tone as if he had been selling a horse:

"Lot 6. Negro wench, Dinah; age twenty-two; with male child. Strong and well made, as you see, gentlemen; fit for field work, or could be made a useful hand about a house; said to be handy and good-tempered. Now, gentlemen, what shall we say for this desirable lot?"

One of the men standing by Andrew Jackson bid a hundred dollars. The bid was raised to a hundred and fifty by a rough-looking fellow standing in front of the platform. For some time the bidding was confined to these two, and it rose until it reached seven hundred and fifty, at which point the man near the platform retired, and there was a pause.

Vincent felt uncomfortable. He had already been round to Mr. Renfrew, who had told him that he had deputed an agent to buy; and until the man near the platform stopped he had supposed that he was the solicitor's agent.

"Now, gentlemen," the auctioneer said, "surely you are not going to let this desirable piece of property go for seven fifty? She would be cheap at double the price. I have sold worse articles for three thousand."

"I will go another twenty-five dollars," a tall man in homespun and a broad planter's straw hat said quietly.

The contest now recommenced, and by bids of twenty-five dollars at a time the amount was raised to twelve hundred and fifty dollars.

"That's enough for me," the man standing by Andrew Jackson said; "he may have her at twelve fifty, and dear enough, too, as times go."

"Will any one else make an offer?" the auctioneer asked. There was no response, and the hammer fell.

"What name?"

"Nathaniel Forster," the tall man said; and advancing to the table he counted out a roll of notes and gave them to the auctioneer, who handed to him a formal note certifying to his having duly and legally purchased Dinah Moore and her infant, late the property of Andrew Jackson, Esquire, of the Cedars, State of Virginia.

The purchaser had evidently made up his mind beforehand to secure the lot, for he handed a parcel he had been holding to Dinah, and said briefly, "Slip those things on, my lass."

The poor girl, who had before been simply attired in the scantiest of petticoats, retired to a corner of the yard, and speedily came forward again dressed in a neat cotton gown. There were several joking remarks made by the bystanders, but Dinah's new master took no notice of them, but with a motion of his hand to her to follow him, walked out of the yard.

A minute later Vincent followed, and although he had no doubt that the man was the agent Mr. Renfrew had employed, he did not feel thoroughly satisfied until he saw them enter the lawyer's office. He quickly followed. They had just entered the private room of Mr. Renfrew.

"That's right, Wingfield," the lawyer said. "You see we have settled the business satisfactorily, and I think you have got a fairly cheap bargain. Just wait a moment and we will complete the transaction."

Dinah gave a start as Vincent entered, but with the habitual self-repression of a slave she stood quietly in the corner to which she had withdrawn at the other end of the room.

The lawyer was busy drawing up a document, and touching the bell ordered a clerk to go across to Mr. Rawlins, justice of the peace, and ask him to step across the road.

In a minute Mr. Rawlins entered.

"I want you to witness a deed of sale of a slave," Mr. Renfrew said. "Here are the particulars: 'Nathaniel Forster sells to Vincent Wingfield his slave, Dinah Moore and her male infant, for the sum of fourteen hundred dollars.' These are the parties. Forster sign this receipt."

The man did so. The justice put his signature as witness to the transaction, dropped into his pocket the fee of five dollars that the lawyer handed to him, and without a word strolled out again.

"There, Dinah," Mr. Renfrew said, "Mr. Wingfield is now your master."

The girl ran forward, fell on her knees before Vincent, seized his hand and kissed it, sobbing out her thanks as she did so.

"There, that will do, Dinah," the lawyer said, seeing that Vincent was confused by her greeting. "I think you are a lucky girl, and have made a good exchange for the Orangery instead of the Cedars. I don't suppose you will find Mr. Wingfield a very hard master. What he is going to do with you I am sure I don't know."

Vincent now went to the door and called in Dan and told him to take Dinah to the Orangery, then mounting his horse he rode off home to prepare his mother for the reception of his new purchase.

## CHAPTER III. AIDING A RUNAWAY.

"Well, you are an extraordinary boy, Vincent," Mrs. Wingfield said as her son told her the story, while his sisters burst into fits of laughter at the idea of Vincent owning a female slave with a baby. "Why did you not tell me that you wanted the money instead of going to Mr. Renfrew? I shall tell him I am very angry with him for letting you have it for such a purpose."

"I was not sure whether you would let me have it, mother; and if you had refused, and I had got it afterward from Mr. Renfrew, I should not have liked to bring her home here."

"That would have been fun," Annie said. "Fancy Vincent's troubles with a female slave on his hands and nowhere to put her. What would you have done, Vincent?"

"I suppose I could have got a home for her somewhere," Vincent said quietly. "I don't think there would have been any difficulty about that. Still I am glad I didn't have to do so, and one slave more or less can make no difference here."

"Not at all," Mrs. Wingfield said; "I dare say Chloe will find something for her to do in the way of washing, and such other light work that she is fit for about the house. It is not that, but it is years since a slave was brought into the Orangery; never since I can remember. We raise more than we want ourselves; and when I see all those children about, I wonder sometimes what on earth we are to find for them all to do. Still, it was a scandalous thing of that man Jackson selling the girl to punish her husband; and as you say it was your foolish interference in the matter that brought it about, so I do not know that I can blame you for doing what you can to set the matter straight. Still, except that the knowledge that she is here and will be well treated will be a comfort to the man, I do not see that he will be much the better off, unless indeed the Jacksons should try to sell him also, in which case

I suppose you would want to buy him."

"I am afraid they won't do that, mother. Still, somehow or other, in time they may come together again."

"I don't see how they can, Vincent. However we need not think of that now. At any rate I hope there will be no further opportunity for your mixing yourself up in this business. You have made two bitter enemies now, and although I do not see that such people as these can do you any harm, it is always well not to make enemies, especially in times like these when no one can foresee exactly what may occur."

And so Dinah Moore became an inmate of the Orangery; and though the girls had laughed at their brother, they were very kind to her when she arrived with Dan, and made much of her and of her baby. The same night Dan went over to the Cedars, and managed to have an interview with Tony, and to tell him that his wife had been bought by Vincent. The joy of the negro was extreme. The previous message had raised his hopes that Vincent would succeed in getting her bought by some one who would be kind to her, but he knew well that she might nevertheless fall to the lot of some higher bidder and be taken hundreds of miles away, and that he might never again get news of her whereabouts. He had then suffered terrible anxiety all day, and the relief of learning that Vincent himself had bought her, and that she was now installed as a house servant at the Orangery, but a few miles away, was quite overpowering, and for some minutes he could only gasp out his joy and thankfulness. He could hope now that when better times came he might be able to steal away some night and meet her, and that some day or other, though how he could not see, they might be reunited. The Jacksons remained in ignorance that their former slave was located so near to them.

It was for this reason that Mr. Renfrew had instructed his agent to buy her in his own name instead of that of Vincent; and the Jacksons, having no idea of the transfer that had subsequently taken place, took no further interest in the matter, believing that they had achieved their object of torturing Tony, and avenging upon him the humiliation that Andrew had suffered at Vincent's hands. Had they questioned their slaves, and had these answered them truly, they would have discovered the facts. For although Tony himself said no word to any one of what he had learned from Dan, the fact that Dinah was at the Orangery was speedily known among the slaves; for the doings at one plantation were soon conveyed to the negroes on the others by the occasional visits which they paid at night to each other's quarters, or to some common rendezvous far removed from interruption.

Occasionally Tony and Dinah met. Dan would come up late in the evening to the house, and a nod to Dinah would be sufficient to send her flying down the garden to a clump of shrubs, where he would be waiting for her. At these stolen meetings they were perfectly happy; for Tony said no word to her of the misery of his life--how he was always put to the hardest work and beaten on the smallest pretext, how in fact his life was made so unendurable that the idea of running away and taking to the swamps was constantly present to him.

As to making his way north, it did not enter his mind as possible. Slaves did indeed at times succeed in traveling through the Northern States and making their way to Canada, but this was only possible by means of the organization known as the underground railway, an association consisting of a number of good people who devoted themselves to the purpose, giving shelter to fugitive slaves during the day, and then passing them on to the next refuge during the night. For in the Northern States as well as the Southern any negro unprovided with papers showing that he was a free man was liable to be arrested and sent back to the South a prisoner, large rewards being given to those who arrested them.

As he was returning from one of these interviews with his wife, Tony was detected by the overseer, who was strolling about round the slaves' quarters, and was next morning flogged until he became insensible. So terrible was the punishment that for some days he was unable to walk. As soon as he could get about he was again set to work, but the following morning he was found to be missing. Andrew Jackson at once rode into Richmond, and in half an hour placards and handbills were printed offering a reward for his capture. These were not only circulated in the neighborhood, but were sent off to all the towns and villages through which Tony might be expected to pass in the endeavor to make his way north. Vincent soon learned from Dan what had taken place.

"You have no idea, I suppose, Dan, as to which way he is likely to go?"

Dan shook his head.

"Me suppose, massa, dat most likely he gone and hidden in de great woods by de James River. Berry difficult to find him dere."

"Difficult to find him, no doubt," Vincent agreed. "But he could not stop there long--he would find nothing to eat in the woods; and though he might perhaps support himself for a time on corn or roots from the clearings scattered about through the James Peninsula, he must sooner or later be caught."

"Dar are runaways in de woods now, Massa Vincent," Dan said; "some ob dem hab been dar for month."

"But how do they live, Dan?"

"Well, sah, you see dey hab friends on de plantations, and sometimes at night one of de slaves will steal away wid a basket ob yams and corn-cakes and oder things and put dem down in a certain place in de forest, and next morning, sure enough, dey will be gone. Dangerous work dat, massa; because if dey caught with food, it known for sure dat dey carry it to runaway, and den you know dey pretty well flog the life out of dem."

"Yes, I know, Dan; it is a very serious matter hiding a runaway slave, and even a white man would be very heavily punished, and perhaps lynched, if caught in the act. Well, make what inquiries you can among the slaves, and find out if you can whether any of those Jacksons have an idea which way Tony has gone. But do not go yourself on to Jackson's place; if you were caught there now it would be an awkward matter for both of us."

"I will find out, Massa Vincent; but I don't s'pose Tony said a word to any of the others. He know well enough dat de Jacksons question ebery one pretty sharp, and perhaps flog dem all round to find out if dey know anything. He keep it to himself about going away for suah."

The Jacksons kept up a vigorous hunt after their slave and day after day parties of men ranged through the woods but without discovering any traces of him. Bloodhounds were employed the first day, but before these could be fetched from Richmond the scent had grown cold; for Tony had gone off as soon as the slaves had been shut up for the night and had, directly he left the hut, wrapped leaves round his feet, therefore the hounds, when they arrived from Richmond, were unable to take up the scent.

A week after Tony's escape, Vincent returned late one evening from a visit to some friends. Dan, as he took his horse, whispered to him: "Stop a little on your way to house, Massa Vincent; me hab something to tell you."

"What is it, Dan?" Vincent asked, as the lad, after putting up his horse in the stable, came running up to him.

"Me have seen Tony, sah. He in de shrubs ober dar. He want to see Dinah, but me no take message till me tell you about him. He half starved, sah; me give him some yams."

"That's right, Dan."

"He pretty nigh desperate, sah; he say dey hunt him like wild beast."

"I will see him, Dan. If I can help him in any way I will do so. Unfortunately I do not know any of the people who help to get slaves away, so I can give him no advice as to the best way to proceed. Still I might talk it over with him. When I have joined him, do you go up to the house and tell Chloe from me to give you a pile of corn-cake--it's no use giving him flour, for he would be afraid to light a fire to cook it. Tell her to give you, too, any cold meat there may be in the house. Don't tell Dinah her husband is here till we have talked the matter over."

Dan led Vincent up to a clump of bushes.

"It am all right, Tony," he said; "here is Massa Vincent come to see you."

The bushes parted and Tony came out into the full moonlight. He looked haggard and worn; his clothes were torn into strips by the bushes.

"My poor fellow," Vincent said kindly, "I am sorry to see you in such a state."

A great sob broke from the black

"De Lord bress you, sah, for your goodness and for saving Dinah from de hands of dose debils! Now she safe wid you and de child, Tony no care berry much what come to him--de sooner he dead de better. He wish dat one day when dey flog him dey had kill him altogether; den all de trouble at an end. Dey hunt him ebery day with dogs and guns, and soon dey catch him. No can go on much longer like dis. To-day me nearly gib myself up. Den me thought me like to see Dinah once more to say good-by, so make great effort and ran a bit furder."

"I have been thinking whether it would be possible to plan some way for your escape, Tony."

The negro shook his head.

"Dar never escape, sah, but to get to Canada; dat too far any way. Not possible to walk all dat way and get food by de road. Suah to be caught."

"No, I do not think it will be possible to escape that way, Tony. The only possible plan would be to get you on board some ship going to England."

"Ships not dare take negro on board," Tony said. "Me heard dat said many times--dat against de law."

"Yes, I know it's against the law," Vincent said, "and it's against the law my talking to you here, Tony; but you see it's done. The difficulty is how to do it. All vessels are searched before they start, and an officer goes down with them past Fortress Monroe to see that they take no one on board. Still it is possible. Of course there is risk in the matter; but there is risk in everything. I will think it over. Do not lose heart. Dan will be back directly with enough food to last you for some days. If I were you I would take refuge this time in White Oak Swamp. It is much nearer, and I hear it has already been searched from end to end, so they are not likely to try again; and if you hear them you can, if you are pressed, cross the Chickahominy and make down through the woods. Do you come again on Saturday evening--that will give me four days to see what I can do. I may not succeed, you know; for the penalty is so severe against taking negroes on board that I may not be able to find any one willing to risk it. But it is worth trying."

"De Lord bless you, sah!" Tony said. "I will do juss what you tole me; but don't you run no risks for me, my life ain't worth dat."

"I will take care, Tony. And now here comes Dan with the provisions."

"Can I see Dinah, sah?" Tony pleaded.

"I think you had better not," Vincent replied. "You see the Jacksons might at any moment learn that she is here, and then she might be questioned whether she had seen you since your escape; and it would be much better for her to be able to deny having done so. But you shall see her next time you come, whether I am able to make any arrangements for your escape or not. I will let her know to-morrow morning that I have seen you, and that you are safe at present."

The next morning Vincent rode over to City Point, where ships with a large draught of water generally brought up, either transferring their goods into smaller craft to be sent up by river to Richmond, or to be carried on by rail through the town of Petersburg. Leaving his horse at a house near the river, he crossed the James in a boat to City Point. There were several vessels lying here, and for some hours he hung about the wharf watching the process of discharging. By the end of that time he had obtained a view of all the captains, and had watched them as they gave their orders, and had at last come to the conclusion as to which would be the most likely to suit his purpose. Having made up his mind, he waited until the one he had fixed upon came ashore. He was a man of some five-and-thirty years old, with a pleasant face and good-natured smile. He first went into some offices on the wharf, and half an hour later came out and walked toward the railway-station. Vincent at once followed him, and as he overtook him said:

"I want very much to speak to you, sir, if you could spare me a minute or two."

"Certainly," the sailor said with some surprise. "The train for Petersburg does not go for another half hour. What can I do for you?"

"My name is Vincent Wingfield. My father was an English officer, and my mother is the owner of some large estates near Richmond. I am most anxious to get a person in whom I am interested on board ship, and I do not know how to set about it."

"There's no difficulty about that," the captain said smiling; "you have only to go to an office and pay for his passage to where he wants to go."

"I can't do that," Vincent replied; "for unfortunately it is against the law for any captain to take him."

"You mean he is a negro?" the captain asked, stopping short in his walk and looking sharply at Vincent.

"Yes, that is what I mean," Vincent said. "He is a negro who has been brutally ill-treated and has run away from his master, and I would willingly give five hundred dollars to get him safely away."

"This is a very serious business in which you are meddling, young sir," the sailor said. "Putting aside the consequences to yourself, you are asking me to break the law and to run the risk of the confiscation of my ship. Even if I were willing to do what you propose it would be impossible, for the ship will be searched from end to end before the hatches are closed, and an official will be on board until we discharge the pilot after getting well beyond the mouth of the river."

"Yes, I know that," Vincent replied; "but my plan was to take a boat and go out beyond the sight of land, and then to put him on board after you have got well away."

"That might be managed, certainly," the captain said. "It would be contrary to my duty to do anything that would risk the property of my employers; but if when I am out at sea a boat came alongside, and a passenger came on board, it would be another matter. I suppose, young gentleman, that you would not interfere in such a business, and run the risk that you certainly would run if detected, unless you were certain that this was a deserving case, and that the man has committed no sort of crime; for I would not receive on board my ship a fugitive from justice, whether he was black or white."

"It is indeed a deserving case," Vincent said earnestly. "The poor fellow has the misfortune of belonging to one of the worst masters in the State. He has been cruelly flogged on many occasions, and was finally driven to run away by their selling his wife and child."

"The brutes!" the sailor said. "How you people can allow such things to be done is a mystery to me. Well, lad, under those circumstances I will agree to do what you ask me, and if your boat comes alongside when I am so far away from land that it cannot be seen, I will take the man to England."

"Thank you very much indeed," Vincent said; "you will be doing a good action. Upon what day do you sail?"

"I shall drop down on Monday into Hampton Roads, and shall get up sail at daylight next morning. I shall pass Fortress Monroe at about seven in the morning, and shall sail straight out."

"And how shall I know your ship?" Vincent asked. "There may be others starting just about the same time."

The sailor thought for a moment. "When I am four or five miles out I will hoist my owner's flag at the foremast-head. It is a red flag with a white ball, so you will be able to make it out a considerable distance away. You must not be less than ten or twelve miles out, for the pilot often does not leave the ship till she is some miles past Fortress Monroe, and the official will not leave the ship till he does. I will keep a sharp lookout for you, but I cannot lose my time in waiting. If you do not come alongside I shall suppose that you have met with some interruption to your plans."

"Thank you very much, sir. Unless something goes wrong I shall be alongside on Tuesday."

"That's settled, then," the captain said, "and I must be off, or else I shall lose my train. By the way, when you come alongside do not make any sign that you have met me before. It is just as well that none of my crew should know that it is a planned thing, for if we ever happened to put in here again they might blab about it, and it is just as well not to give them the chance. Good-by, my lad; I hope that all will go well. But, you know, you are doing a very risky thing; for the assisting of a runaway slave to escape is about as serious an offense as you can commit in these parts. You might shoot half a dozen men and get off scot free, but if you were caught aiding a runaway to escape there is no saying what might come of it."

After taking leave of the captain, Vincent recrossed the river and rode home. He had friends whose fathers' estates bordered some on the James and others on the York River, and all of these had pleasure-boats. It was obviously better to go down the York River, and thence round to the mouth of the James at Fortress Monroe, as the traffic on the York was comparatively small, and it was improbable that he would be noticed either going down or returning. He had at first thought of hiring a fishing-boat from some of the free negroes who made their living on the river. But he finally decided against this; for the fact of the boat being absent so long would attract its owner's attention, and in case any suspicion arose that the fugitive had escaped by water, the hiring of a boat by one who had already befriended the slave, and its absence for so long a time, would be almost certain to cause suspicion to be directed toward him. He therefore decided upon borrowing a boat from a friend, and next morning rode to the plantation of the father of Harry Furniss, this being situated on a convenient position on the Pamunkey, one of the branches of the York River.

"Are you using that sailing-boat of yours at present, Harry? Because, if not, I wish you would let me have the use of it for a week or so."

"With pleasure, Vincent; and my fishing-lines and nets as well, if you like. We very seldom use the boat. Do you mean to keep it here or move it higher up the river, where it would be more handy for you, perhaps?"

"I think I would rather leave it here, Furniss. A mile or two extra to ride makes no difference. I suppose it's in the water?"

"Yes; at the foot of the boathouse stairs. There is a padlock and chain. I will give you the key, so you can go off whenever you like without bothering to come up to the house. If you just call in at the stable as you ride by, one of the boys will go down with you and take your horse and put him up till you come back again."

"That will do capitally," Vincent replied. "It is some time since I was on the water, and I seem to have a fancy for a change at present. One is sick of riding into Richmond and hearing nothing but politics talked of all day. Don't be alarmed if you hear at any time that the boat has not come back at night, for if tide and wind are unfavorable at any time I might stop at Cumberland for the night."

"I have often had to do that," Furniss said. "Besides, if you took it away for a week, I don't suppose any one would notice it; for no one goes down to the boathouse unless to get the boat ready for a trip."

The next day Vincent rode over to his friend's plantation, sending Dan off an hour beforehand to bail out the boat and get the masts and sails into her from the boathouse. The greater part of the next two days was spent on the water, sometimes sailing, sometimes fishing. The evening of the second of these days was that upon which Vincent had arranged to meet Tony again, and an hour after dark he went down through the garden to the stable; for that was the time the fugitive was to meet him, for he could not leave his place of concealment until night fell. After looking at the horses, and giving some instructions to the negroes in charge, he returned to the shrubbery, and, sending Dan up to summon Dinah, he went to the bushes where he had before met Tony. The negro came out as he approached.

"How are you, Tony?"

"Much better dan I was, massa. I hab not been disturbed since I saw you, and, thanks to dat and to de good food and to massa's kind words, I'm stronger and better now, and ready to do whatever massa think best."

"Well, Tony, I am glad to say that I think I have arranged a plan by which you will be got safely out of the country. Of course, it may fail; but there is every hope of success. I have arranged for a boat, and shall take you down the river, and put you on board a ship bound for England."

The black clapped his hands in delight at the news.

"When you get there you will take another ship out to Canada, and as soon as I learn from you that you are there, and what is your address, I will give Dinah her papers of freedom and send her on to you."

"Oh, massa, it is too much," Tony said, with the tears running down his cheeks; "too much joy altogeder."

"Well, I hope it will all come right, Tony. Dinah will be here in a minute or two. Do not keep her long, for I do not wish her absence from the house to be observed just now. Now, listen to my instructions. Do you know the plantation of Mr. Furniss, on the Pamunkeyunky, near Coal harbor?"

"No, sir; but me can find out."

"No, you can't; because you can't see any one or ask questions. Very well, then, you must be here again to-morrow night at the same hour. Dan will meet you here, and act as your guide. He will presently bring you provisions for to-morrow. Be sure you be careful, Tony, and get back to your hiding-place as soon as you can, and be very quiet to-morrow until it is time to start. It would be terrible if you were to be caught now, just as we have arranged for you to get away."

On the following afternoon Vincent told his mother that he was going over that evening to his friend Furniss, as an early start was to be made next morning; they intended to go down the river as far as Yorktown, if not further; that he certainly should not be back for two days, and probably might be even longer.

"This new boating freak of yours, Vincent, seems to occupy all your thoughts. I wonder how long it will last."

"I don't suppose it will last much longer, mother," Vincent said with a laugh. "Anyhow, it will make a jolly change for a week. One had got so sick of hearing nothing talked about but secession that a week without hearing the word mentioned will do one lots of good, and I am sure I felt that if one had much more of it, one would be almost driven to take up the Northern side just for the sake of a change."

"We should all disown you, Vin," Annie said, laughing; "we should have nothing to say to you, and you would be cut by all your friends."

"Well, you see, a week's sailing and fishing will save me from all that, Annie; and I be all be able to begin again with a fresh stock of patience."

"I believe you are only half in earnest in the cause, Vincent," his mother said gravely.

"I am not indeed, mother. I quite agree with what you and every one say as to the rights of the State of Virginia, and if the North should really try to force us and the other Southern States to remain with them, I shall be just as ready to do everything I can as any one else; but I can't see the good of always talking about it, and I think it's very wrong to ill-treat and abuse those who think the other way. In

England in the Civil War the people of the towns almost all thought one way, and almost all those of the counties the other, and even now opinions differ almost as widely as to which was right. I hate to hear people always laying down the law as if there could not possibly be two sides of the case, and as if every one who differed from them must be a rascal and a traitor. Almost all the fellows I know say that if it comes to fighting they shall go into the State army, and I should be quite willing, if they would really take fellows of my age for soldiers, to enlist too; but that is no reason why one should not get sick of hearing nothing but one subject talked of for weeks."

It was nearly dark when Vincent started for his walk of ten miles; for he had decided not to take his horse with him, as he had no means of sending it back, and its stay for three days in his friend's stables would attract attention to the fact of his long absence.

After about three hours' walking he reached the boat house, having seen no one as he passed through the plantation. He took the oars and sails from the boathouse and placed them in the boat, and then sat down in the stern to await the coming of the negroes. In an hour they arrived; Tony carrying a bundle of clothes that Dan had by Vincent's orders bought for him in Richmond, while Dan carried a large basket of provisions. Vincent gave an exclamation of thankfulness as he saw the two figures appear, for the day having been Sunday he knew that a good many men would be likely to join the search parties in hopes of having a share in the reward offered for Tony's capture, and he had felt very anxious all day.

"You sit in the bottom of the boat, Tony, and do you steer, Dan. You make such a splashing with your oar that we should be heard a mile away. Keep us close in shore in the shadow of the trees; the less we are noticed the better at this time of night."

Taking the sculls, Vincent rowed quietly away. He had often been out on boating excursions with his friends, and had learned to row fairly. During the last two days he had diligently instructed Dan, and after two long days' work the young negro had got over the first difficulties, but he was still clumsy and awkward. Vincent did not exert himself. He knew he had a long night's row before him, and he paddled quietly along with the stream. The boat was a good-sized one, and when not under sail was generally rowed by two strong negroes accustomed to the work.

Sometimes for half an hour at a time Vincent ceased rowing, and let the boat drift along quietly. There was no hurry, for he had a day and two nights to get down to the mouth of the river, a distance of some seventy miles, and out to sea far enough to intercept the vessel. At four o'clock they arrived at Cumberland, where the Pamunkey and Mattapony Rivers unite and form the York River. Here they were in tidal waters; and as the tide, though not strong, was flowing up, Vincent tied the boat to the branch of a tree, and lay down in the bottom for an hour's sleep, telling Dan to wake him when the tide turned, or if he heard any noise. Day had broken when the boat drifted round, and Dan aroused him.

The boat was rowed off to the middle of the river, as there could be no longer any attempt at concealment. Dan now took the bow oar, and they rowed until a light breeze sprang up. Vincent then put up the mast, and, having hoisted the sail, took his place at the helm, while Dan went forward into the bow. They passed several fishing-boats, and the smoke was seen curling up from the huts in the clearings scattered here and there along the shore. The sun had now risen, and its heat was pleasant after the damp night air.

Although the breeze was light, the boat made fair way with the tide, and when the ebb ceased at about ten o'clock the mouth of the river was but a few miles away. The mast was lowered and the sails stowed. The boat was then rowed into a little creek and tied up to the bushes. The basket of provisions was opened, and a hearty meal enjoyed, Tony being now permitted for the first time to sit up in the boat. After the meal Vincent and Dan lay down for a long sleep, while Tony, who had slept some hours during the night, kept watch.

At four in the afternoon tide again slackened, and as soon as it had fairly turned they pushed out from the creek and again set sail. In three hours they were at the mouth of the river. A short distance out they saw several boats fishing, and dropping anchor a short distance away from these, they lowered their sail, and taking the fishing-lines from the locker of the boat, set to to fish. As soon as it was quite dark the anchor was hauled up, and Vincent and Dan took the oars, the wind having now completely dropped. For some time they rowed steadily, keeping the land in sight on their right hand.

Tony was most anxious to help, but as he had never had an oar in his hand in his life, Vincent thought that he would do more harm than good. It was, he knew, some ten miles from the mouth of the York River to Fortress Monroe, at the entrance to Hampton Roads, and after rowing for three hours he thought that he could not be far from that point, and therefore turned the boat's head out toward the sea. They rowed until they could no longer make out the land astern, and then laying in their oars waited till the morning, Vincent sitting in the stern and often nodding off to sleep, while the two negroes kept up a constant conversation in the bow.

As soon as it was daylight the oars were again got out. They could clearly make out the outline of the coast, and saw the break in the shore that marked the entrance to Hampton Roads. There was a light breeze now, but Vincent would not hoist the sail lest it might attract the attention of some one on shore. He did not think the boat itself could be seen, as they were some eight or nine miles from the land. They rowed for a quarter of an hour, when Vincent saw the white sails of a ship coming out from the entrance.

The breeze was so light that she would, he thought, be nearly three hours before she reached the spot where they were now, and whether she headed to the right or left of it he would have plenty of time to cut her off. For another two hours he and Dan rowed steadily. The wind had freshened a good deal, and the ship was now coming up fast to them. Two others had come out after her, but were some miles astern. They had already made out that the ship was flying a flag at her masthead, and although they had not been able to distinguish its colors, Vincent felt sure that it was the right ship; for he felt certain that the captain would get up sail as soon as possible, so as to come up with them before any other vessels came out. They had somewhat altered their course, to put themselves in line with the vessel. When she was within a distance of about a mile and a half Vincent was able to make out the flag, and knew that it was the right one.

"There's the ship, Tony," he said; "it is all right, and in a few minutes you will be on your way to England."

Tony had already changed his tattered garments for the suit of sailor's clothes that at Dan had bought for him. Vincent had given him full instructions as to the course he was to pursue. The ship was bound for Liverpool; on his arrival there he was at once to go round the docks and take a passage in the steerage of the next steamer going to Canada.

"The fare will be about twenty-five dollars," he said. "When you get to Canada you will land at Quebec, and you had better go on by rail to Montreal, where you will, I think, find it easier to get work than at Quebec. As soon as you get a place you are likely to stop in, get somebody to write for you to me, giving me your address. Here are a hundred dollars, which will be sufficient to pay your expenses to Montreal and leave you about fifty dollars to keep you till you can get something to do."

## CHAPTER IV. SAFELY BACK.

WHEN the ship came within a few hundred yards, Vincent stood up and waved his cap, and a minute later the ship was brought up into the wind and her sails thrown aback. The captain appeared at the side and shouted to the boat now but fifty yards away:

"What do you want there?"

"I have a passenger for England," Vincent replied. "Will you take him?"

"Come alongside," the captain said. "Why didn't he come on board before I started?"

The boat was rowed alongside, and Vincent climbed on board. The captain greeted him as a stranger and led the way to his cabin.

"You have managed that well," he said when they were alone, "and I am heartily glad that you have succeeded. I made you out two hours ago. We will stop here another two or three minutes so that the men may think you are bargaining for a passage for the negro, and then the sooner he is on board and you are on your way back the better, for the wind is rising, and I fancy it is going to blow a good deal harder before night."

"And won't you let me pay for the man's passage, captain? It is only fair anyhow that I should pay for what he will eat."

"Oh, nonsense!" the captain replied. "He will make himself useful and pay for his keep. I am only too glad to get; the poor fellow off. Now, we will have a glass of wine together and then say good-by."

Two minutes later they returned to the deck. Vincent went to the side.

"Jump on board, Tony. I have arranged for your passage."

The negro climbed up the side.

"Good-by, captain, and thank you heartily. Good-by, Tony."

The negro could not speak, but he seized the hand Vincent held out to him and pressed it to his lips. Vincent dropped lightly into his boat; and pushed off from the side of the vessel. As he did so he heard orders shouted, the yards swung round, and the vessel almost at once began to move through the water.

"Now, Dan, up with the mast; and sail again; but let me put two reefs in first, the wind is getting up."

In five minutes the sail was hoisted, and with Vincent at the helm and Dan sitting up to windward, was dashing through the water. Although Vincent understood the management of a sailing-boat on the calm waters of the rivers, this was his first experience of sea-sailing; and although the waves were still but small, he felt at first somewhat nervous as the boat dashed through them, sending up at times a sheet of spray from her bows. But he soon got over this sensation, and enjoyed the lively motion and the fresh wind. The higher points of the land were still visible; but even had they not been so it would have mattered little, as he had taken the precaution to bring with him a small pocket-compass. The wind was from the southwest; and he was therefore able, with the sheet hauled in, to make for a point where he judged the mouth of the York River lay.

"Golly, massa! how de boat do jump up and down."

"She is lively, Dan, and it would be just as well if we had some ballast on board; however, she has a good beam and walks along splendidly. If the wind keeps as it is, we shall be back at the mouth of the York in three or four hours. You may as well open that basket again and hand me that cold chicken and a piece of bread; cut the meat off the bones and put it on the bread, for I have only one hand disengaged; and hand me that bottle of cold tea. That's right. Now you had better take something yourself. You must be hungry. We forgot all about the basket in our interest in the ship."

Dan shook his head.

"A little while ago, massa, me seem berry hungry, now me doesn't feel hungry at all."

"That's bad, Dan. I am afraid you are going to be seasick."

"Me no feel seasick, massa; only me don't feel hungry." But in a few minutes Dan was forced to confess that he did feel ill, and a few moments afterward was groaning in the agonies of seasickness.

"Never mind, Dan," Vincent said cheerfully. "You will be better after this."

"Me not seasick, massa; de sea have nuffin to do with it. It's de boat dat will jump up and down instead of going quiet."

"It's all the same thing, Dan; and I hope she won't jump about more before we get into the river."

But in another half hour Vincent had to bring the boat's head up to the wind, lower the lug, and tie down the last reef.

"There, she goes easier now, Dan," he said, as the boat resumed her course; but Dan, who was leaning helplessly over the side of the boat, could see no difference.

Vincent, however, felt that; under her close sail the boat was doing better, and rising more easily on the waves, which were now higher and farther apart than before. In another hour the whole of the shore-line was visible; but the wind had risen so much that, even under her reduced sail, the boat had as much as she could carry, and often heeled over until her gunwale was nearly under water. Another hour and the shore was but some four miles away, but Vincent felt he could no longer hold on.

In the hands of an experienced sailor, who would have humored the boat and eased her up a little to meet the seas, the entrance to the York River could no doubt have been reached with safety; but Vincent was ignorant of the art of sailing a boat in the sea, and she was shipping water heavily. Dan had for some time been bailing, having only undertaken the work in obedience to Vincent's angry orders, being too ill to care much what became of them.

"Now, Dan, I am going to bring her head up to the wind, so get ready to throw off that halyard and gather in the sail as it; comes down. That's right, man; now down with the mast."

Vincent had read that the best plan when caught in an open boat in a gale, was to tie the oars and mast, if she had one, together, and to throw them overboard with the head rope tied to them, as by that means the boat would ride head to sea. The oars, sculls, mast, and sail were firmly tied together and launched overboard, the rope being first taken off the anchor and tied round the middle of the clump of spars.

Vincent carefully played out the rope till some fifteen yards were over, then he fastened it to the ring of the head rope, and had the satisfaction of finding that the boat rode easily to the floating anchor, rising lightly over the waves, and not shipping a drop of water. He then took the bailer and got rid of the water that had found its way on board, Dan, after getting down the sail, having collapsed utterly.

"Now, Dan, sit up; there, man, the motion is much easier now, and we are taking no water on board. I will give you a glass of rum, that will put new strength into you. It's lucky we put it in the basket in case of emergency."

The negro, whose teeth were chattering from cold, fright, and exhaustion, eagerly drank off the spirit. Vincent, who was wet to the skin with the spray, took a little himself, and then settled himself as comfortably as he could on the floor-boards in the stern of the boat, and quietly thought out the position. The wind was still rising, and a thick haze obscured the land. He had no doubt that by night it would be blowing a gale; but the boat rode so easily and lightly that he believed she would get through it.

They might, it was true, be blown many miles off the shore, and not be able to get back for some time, for the gale might last two or three days. The basket of provisions was, however, a large one. Dan had received orders to bring plenty and had obeyed them literally, and Vincent saw that the supply of food, if carefully husbanded, would last; without difficulty for a week. The supply of liquor was less satisfactory. There was the bottle of rum, two bottles of claret, and a two-gallon jar, nearly half empty, of water. The cold tea was finished.

"That would be a poor supply for a week for two of us," Vincent; muttered, as he removed the contents of the basket and stored them carefully in the locker; "however, if it's going to be a gale there is sure to be some rain with it, so I think we shall manage very well."

By night it was blowing really heavily, but although the waves were high the boat shipped but little water. Dan had fallen off to sleep, and Vincent had been glad to wrap himself in the thick coat he had brought with him as a protection against the heavy dews when sleeping on the river. At times sharp rain squalls burst upon them, and Vincent had no difficulty in filling up the water-bottle again with the bailer.

The water was rather brackish, but not sufficiently so to be of consequence. All night the boat was tossed heavily on the waves. Vincent dozed off at times, rousing himself occasionally and bailing out the water, which came in the shape of spray and rain. The prospect in the morning was not cheering. Gray clouds covered the sky and seemed to come down almost on to the water, the angry sea was crested with white heads, and it seemed to Vincent wonderful that the boat should live in such a sea.

"Now, Dan, wake yourself up and get some breakfast," Vincent said, stirring up the negro with his foot.

"Oh Lor'!" Dan groaned, raising himself into a sitting position from the bottom of the boat, "dis am awful; we neber see the shore no more, massa."

"Nonsense, man," Vincent said cheerily; "we are getting on capitally."

"It hab been an awful night, sah."

"An awful night! You lazy rascal, you slept like a pig all night, while I have been bailing the boat and looking out for you. It is your turn now, I can tell you. Well, do you feel ready for your breakfast?"

Dan, after a moment's consideration, declared that he was. The feeling of sea-sickness had passed off, and except that he was wet through and miserable, he felt himself again, and could have eaten four times the allowance of food that Vincent handed him. A pannikin of rum and water did much to restore his life and vitality, and he was soon, with the light-heartedness of his race, laughing and chatting cheerfully.

"How long dis go on, you tink, sah?"

"Not long, I hope, Dan. I was afraid last night it was going to be a big gale, but I do not think it is blowing so hard now as it was in the night."

"Where have we get to now, sah?"

"I don't exactly know, Dan; but I do not suppose that we are very many miles away from shore. The mast and oars prevent our drifting fast, and I don't think we are further off now than we were when we left that ship yesterday. But even if we were four or five times as far as that, we should not take very long in sailing back again when the wind drops, and as we have got enough to eat for a week we need not be uncomfortable about that."

"Not much food for a week, Massa Vincent."

"Not a very great deal, Dan; but quite enough to keep us going. You can make up for lost time when you get to shore again."

In a few hours it was certain that the wind was going down. By midday the clouds began to break up, and an hour later the sun was shining brightly. The wind was still blowing strongly, but the sea had a very different appearance in the bright light of the sun to that which it had borne under the canopy of dark gray clouds. Standing up in the boat two hours later, Vincent could see no signs of land.

"How shall we find our way back, Massa Vincent?"

"We have got a compass; besides, we should manage very well even if we had not. Look at the sun, Dan. There it is right ahead of us. So, you know, that's the west--that's the way we have to go."

"That very useful ob de sun, sah; but suppose we not live in de west de sun not point de way den."

"Oh, yes, he would, just the same, Dan. We should know whether to go away from him, or to keep him on the right hand or on the left."

This was beyond Dan. "And I s'pose the moon will show de way at night, massa?"

"The moon would show the way if she were up, but she is not always up; but I have got a compass here, and so whether we have the sun or the moon, or neither of them, I can find my way back to land."

Dan had never seen a compass, and for an hour amused himself turning it round and round and trying to get it to point in some other direction than the north.

"Now, Dan," Vincent said at last, "give me that compass, and get out the food. We will have a better meal than we did this morning, for now that the wind is going down there's no chance of food running short. When we have had dinner we will get up the sail again. The sea is not so rough as it was, and it is certainly not so high as it was before we lowered the sail yesterday."

"De waves berry big, massa."

"They are big, Dan; but they are not so angry. The heads are not breaking over as they did last night, and the boat will go better over those long waves than she did through the choppy sea at the beginning of the gale."

Accordingly the bundle of spars was pulled up alongside and lifted. The mast was set up and the sail hoisted. Dan in a few minutes forgot his fears and lost even his sense of uneasiness as he found the boat mounted wave after wave without shipping water. Several times, indeed, a shower of spray flew high up in the air, but the gusts no longer buried her so that the water came over the gunwale, and it was a long time before there was any occasion to use the bailer. As the sun set it could be seen that there was a dark line between it and the water.

"There is the land, Dan; and I do not suppose it is more than twenty miles away, for most of the coast lies low."

"But how we find de York River, massa? Will de compass tell you dat?"

"No, Dan. I don't know whether we have drifted north or south of it. At ordinary times the current runs up the coast, but the wind this morning was blowing from the north of west, and may have been doing so all through the night for anything I know. Well, the great thing is to make land. We are almost sure to come across some fishing-boats, but, if not, we must run ashore and find a house."

They continued sailing until Vincent's watch told him it was twelve o'clock, by which time the coast was quite close. The wind now almost dropped, and, lowering their sail, they rowed in until, on lowering the anchor, they found that it touched the ground. Then they lay down and slept till morning. Dan was the first to waken.

"Dar are some houses dere close down by the shore, sah, and some men getting out a boat."

"That's all right, Dan," Vincent said as he roused himself and looked over. "We shall learn soon where we are."

In a quarter of an hour the fishing-boat put off, and the lads at once rowed to it.

"How far are we from the mouth of the York River?" Vincent asked the two negroes on board.

"About twenty miles, sah. Where you come from?"

"We were off the mouth of the river, and were blown off in the gale."

"You tink yourself berry lucky you get back," one of them said. "Berry foolish to go out like dat when not know how to get back."

"Well, we have managed to get back now, you see, and none the worse for it. Now, Dan, up with the sail again."

There was a light wind off shore, and all the reefs being shaken out the boat ran along fast.

"I should think we are going about five miles an hour, Dan. We ought to be off the mouth of the river in four hours. We must look out sharp or else we shall pass it, for many of these islets look just like the mouth of the river. However, we are pretty sure to pass several fishing-boats on our way, and we shall be able to inquire from them."

There was no need, however, to do this. It was just the four hours from the time of starting when they saw some eight or ten fishing-boats ahead of them.

"I expect that that is the entrance to the river. When we get half a mile further we shall see it open."

On approaching the fishing-boats they recognized at once the appearance of the shore, as they had noticed it when fishing there before, and were soon in the entrance to the river.

"It will be high tide in about two hours," Vincent said, "according to the time it was the other day. I am afraid when it turns we shall have to get down our sails; there will be no beating against both wind and tide. Then we must get out oars and row. There is very little tide close in by the bank, and every little gain will be a help. We have been out four days. It is Thursday now, and they will be beginning to get very anxious at home, so we must do our best to get back."

Keeping close under the bank, they rowed steadily, making on an average about two miles an hour. After five hours' rowing they tied up to the bank, had a meal, and rested until tide turned; then they again hoisted their sail and proceeded on their way. Tide carried them just up to the junction of the two rivers, and landing at Cumberland they procured beds and slept till morning.

Another long day's work took them up to the plantation of Mr. Furniss, and fastening up the boat, and carrying the sails and oars on shore, they started on their walk home.

"Why, Vincent, where on earth have you been all this time?" Mrs. Wingfield said as her son entered. "You said you might be away a couple of nights; and we expected you back on Wednesday at the latest, and now it is Friday evening."

"Well, mother, we have had great fun. We went sailing about right down to the mouth of the York River. I did not calculate that it would take me more than twice as long to get back as to get down; but as the wind blew right down the river it was precious slow work, and we had to row all the way. However, it has been a jolly trip, and I feel a lot better for it."

"You don't look any better for it," Annie said. "The skin is all off your face, and you are as red as fire. Your clothes look shrunk as well as horribly dirty. You are quite an object, Vincent."

"We got caught in a heavy gale," Vincent said, "and got a thorough ducking. As to my face, a day or two will set it all to rights again; and so they will my hands, I hope, for I have got nicely blistered tugging at those oars. And now, mother, I want some supper, for I am as hungry as a hunter. I told Dan to go into the kitchen and get a good square meal."

The next morning, just after breakfast, there was the sound of horses' hoofs outside the house, and, looking out, Vincent saw Mr. Jackson, with a man he knew to be the sheriff, and four or five others. A minute later one of the servants came in, and said that the sheriff wished to speak to Mrs. Wingfield.

"I will go out to him," Mrs. Wingfield replied. Vincent followed her to the door.

"Mrs. Wingfield," the sheriff said, "I am the holder of a warrant; to search your slave-huts and grounds for a runaway negro named Anthony Moore, the property of Mr. Jackson here."

"Do you suppose, sir," Mrs. Wingfield asked angrily, "that I am the sort of person to give shelter to runaway slaves?"

"No, madam, certainly not," the sheriff replied; "no one would suppose for a moment that Mrs. Wingfield of the Orangery would have anything to do with a runaway, but Mr. Jackson here learned only yesterday that the wife of this slave was here, and every one knows that where the wife is the husband is not likely to be far off."

"I suppose, sir," Mrs. Wingfield said coldly, "that there was no necessity for me to acquaint Mr. Jackson formerly with the fact that I had purchased through my agent the woman he sold to separate her from her husband."

"By no means, madam, by no means; though, had we known it before, it might have been some aid to us in our search. Have we your permission to see this woman and to question her?"

"Certainly not," Mrs. Wingfield said; "but if you have any question to ask I will ask her and give you her answer."

"We want to know whether she has seen her husband since the day of his flight from the plantation?"

"I shall certainly not ask her that question, Mr. Sheriff. I have no doubt that, as the place from which he has escaped is only a few miles from here, he did come to see his wife. It would have been very strange if he did not. I hope that by this time the man is hundreds of miles away. He was brutally treated by a brutal master, who, I believe, deliberately set to work to make him run away, so that he could hunt him down and punish him. I presume, sir, you do not wish to search this house, and you do not suppose that the man is hidden here. As to the slave-huts and the plantation, you can, of course, search them thoroughly; but as it is now more than a fortnight since the man escaped, it is not likely you will find him hiding within a few miles of his master's plantation."

So saying she went into the house and shut the door behind her.

Mr. Jackson ground his teeth with rage, but the sheriff rode off toward the slave-huts without a word. The position of Mrs. Wingfield of the Orangery, connected as she was with half the old families of Virginia, and herself a large slave-owner, was beyond suspicion, and no one would venture to suggest that such a lady could have the smallest sympathy for a runaway slave.

"She was down upon you pretty hot, Mr. Jackson," the sheriff said as they rode off. "You don't seem to be in her good books." Jackson muttered an imprecation.

"It is certainly odd," the sheriff went on, "after what you were telling me about her son pitching into Andrew over flogging this very slave, that she should go and buy his wife. Still, that's a very different thing from hiding a runaway. I dare say that, as she says, the fellow came here to see his wife when he first ran away; but I don't think you will find him anywhere about here now. It's pretty certain from what we hear that he hasn't made for the North, and where the fellow can be hiding I can't think. Still the woods about this country are mighty big, and the fellow can go out on to the farms and pick corn and keep himself going for a long time. Still, he's sure to be brought up sooner or later."

A thorough search was made of the slave-huts, and the slaves were closely questioned, but all denied any knowledge of the runaway. Dan escaped questioning, as he had taken up Vincent's horse to the house in readiness for him to start as soon as he had finished breakfast.

All day the searchers rode about the plantation examining every clump of bushes, and assuring themselves that none of them had been used as a place of refuge for the runaway.

"It's no good, Mr. Jackson," the sheriff said at last. "The man may have been here; he ain't here now. The only place we haven't; searched is the house, and you may be quite sure the slaves dare not conceal him there. Too many would get to know it. No, sir, he's made a bolt of it, and you will have to wait now till he is caught by chance, or shot by some farmer or other in the act of stealing."

"I would lay a thousand dollars," Andrew Jackson exclaimed passionately, "that young Wingfield knows something about his whereabouts, and has lent him a hand!"

"Well, I should advise you to keep your mouth shut about it till you get some positive proof," the sheriff said dryly. "I tell you it's no joke to accuse a member of a family like the Wingfields of helping runaway slaves to escape."

"I will bide my time," the planter said. "You said that some day you would lay hands on Tony dead or alive. You see if some day I don't lay hands on young Wingfield."

"Well, it seems, Mr. Jackson," the sheriff remarked with a sneer, for he was out of temper at the ill success of the day's work, "that he has already laid hands on your son. It seems to me quite as likely that he will lay hands on you as you on him."

Two days afterward as Vincent was riding through the streets of Richmond he saw to his surprise Andrew Jackson in close conversation with Jonas Pearson.

"I wonder what those two fellows are talking about?" he said to himself. "I expect Jackson is trying to pump Pearson as to the doings at the Orangery. I don't like that fellow, and never shall, and he is just the sort of man to do one a bad turn if he had the chance. However, as I have never spoken to him about that affair from beginning to end, I don't see that he can do any mischief if he wants to."

Andrew Jackson, however, had obtained information which he considered valuable. He learned that Vincent had been away in a boat for five days, and that his mother had been very uneasy about him. He also learned that the boat was one belonging to Mr. Furniss, and that it was only quite lately that Vincent had taken to going out sailing.

After considerable trouble he succeeded in getting at one of the slaves upon Mr. Furniss' plantation. But he could only learn from him that Vincent had been unaccompanied when he went out in the boat either by young Furniss or by any of the plantation hands; that he had taken with him only his own slave, and had come and gone as he chose, taking out and fastening up the boat himself, so that no one could say when he had gone out, except that his horse was put up at the stables. The slave said that certainly the horse had only stood there on two or three occasions, and then only for a few hours, and that unless Mr. Wingfield had walked over he could never have had the boat out all night, as the horse certainly had not stood all night in the stables.

Andrew Jackson talked the matter over with his son, and both agreed that Vincent's conduct was suspicious. His own people said he had been away for five days in the boat. The people at Furniss' knew nothing about this, and therefore there must be some mystery about it, and they doubted not that that mystery was connected with the runaway slave, and they guessed that he had either taken Tony and landed him near the mouth of the York River on the northern shore, or that he had put him on board a ship. They agreed, however, that whatever their suspicions, they had not sufficient grounds for openly accusing Vincent of aiding their runaway.

# CHAPTER V. SECESSION.

WHILE Vincent had been occupied with the affairs of Tony and his wife, public events had moved forward rapidly. The South Carolina Convention met in the third week in December, and on the 20th of that month the Ordinance of Secession was passed. On the 10th of January, three days after Vincent returned home from his expedition, Florida followed the example of South Carolina and seceded. Alabama and Mississippi passed the Ordinance of Secession on the following day; Georgia on the 18th, Louisiana on the 23d, and Texas on the 1st of February.

In all these States the Ordinance of Session was received with great rejoicing: bonfires were lit, the towns illuminated, and the militia paraded the streets, and in many cases the Federal arsenals were seized and the Federal forts occupied by the State troops. In the meantime the Northern Slave States, Virginia, North Carolina, Tennessee, Kentucky, and Missouri, remained irresolute. The general feeling was strongly in favor of their Southern brethren; but they were anxious for peace, and for a compromise being arrived at. Whether the North would agree to admit the constitutional rights of secession, or whether it would use force to compel the Seceding States to remain in the Union, was still uncertain; but the idea of a civil war was so terrible a one that the general belief was that some arrangement to allow the States to go their own way would probably be arrived at.

For the time the idea of Vincent going to West Point was abandoned. Among his acquaintances were several young men who were already at West Point, and very few of these returned to the academy. The feeling there was very strongly on the side of secession. A great majority of the students came from the Southern States, as while the sons of the Northern men went principally into trade and commerce, the Southern planters sent their sons into the army, and a great proportion of the officers of the army and navy were Southerners.

As the professors at West Point were all military men, the feeling among them, as well as among the students, was in favor of State rights; they considering that, according to the constitution, their allegiance was due first to the States of which they were natives, and in the second place to the Union. Thus, then, many of the professors who were natives of the seven States which had seceded resigned their appointments, and returned home to occupy themselves in drilling the militia and the levies, who were at once called to arms.

Still all hoped that peace would be preserved, until on the 11th of April General Beauregard, who commanded the troops of South Carolina, summoned Major Anderson, who was in command of the Federal troops in Fort Sumter, to surrender, and on his refusal opened fire upon the fort on the following day.

On the 13th, the barracks of the fort being set on fire, and Major Anderson seeing the hopelessness of a prolonged resistance, surrendered. The effect of the news throughout the United States was tremendous, and Mr. Lincoln at once called out 75,000 men of the militia of the various States to put down the rebellion--the border States being ordered to send their proportion. This brought matters to a climax. Virginia, North Carolina, Kentucky, Tennessee, and Missouri all refused to furnish contingents to act against the Southern States; and Virginia, North Carolina, and Kansas a few days later passed Ordinances of Secession and joined the Southern States. Missouri, Maryland, and Delaware were divided in their counsels.

The struggle that was about to commence was an uneven one. The white population of the Seceding States was about 8,000,000; while that the Northern States were 19,614,885. The North possessed an immense advantage, inasmuch as they retained the whole of the Federal navy, and were thereby enabled at once to cut off all communication between the Southern States and Europe, while they themselves could draw unlimited supplies of munitions of war of all kinds from across the Atlantic.

Although the people of Virginia had hoped to the last that some peaceful arrangement might be effected, the Act of Secession was received with enthusiasm. The demand of Mr. Lincoln that they should furnish troops to crush their Southern brethren excited the liveliest indignation, and Virginia felt that there was no course open to her now but to throw in her lot with the other Slaves States. Her militia was at once called out, and volunteers called for to form a provisional army to protect the State from invasion by the North.

The appeal was answered with enthusiasm; men of all ages took up arms; the wealthy raised regiments at their own expense, generally handing over the commands to experienced army officers, and themselves taking their places in the ranks; thousand of lads of from fifteen to sixteen years of age enrolled themselves, and men who had never done a day's work in their life prepared to suffer all the hardships of the campaign as private soldiers.

Mrs. Wingfield was an enthusiastic supporter of State rights; and when Vincent told her that numbers of his friends were going to enroll themselves as soon as the lists were opened, she offered no objection to his doing the same.

"Of course you are very young, Vincent; but no one thinks there will be any serious fighting. Now that Virginia and the other four States have cast in their lot with the seven that have seceded, the North can never hope to force the solid South back into the Union. Still it is right you should join. I certainly should not like an old Virginian family like ours to be unrepresented; but I should prefer your joining one of the mounted corps.

"In the first place it will be much less fatiguing than carrying a heavy rifle and knapsack; and in the second place, the cavalry will for the most part be gentlemen. I was speaking only yesterday when I went into Richmond to Mr. Ashley, who is raising a corps. He is one of the best riders in the country, and a splendid specimen of a Virginian gentleman. He tells me that he has already received a large number of applications from young volunteers, and that he thinks he shall be able without any difficulty to get as many as he wants. I said that I had a son who would probably enroll himself, and that I should like to have him in his corps.

"He said that he would be glad to put down your name, and that he had had many applications from lads no older than yourself. He considered that for cavalry work, scouting, and that sort; of thing age mattered little, and that; a lad who was at once a light weight, a good rider, and a good shot was of as much good as a man."

"Thank you, mother. I will ride into Richmond to-morrow morning and see Ashley. I have often met him at one house or another, and should like to serve under him very much. I should certainly prefer being in the cavalry to the infantry."

Rosie and Annie, who were of course enthusiastic for the South, were almost as pleased as was Vincent when they heard that their mother had consented to his enrolling himself. So many of the girls of their acquaintance had brothers or cousins who were joining the army, that they would have felt it as something like a slur upon the family name had Vincent remained behind.

On the following morning Vincent rode over and saw Mr. Ashley, who had just; received his commission as major. He was cordially received.

"Mrs. Wingfield was speaking to me about you, and I shall be glad to have you with me--the more so as you are a capital rider and a good shot. I shall have a good many in my ranks no older than you are. Did I not hear a few months since that you bought Wildfire? I thought when I heard it; that you would be lucky if you did not get your neck broken in the course of a week. Peters, who owns the next estate to mine, had the horse for about three weeks, and was glad enough to get rid of it for half what he had given for it. He told me the horse was the most savage brute he ever saw. I suppose you did not keep it many days?"

"I have got it still, and mean to ride it with you. The horse was not really savage. It was hot-tempered, and had, I think, been badly treated by its first owner. Who-ever it had belonged to, I found no difficulty with it. It only wanted kindness and a little patience; and as soon as it found that it could not get rid of me, and that I had no intention of ill-treating it, it settled down quietly, after running away a few times and giving me some little trouble at starting. And now I would not change it for any horse in the State."

"You must be a first-rate rider," Major Ashley said, "to be able to tame Wildfire. I never saw the horse, for I was away when Peters had him, but from his description it was a perfect savage."

"Are we allowed to bring a servant with us?" Vincent asked.

"Yes, if you like. I know that a good many are going to do so, but you must not make up your mind that you will get much benefit from one. We shall move rapidly, and each man must shift for himself, but at the same time we shall of course often be stationary; and then servants will be useful. At any rate I can see no objection to men having them. We must be prepared to rough it to any extent when it is necessary, but I see no reason why at other times a man should not make himself comfortable. I expect the order to-morrow or next day to begin formally to enroll volunteers. As I have now put down your name there will be no occasion for you to come in then. You will receive a communication telling you when to report yourself.

"I shall not trouble much about uniform at first. High boots and breeches, a thick felt hat that will turn the edge of a sword, and a loose coat-jacket of dark-gray cloth. That is the name of the tailor who has got the pattern, and will make them. So I should advise you to go to him at once, for he will be so busy soon that; there is no saying when the whole troop will get their uniforms."

Upon his return home Vincent related to his mother and sisters the conversation that he had had with Major Ashley.

"Certainly you had better take a servant with you," his mother said. "I suppose when you are riding about; you will have to clean your horse, and cook your dinner, and do everything for yourself; but when you are in a town you should have these things done for you. Who would you like to take?

"I should like to take Dan, mother, if you have no objection. He is very strong and active, and I think would generally be able to keep up with us; besides, I know he would always stick to me."

"You shall have him certainly, Vincent; I will make him over formally to you."

"Thank you, mother," Vincent said joyfully; for he had often wished that Dan belonged to him, as he would then be able to prevent any interference with him by the overseer or any one else, and could, if he liked, give him his freedom--although this would, he knew, be of very doubtful advantage to the lad as long as he remained in the South.

The next morning the necessary papers were drawn up, and the ownership of Dan was formally transferred to Vincent. Dan was wild with delight when he heard that Vincent was now his master, and that he was to accompany him to the war. It had been known two days before that Vincent was going, and it seemed quite shocking to the negroes that the young master should go as a private soldier, and have to do everything for himself-"just," as they said, "like de poor white trash;" for the slaves were proud to belong to an old family, and looked down with almost contempt upon the poorer class of whites, regarding their own position as infinitely superior.

Four days later Vincent received an official letter saying that the corps would be mustered in two days' time. The next day was spent in a long round of farewell visits, and then Vincent mounted Wildfire, and, with Dan trotting behind, rode off from the Orangery amid a chorus of blessings and good wishes from all the slaves who could on any pretext get away from their duties, and who had assembled in front of the house to see him start.

The place of meeting for the regiment was at Hanover Courthouse--a station on the Richmond and Fredericksburg Railway, close to the Pamunkey River, about eighteen miles from the city.

The Orangery was a mile from the village of Gaines, which lay to the northeast of Richmond, and was some twelve miles from Hanover Courthouse.

A month was spent in drill, and at the end of that time the corps were able to execute any simple maneuver. More than this Major Ashley did not care about their learning. The work in which they were about to engage was that of scouts rather than that of regular cavalry, and the requirements were vigilance and attention to orders, good shooting and a quick eye. Off duty there was but little discipline. Almost the whole of the men were in a good position in life, and many of them very wealthy; and while strict discipline and obedience were expected while on duty, at all other times something like equality existed between officers and men, and all were free to live as they chose.

The rations served out were simple and often scanty, for at present the various departments were not properly organized, and such numbers of men were flocking to the standards that the authorities were at their wit's end to provide them with even the simplest food. This mattered but little, however, to the regiment, whose members were all ready and willing to pay for everything they wanted, and the country people round found a ready market for all their chickens, eggs, fruit, and vegetables at Hanover Courthouse, for here there were also several infantry regiments, and the normally quiet little village was a scene of bustle and confusion.

The arms of the cavalry were of a very varied description. Not more than a dozen had swords; the rest were armed with rifles or shot-guns, with the barrels cut short to enable them to be carried as carbines. Many of them were armed with revolvers, and some carried pistols so antiquated that they might have been used in the revolutionary war. A certain number of tents had been issued for the use of the corps. These, however, were altogether insufficient for the numbers, and most of the men preferred to sleep in shelters composed of canvas, carpets, blankets, or any other material that came to hand, or in arbors constructed of the boughs of trees, for it was now April and warm enough to sleep in the open air.

In the third week in May the order came that the corps was to march at once for Harper's Ferry--an important position at the point where the Shenandoah River runs into the Potomac, at the mouth of the Shenandoah Valley. The order was received with the greatest satisfaction. The Federal forces were gathering rapidly upon the northern banks of the Potomac, and it was believed that, while the main army would march down from Washington through Manassas Junction direct upon Richmond, another would enter by the Shenandoah Valley, and, crossing the Blue Ridge Mountains, come down on the rear of the Confederate army, facing the main force at Manassas. The cavalry marched by road, while the infantry were despatched by rail as far as Manassas Junction, whence they marched to Harper's Ferry. The black servants accompanied the infantry.

The cavalry march was a pleasant one. At every village through which they passed the people flocked out with offerings of milk and fruit. The days were hot, but the mornings and evenings delightful; and as the troops always halted in the shade of a wood for three or four hours in the middle of the day, the marches although long were not fatiguing. At Harper's Ferry General Johnston had just superseded Colonel Jackson in command. The force there consisted of 11 battalions of infantry, 16 guns, and after Ashley's force arrived, 300 cavalry. Among the regiments there Vincent found many friends, and learned what was going on.

He learned that Colonel Jackson had been keeping them hard at work. Some of Vincent's friends had been at the Virginia Military Institute at Lexington, where Jackson was professor of natural philosophy and instructor of artillery.

"He was the greatest fun," one of the young men said; "the stiffest and most awkward-looking fellow in the institute. He used to walk about as if he never saw anything or anybody. He was always known as Old Tom, and nobody ever saw him laugh. He was awfully earnest in all he did, and strict, I can tell you, about everything. There was no humbugging him. The fellows liked him because he was really so earnest about everything, and always just and fair. But he didn't look a bit like a soldier except as to his stiffness, and when the fellows who had been at Lexington heard that he was in command here they did not think he would have made much hand at it; but I tell you, he did. You never saw such a fellow to work.

"Everything had to be done, you know. There were the guns, but no horses and no harness. The horses had to be got somehow, and the harness manufactured out of ropes; and you can imagine the confusion of nine battalions of infantry, all recruits, with no one to teach them except a score or two of old army and militia officers. Old Tom has done wonders, I can tell you. You see, he is so fearfully earnest himself every one else has got to be earnest. There has been no playing about anything, but just fifteen hours' hard work a day. Fellows grumbled and growled and said it was absurd, and threatened to do all sorts of things. You see, they had all come out to fight if necessary, but hadn't bargained for such hard work as this.

"However, Jackson had his way, and I don't suppose any one ever told him the men thought they were too hard worked. He is not the sort of man one would care about remonstrating with. I don't know yet whether he is as good at fighting as he is at working and organizing; but I rather expect a fellow who is so earnest about everything else is sure to be earnest about fighting, and I fancy that when he once gets into the thick of it he will go through with it. He had such a reputation as an oddity at Lexington that there were a lot of remarks when he was made colonel and sent here; but there is no doubt that he has proved himself the right man so far, and although his men may grumble they believe in him.

"My regiment is in his brigade, and I will bet any money that we have our share of fighting. What sort of man is Johnston? He is a fine fellow--a soldier, heart and soul. You could tell him anywhere, and we have a first-rate fellow in command of the cavalry--Colonel Stuart--a splendid dashing fellow, full of life and go. His fellows swear by him. I quite envy you, for I expect you will astonish the Yankee horsemen. They are no great riders up there, you know, and I expect the first time you meet them you will astonish them."

Here he suddenly stopped, stood at attention, and saluted.

Vincent at once did the same, although, had he not been set the example by his friend, he would never have thought of doing so to the figure who passed.

"Who is it?" he asked, as his companion resumed his easy attitude.

"Why, that's Old Tom."

"What! Colonel Jackson!" Vincent said in surprise. "Well, he is an odd-looking fellow."

The figure that had passed was that of a tall, gaunt man, leaning awkwardly forward in his saddle. He wore an old gray coat, and there was no sign of rank, nor particle of gold lace upon the uniform. He wore on his head a faded cadet cap, with the rim coming down so far upon his nose that he could only look sideways from under it. He seemed to pay but little attention to what was going on around him, and did not enter into conversation with any of the officers he met.

The brigade commanded by Jackson was the first of the army of the Shenandoah, and consisted of the 2d, 4th, 5th, and 27th Virginians, to which was shortly afterward added the 33d. They were composed of men of all ranks and ages, among them being a great number of lads from fifteen and upward; for every school had been deserted. Every boy capable of carrying a musket had insisted upon joining, and among them were a whole company of cadets from Lexington. The regiments selected their own officers, and among these were many who were still lads. Many of the regiments had no accouterments, and were without uniforms, and numbers carried no better arms than a double-barreled shot-gun; but all were animated with the same spirit of enthusiasm in their cause, and a determination to die rather than to allow the invaders to pass on through the fertile valleys of their native land.

Of all these valleys that of Shenandoah was the richest and most beautiful. It was called the Garden of Virginia; and all writers agreed in their praises of the beauties of its fields and forests, mountains and rivers, its delicious climate, and the general prosperity which prevailed among its population.

It was a pleasant evening that Ashley's horse spent at Harper's Ferry on the day they marched in. All had many friends among the other Virginian regiments, and their camp-fires were the center toward which men trooped by scores. The rest was pleasant after their hard marches; and, although ready to do their own work when necessary, they appreciated the advantage of having their servants again with them to groom their horses and cook their food.

The negroes were not less glad at being again with their masters. Almost all were men who had, like Dan, been brought up with their young owners, and felt for them a strong personal attachment, and, if it had been allowed, would gladly have followed them in the field of battle, and fought by their side against the "Yankees." Their stay at Harper's Ferry was to be a short one. Colonel Stuart, with his 200 horse, was scouting along the whole bank of the Potomac, watching every movement of the enemy, and Ashley's horse was to join them at once.

It was not difficult for even young soldiers to form an idea of the general nature of the operations. They had to protect the Shenandoah Valley, to guard the five great roads by which the enemy would advance against Winchester, and not only to save the loyal inhabitants and rich resources of the valley from falling into the hands of the Federals, but what was of even greater importance, to prevent the latter from marching across the Blue Ridge Mountains, and falling upon the flank of the main Confederate army at Manassas.

The position was a difficult one, for while "the grand army" was assembling at Alexandria to advance against Manassas Junction, McClellan was advancing from the northwest with 20,000 men, and Patterson from Pennsylvania with 18,000.

In the morning before parading his troop, 100 strong, Ashley called them together and told them that, as they would now be constantly on the move and scattered over a long line, it was impossible that they could take their servants with them.

"I should never have allowed them to be brought," he said, "had I known that we should be scouting over such an extensive country; at the same time, if we can manage to take a few on it would certainly add to our comfort. I propose that we choose ten by lot to go on with us. They must be servants of the troop and not of individuals. We can scatter them in pairs at five points, with instructions to forage as well as they can, and to have things in readiness to cook for whoever may come in off duty or may for the time be posted there. Henceforth every man must groom and see to his own horse, but I see no reason, military or otherwise, why we shouldn't get our food cooked for us; and it will be just as well, as long as we can, to have a few bundles of straw for us to lie on instead of sleeping on the ground.

"Another ten men we can also choose by lot to go to Winchester; which is, I imagine, the point we shall move to if the enemy advance, as I fancy they will, from the other side of the Shenandoah Valley. The rest must be sent home."

Each man accordingly wrote his name on a piece of paper, and placed them in a haversack. Ten were then drawn out; and their servants were to accompany the troop at once. The servants of the next ten were to proceed by train to Winchester, while the slaves of all whose names remained in the bag were to be sent home at once, provided with passes permitting them to travel. To Vincent's satisfaction his name was one of the first ten drawn, and Dan was therefore to go forward. The greater part of the men evaded the obligation to send their servants back to Richmond by despatching them to friends who had estates in the Shenandoah Valley, with letters asking them to keep the men for them until the troop happened to come into their neighborhood.

At six o'clock in the morning the troop mounted and rode to Bath, thirty miles away. It was here that Stuart had his headquarters, whence he sent out his patrols up and down the Potomac, between Harper's Ferry on the east and Cumberland on the west. Stuart was away when they arrived, but he rode in a few hours afterward.

"Ah! Ashley, I am glad you have arrived," he said, as he rode up to the troop, who had hastily mounted as he was seen approaching. "There is plenty for you to do, I can tell you; and I only wish that you had brought a thousand men instead of a hundred. I am heartily glad to see you all, gentlemen," he said to the troop. "I am afraid just at first that the brightness of your gray jackets will put my men rather to shame; but we shall soon get rid of that. But dismount your men, Ashley; there is plenty for them and their horses to do without wasting time in parade work. There is very little of that here, I can tell you. I have not seen a score of my men together for the last month."

Vincent gazed with admiration at the young leader, whose name was soon to be celebrated throughout America and Europe. The young Virginian--for he was not yet twenty-eight years old--was the beau ideal of a cavalry officer. He was singularly handsome, and possessed great personal strength and a constitution which enabled him to bear all hardships. He possessed unfailing good spirits, and had a joke and laugh for all he met; and while on the march at the head of his regiment he was always ready to lift up his voice and lead the songs with which the men made the woods resound.

He seemed to live in his saddle, and was present at all hours of the night and day along the line he guarded seeing that the men were watchful and on the alert, instructing the outposts in their duty, and infusing his own spirit and vigilance among them. He had been educated at West Point, and had seen much service with the cavalry against the Indians in the West. Such was the man who was to become the most famous cavalry leader of his time. So far he had not come in contact with the enemy, and his duties were confined to obtaining information regarding their strength and intentions, to watching every road by which they could advance, and to seeing that none passed north to carry information to the enemy as to the Confederate strength and positions, for even in the Shenandoah Valley there were some whose sympathies were with the Federals.

These were principally Northern men settled as traders in the towns, and it was important to prevent them from sending any news to the enemy. So well did Stuart's cavalry perform this service, and so general was the hostility of the population against the North, that throughout the whole of the war in Virginia it was very seldom that the Northern generals could obtain any trustworthy information as to the movements and strength of the Confederates, while the latter were perfectly informed of every detail connected with the intentions of the invaders.

The next morning Ashley's troop took up their share of the work at the front. They were broken up into parties of ten, each of which was stationed at a village near the river, five men being on duty night and day. As it happened that none of the other men in his squad had a servant at the front, Vincent was able without difficulty to have Dan assigned to his party. A house in the village was placed at their disposal, and here the five off duty slept and took their meals while the others were in the saddle. Dan was quite in his element, and turned out an excellent cook, and was soon a general favorite among the mess.

## CHAPTER VI. BULL RUN.

THE next fortnight passed by without adventure. Hard as the work was, Vincent enjoyed it thoroughly. When on duty by day he was constantly on the move, riding through the forest, following country lanes, questioning every one he came across; and as the men always worked in pairs, there was no feeling of loneliness. Sometimes Ashley would draw together a score of troopers, and crossing the river in a ferryboat, would ride twenty miles north, and, dashing into quiet villages, astonish the inhabitants by the sight of the Confederate uniform. Then the villagers would be questioned as to the news that had reached them of the movement of the troops; the post office would be seized and the letters broken open; any useful information contained in them being noted. But in general questions were readily answered; for a considerable portion of the people of Maryland were strongly in favor of the South, and were only prevented from joining it by the strong force that held possession of Baltimore, and by the constant movement of Federal armies through the State. Vincent was often employed in carrying despatches from Major Ashley to Stuart, being selected for that duty as being the best mounted man in the troop. The direction was always a vague one. "Take this letter to Colonel Stuart, wherever he may be," and however early he started, Vincent thought himself fortunate if he carried out his mission before sunset; for Stuart's front covered over fifty miles of ground, and there was no saying where he might be. Sometimes after riding thirty or forty miles, and getting occasional news that Stuart had passed through ahead of him, he would learn from some outpost that the colonel had been there but ten minutes before, and had ridden off before he came, and then Vincent had to turn his horse and gallop back again, seldom succeeding in overtaking his active commander until the latter had halted for his supper at one or other of the villages where his men were stationed. Sometimes by good luck he came upon him earlier, and then, after reading the despatch, Stuart would, if he were riding in the direction where Ashley's command lay, bid him ride on with him, and would chat with him on terms of friendly intimacy about people they both knew at Richmond, or as to the details of his work, and sometimes they would sit down together under the shade of some trees, take out the contents of their haversacks, and share their dinners.

"This is the second time I have had the best of this," the colonel laughed one day; "my beef is as hard as leather, and this cold chicken of yours is as plump and tender as one could wish to eat."

"I have my own boy, colonel, who looks after the ten of us stationed at Elmside, and I fancy that in the matter of cold rations he gives me an undue preference. He always hands me my haversack when I mount with a grin, and I quite understand that it is better I should ask no questions as to its contents."

"You are a lucky fellow," Stuart said. "My own servant is a good man, and would do anything for me; but my irregular hours are too much for him. He never knows when to expect me; and as he often finds that when I do return I have made a meal an hour before at one of the outposts, and do not want the food he has for hours been carefully keeping hot for me, it drives him almost to despair, and I have sometimes been obliged to eat rather than disappoint him. But he certainly has not a genius for cooking, and were it not that this riding gives one the appetite of a hunter, I should often have a good deal of difficulty in devouring the meat he puts into my haversack."

But the enemy were now really advancing, and on the 12th of June a trooper rode in from the extreme left, and handed to Vincent a despatch from Colonel Stuart.

"My orders were," he said, "that, if you were here, you were to carry this on at all speed to General Johnston. If not, some one else was to take it on."

"Any news?" Vincent asked, as aided by Dan he rapidly saddled Wildfire.

"Yes," the soldier said; "2,000 of the enemy have advanced up the Western side and have occupied Romney, and they say that all Patterson's force is on the move."

"So much the better," Vincent replied, as he jumped into the saddle. "We have been doing nothing long enough, and the sooner it comes the better."

It was a fifty-mile ride; but it was done in five hours, and at the end of that time

Vincent dismounted in front of General Johnston's quarters.

"Is the general in?" he asked the sentry at the door.

"No, he is not in; but here he comes," the soldier replied, and two minutes later the general, accompanied by three or four officers, rode up.

Vincent saluted, and handed him the despatch. The general opened it and glanced at the contents.

"The storm is going to burst at last, gentlemen," he said to the officers. "Stuart writes me that 2,000 men, supposed to be the advance of McClellan's army, are at Romney, and that he hears Patterson is also advancing from Chambersburg on Williamsport. His despatch is dated this morning at nine o'clock. He writes from near Cumberland. No time has been lost, for that is eighty miles away, and it is but five o'clock now. How far have you brought this despatch, sir?"

"I have brought it from Elmside, general; twenty miles on the other side of Bath. A trooper brought it in just at midday, with orders for me to carry it on at once."

"That is good work," the general said. "You have ridden over fifty miles in five hours. You must be well mounted, sir."

"I do not think there is a better horse in the State," Vincent said, patting Wildfire's neck.

The general called an orderly.

"Let this man picket his horse with those of the staff," he said, "and see that it has forage at once. Take the man to the orderly's quarters, and see that he is well cared for."

Vincent saluted, and, leading Wildfire, followed the orderly. When he had had a meal, he strolled out to see what was going on. Evidently some movement was in contemplation. Officers were riding up or dashing off from the general's headquarters. Two or three regiments were seen marching down from the plateau on which they were encamped into the town. Bells rang and drums beat, and presently long trains of railway wagons, heavily laden, began to make their way across the bridge. Until next morning the movement continued unceasingly; by that time all the military stores and public property, together with as much private property belonging to inhabitants who had decided to forsake their homes for a time rather than to remain there when the town was occupied by the enemy, as could be carried on in the available wagons, had been taken across the bridge. A party of engineers, who had been all night hard at work, then set fire both to the railway bridge across the river and the public buildings in the town. The main body of troops had moved across in the evening. The rear-guard passed when all was in readiness for the destruction of the bridge.

General Johnston had been preparing for the movement for some time; he had foreseen that the position must be evacuated as soon as the enemy began to advance upon either of his flanks, and a considerable portion of his baggage and military stores had some time previously been sent into the interior of Virginia. The troops, formed up on the high grounds south of the river, looked in silence at the dense volumes of smoke rising. This was the reality of war. Hitherto their military work had been no more than that to which many of them were accustomed when called out with the militia of their State; but the scene of destruction on which they now gazed brought home to them that the struggle was a serious one--that it was war in its stern reality which had now begun.

The troops at once set off on their march, and at night bivouacked in the woods around Charlestown. The next day they pushed across the country and took up a position covering Winchester; and then the enemy, finding that Johnston's army was in front of them ready to dispute their advance, recrossed the river, and Johnston concentrated his force round Winchester.

Vincent joined his corps on the same afternoon that the infantry marched out from Harper's Ferry, the general sending him forward with despatches as soon as the troops had got into motion.

"You will find Colonel Stuart in front of the enemy; but more than that I cannot tell you."

This was quite enough for Vincent, who found the cavalry scouting close to Patterson's force, prepared to attack the enemy's cavalry should it advance to reconnoiter the country, and to blow up bridges across streams, fell trees, and take every possible measure to delay the advance of Patterson's army, in its attempt to push on toward Winchester before the arrival of General Johnston's force upon the scene.

"I am glad to see you back, Wingfield," Major Ashley said, as he rode up. "The colonel tells me that in the despatch he got last night from Johnston the general said that Stuart's information had reached in a remarkably short time, having been carried with great speed by the orderly in charge of the duty. We have scarcely been out of our saddles since you left. However, I think we have been of use, for we have been busy all round the enemy since we arrived here in the afternoon, and I fancy he must think us a good deal stronger than we are. At any rate, he has not pushed his cavalry forward at all; and, as you say Johnston will be up to-morrow afternoon. Winchester is safe anyhow."

After the Federals had recrossed the river, and Johnston had taken up his position round Winchester, the cavalry returned to their old work of scouting along the Potomac.

On the 20th of June movements of considerable bodies of the enemy were noticed; and Johnston at once despatched Jackson with his brigade to Martinsburg, with orders to send as much of the rolling-stock of the railroad as could be removed to Winchester, to destroy the rest, and to support Stuart's cavalry when they advanced. A number of locomotives were sent to Winchester along the highroad, drawn by teams of horses. Forty engines and 300 cars were burned or destroyed, and Jackson then advanced and took up his position on the road to Williamsport, the cavalry camp being a little in advance of him. This was pleasant for Vincent, as when off duty he spent his time with his friends and schoolfellows in Jackson's brigade.

On the 2d of July the scouts rode into camp with the news that a strong force was advancing from Williamsport. Jackson at once advanced with the 5th Virginia Infantry, numbering 380 men and one gun, while Stuart, with 100 cavalry, started to make a circuitous route, and harassed the flank and rear of the enemy. There was no intention on the part of Jackson of fighting a battle, his orders being merely to feel the enemy; whose strength was far too great to be withstood even had he brought his whole brigade into action, for they numbered three brigades of infantry, 500 cavalry, and some artillery.

For some hours the little Confederate force skirmished so boldly that they checked the advance of the enemy, whose general naturally supposed that he had before him the advanced guard of a strong force, and therefore moved forward with great caution. Then the Confederates, being threatened on both flanks by the masses of the Federals, fell back in good order. The loss was very trifling on either side, but the fact that so small a force had for hours checked the advance of an army greatly raised the spirits and confidence of the Confederates. Stuart's small cavalry force, coming down upon the enemy's rear, captured a good many prisoners--Colonel Stuart himself capturing forty-four infantry. Riding some distance ahead of his troop to find out the position of the enemy, he came upon a company of Federal infantry sitting down in a field, having no idea whatever that any Confederate force was in the neighborhood. Stuart did not hesitate a moment, but riding up to them shouted the order, "Throw down your arms, or you are all dead men." Believing themselves surrounded, the Federals threw down their arms, and when the Confederate cavalry came up were marched off as prisoners.

Jackson, on reaching his camp, struck his tents and sent them to the rear, and formed up his whole brigade in order of battle. The Federals, however, instead of attacking, continued their flank movement, and Jackson fell back through Martinsburg and halted for the night a mile beyond the town.

Next day he again retired, and was joined six miles further on by Johnston's whole force. For four days the little army held its position, prepared to give battle if the enemy advanced; but the Federals, though greatly superior in numbers, remained immovable at Martinsburg, and Johnston, to the great disgust of his troops, retired to Winchester. The soldiers were longing to meet the invaders in battle, but their general had to bear in mind that the force under his command might at any moment be urgently required to join the main Confederate army and aid in opposing the Northern advance upon Richmond.

Stuart's cavalry kept him constantly informed of the strength of the enemy gathering in his front. Making circuits round Martinsburg, they learned from the farmers what numbers of troops each day came along; and while the Federals knew nothing of the force opposed to them, and believed that it far outnumbered their own, General Johnston knew that Patterson's force numbered about 22,000 men, while he himself had been joined only by some 3,000 men since he arrived at Winchester.

On the 18th of July a telegram from the government at Richmond announced that the Federal grand army had driven in General Beauregard's pickets at Manassas, and had begun to advance, and Johnston was directed if possible to hasten to his assistance. A few earthworks had been thrown up at Winchester, and some guns mounted upon them, and the town was left under the protection of the local militia. Stuart's cavalry was posted in a long line across the country to prevent any news of the movement reaching the enemy. As soon as this was done the infantry, 8,300 strong, marched off. The troops were in high spirits now, for they knew that their long period of inactivity was over, and that, although ignorant when and where, they were on their march to meet the enemy.

They had no wagons or rations, the need for speed was too urgent even to permit of food being cooked. Without a halt they pressed forward steadily, and after two days' march, exhausted and half famished, they reached the Manassas Gap Railroad. There they were put into trains as fast as these could be prepared, and by noon on the 20th joined Beauregard at Manassas. The cavalry had performed their duty of preventing the news of the movement from reaching the enemy until the infantry were nearly a day's march away, and then Stuart reassembled his men and followed Johnston. Thus the Confederate plans had been completely successful. Over 30,000 of the enemy, instead of being in line of battle with the main army, were detained before Winchester, while the little Confederate force who had been facing them had reached Beauregard in time to take part in the approaching struggle.

In the North no doubt as to the power of the grand army to make its way to Richmond was entertained. The troops were armed with the best weapons obtainable, the artillery was numerous and excellent, the army was fed with every luxury, and so confident were the men of success that they regarded the whole affair in the light of a great picnic. The grand army numbered 55,000 men, with 9 regiments of cavalry and 49 rifle-guns. To oppose these, the Confederate force, after the arrival of Johnston's army, numbered 27,833 infantry, 35 smooth-bored guns, and 500 cavalry. Many of the infantry were armed only with shot-guns and old fowling-pieces, and the guns were small and ill-supplied with ammunition. There had been some sharp fighting on the 18th, and the Federal advance across the river of Bull Run had been sharply repulsed; therefore their generals determined, instead of making a direct attack on the 31st against the Confederate position, to take a wide sweep round, cross the river higher up, and falling upon the Confederate left flank, to crumple it up.

All night the Federal troops had marched, and at daybreak on the 21st nearly 40,000 men were in position on the left flank of the Confederates. The latter were not taken by surprise when Stuart's cavalry brought in news of the Federal movement, and General Beauregard, instead of moving his troops toward the threatened point, sent orders to General Longstreet on the right to cross the river as soon as the battle began, and to fall upon the Federal flank and rear.

Had this movement been carried out, the destruction of the Federal army would have been complete; but by one of those unfortunate accidents which so frequently occur in war and upset the best laid plans, the order in some way never came to hand, and when late in the day the error was discovered it was too late to remedy it.

At eight o'clock in the morning two of the Federal divisions reached the river, and while one of them engaged the Confederate force stationed at the bridge, another crossed the river at a ford. Colonel Evans, who commanded the Confederate forces, which numbered but fifteen companies, left 200 men to continue to hold the bridge, while with 800 he hurried to oppose General Hunter's division, which had crossed at the ford.

This consisted of 16,000 infantry, with cavalry and artillery, and another division of equal force had crossed at the Red House ford higher up. To check so great a force with this handful of men seemed all but impossible; but Colonel Evans determined to hold his ground to the last, to enable his general to bring up reinforcements. His force consisted of men of South Carolina and Louisiana, and they contested every foot of the ground.

The regiment which formed the advance of the Federals charged, supported by an artillery fire, but was repulsed. As the heavy Federal line advanced, however, the Confederates were slowly but steadily pressed back, until General Bee, with four regiments and a battery of artillery, came up to their assistance. The newcomers threw themselves into the fight with great gallantry, and maintained their ground until almost annihilated by the fire of the enemy, who outnumbered them by five to one. As, fighting desperately, they fell back before Hunter's division, the Federals who had crossed at Red House Ford suddenly poured down and took them in flank.

Swept by a terrible musketry fire, these troops could no longer resist, and in spite of the efforts of their general, who rode among them imploring them to stand firm until aid arrived, they began to fall back. Neither entreaties nor commands were of avail; the troops had done all that they could, and broken and disheartened they retreated in great confusion. But at this moment, when all seemed lost, a line of glittering bayonets was seen coming over the hill behind, and the general, riding off in haste toward them, found Jackson advancing with the first brigade.

Unmoved by the rush of the fugitives of the brigades of Bee and Evans, Jackson moved steadily forward, and so firm and resolute was their demeanor, that Bee rode after his men, and pointing with his sword to the first brigade, shouted, "Look, there is Jackson standing like a stone wall." The general's words were repeated, and henceforth the brigade was known as the Stonewall Brigade, and their general by the nickname of Stonewall Jackson, by which he was ever afterward known. The greater part of the fugitives rallied, and took up their position on the right of Jackson, and the Federal forces, who were hurrying forward assured of victory, found themselves confronted suddenly by 2,000 bayonets. After a moment's pause they pressed forward again, the artillery preparing a way for them by a tremendous fire.

Jackson ordered his men to lie down until the enemy arrived within fifty yards, and then to charge with the bayonet. Just at this moment Generals Johnston and Beauregard arrived on the spot, and at once seeing the desperate nature of the situation, and the whole Federal army pressing forward against a single brigade, they did their best to prepare to meet the storm. First they galloped up and down the disordered lines of Bee, exhorting the men to stand firm; and seizing the colors of the 4th Alabama, Johnston led them forward and formed them up under fire.

Beauregard hurried up some reinforcements and formed them on the left of Jackson, and thus 6,500 infantry and artillery, and Stuart's two troops of cavalry, stood face to face with more than 20,000 infantry and seven troops of regular cavalry, behind whom at the lower fords were 35,000 men in reserve. While his men were lying down awaiting the attack, Jackson rode backward and forward in front of them as calm and as unconcerned to all appearance as if on the parade ground, and his quiet bravery greatly nerved and encouraged the young troops.

All at once the tremendous artillery fire of the enemy ceased, and their infantry came on in massive lines. The four Confederate guns poured in their fire and then withdrew behind the infantry. When the line came within fifty yards of him, Jackson gave the word, his men sprang to their feet, poured in a heavy volley, and then charged. A wild yell rose from both ranks as they closed, and then they were mingled in a desperate conflict. For a time all was in wild confusion, but the ardor and courage of Jackson's men prevailed, and they burst through the center of the Federal line.

Immediately Jackson had charged, Beauregard sent forward the rest of the troops, and for a time a tremendous struggle took place along the whole line. Generals Bee and Barlow fell mortally wounded at the head of their troops. General Hampton was wounded, and many of the colonels fell. So numerous were the Federals, that although Jackson had pierced their center, their masses drove back his flanks and threatened to surround him. With voice and example he cheered on his men to hold their ground, and the officers closed up their ranks as they were thinned by the enemy's fire, and for an hour the struggle continued without marked advantage on either side.

Jackson's calmness was unshaken even in the excitement of the fight. At one time an officer rode up to him from another portion of the field and exclaimed, "General, I think the day is going against us!" To which Jackson replied in his usual curt manner, "If you think so, sir, you had better not say anything about it."

The resolute stand of the Confederates enabled General Beauregard to bring up fresh troops, and he at last gave the word to advance.

Jackson's brigade rushed forward on receiving the order, burst through the Federals with whom they were engaged, and, supported by the reserves, drove the enemy from the plateau. But the Federals, still vastly superior in force, brought up the reserves, and prepared to renew the attack; but 1,700 fresh men of the army of the Shenandoah came upon the field of battle, Smith and Early brought up their division from the river, and the whole Southern line advanced at the charge, drove the enemy down the slopes and on toward the fords.

A panic seized them, and their regiments broke up and took to headlong flight, which soon became an utter rout. Many of them continued their flight for hours, and for a time the Federal army ceased to exist; and had the Confederates advanced, as Jackson desired that they should do, Washington would have fallen into their hands without a blow being struck in its defense.

This, the first great battle of the war, is sometimes known as the battle of Manassas, but more generally as Bull Run.

With the exception of one or two charges, the little body of Confederate horse did not take any part in the battle of Bull Run. Had they been aware of the utter stampede of the Northern troops, they could safely have pressed forward in hot pursuit as far as Washington, but being numerically so inferior to the Federal cavalry, and in ignorance that the Northern infantry had become a mere panic-stricken mob, it would have been imprudent in the extreme for such a handful of cavalry to undertake the pursuit of an army.

Many of the Confederates were of opinion that this decisive victory would be the end of the war, and that the North, seeing that the South was able as well as willing to defend the position it had taken up, would abandon the idea of coercing it into submission. This hope was speedily dissipated. The North was indeed alike astonished and disappointed at the defeat of their army by a greatly inferior force, but instead of abandoning the struggle, they set to work to retrieve the disaster, and to place in the field a force which would, they believed, prove irresistible.

Vincent Wingfield saw but little of the battle at Bull Run. As they were impatiently waiting the order to charge while the desperate conflict between Jackson's brigade and the enemy was at its fiercest, a shell from one of the Federal batteries burst a few yards in front of the troop, and one of the pieces striking Vincent on the side hurled him insensible from his horse. He was at once lifted and carried by Dan and some of the other men-servants, who had been told off for this duty, to the rear, where the surgeons were busily engaged in dressing the wounds of the men who straggled back from the front. While the conflict lasted those unable to walk lay where they fell, for no provision had at present been made for ambulance corps, and not a single man capable of firing a musket could be spared from the ranks. The tears were flowing copiously down Dan's cheeks as he stood by while the surgeons examined Vincent's wound.

"Is he dead, sah?" he sobbed as they lifted him up from his stooping position.

"Dead." the surgeon repeated. "Can't you see he is breathing, and did you not hear him groan when I examined his side? He is a long way from being a dead man yet. Some of his ribs are broken, and he has had a very nasty blow; but I do not think there is any cause for anxiety about him. Pour a little wine down his throat, and sprinkle his face with water. Raise his head and put a coat under it, and when he opens his eyes and begins to recover, don't let him move. Then you can cut up the side of his jacket and down the sleeve, so as to get it off that side altogether. Cut his shirt open, and bathe the wound with some water and bit of rag of any sort; it is not likely to bleed much. When it has stopped bleeding put a pad of linen upon it, and keep it wet. When we can spare time we will bandage it properly."

But it was not until late at night that the time could be spared for attending to Vincent; for the surgeons were overwhelmed with work, and the most serious cases were, as far as possible, first attended to. He had soon recovered consciousness. At first he looked with a feeling of bewilderment at Dan, who was copiously sprinkling his face with water, sobbing loudly while he did so. As soon as the negro perceived that his master had opened his eyes he gave a cry of delight.

"Tank de Lord, Marse Vincent; dis child tought you dead and gone for sure."

"What's the matter, Dan? What has happened?" Vincent said, trying to move, and then stopping suddenly with a cry of pain.

"You knocked off your horse, sah, wid one of de shells of dem cussed Yanks."

"Am I badly hurt, Dan?"

"Berry bad, sah; great piece of flesh pretty nigh as big as my hand come out ob your side, and doctor says some of de ribs broken. But de doctor not seem to make much ob it; he hard sort ob man dat. Say you get all right again. No time to tend to you now. Hurry away just as if you some poor white trash instead of Massa Wingfield ob de Orangery."

Vincent smiled faintly.

"It doesn't make much difference what a man is in a surgeon's eyes, Dan; the question is how badly he is hurt, and what can be done for him? Well, thank God it's no worse. Wildfire was not hurt, I hope?"

"No, sah; he is standing tied up by dat tree. Now, sah, de doctor say me cut your jacket off and bave de wound."

"All right, Dan; but be a little careful with the water, you seem to be pretty near drowning me as it is. Just wipe my face and hair, and get the handkerchief from the pocket of my jacket, and open the shirt collar and put the handkerchief inside round my neck. How is the battle going on? The roar seems louder than ever."

Dan went forward to the crest a of slight rise of the ground whence he could look down upon the field of battle, and made haste to return.

"Can't see berry well, sah; too much smoke. But dey in de same place still."

"Look round, Dan, and see if there are any fresh troops coming up."

"Yes, sah; lot of men coming ober de hill behind."

"That's all right, Dan. Now you can see about this bathing my side."

As soon as the battle was over Major Ashley rode up to where Vincent and five or six of his comrades of the cavalry were lying wounded.

"How are you getting on, lads? Pretty well I hope?" he asked the surgeon as he dismounted.

"First rate, major," one of the men answered. "We all of us took a turn as soon as we heard that the Yanks were whipped."

"Yes, we have thrashed them handsomely," the major said. "Ah, Wingfield, I am glad to see you are alive. I thought when you fell it was all over with you."

"I am not much hurt, sir," Vincent replied. "A flesh wound and some ribs are broken, I hear; but they won't be long mending I hope."

"It's a nasty wound to look at," the major said, as Dan lifted the pad of wet linen. "But with youth and health you will soon get round it, never fear."

"Ah, my poor lad, yours is a worse case," he said as he bent over a young fellow who was lying a few paces from Vincent.

"It's all up with me, major," he replied faintly; "the doctor said he could do nothing for me. But I don't mind, now we have beaten them. You will send a line to the old people, major, won't you, and say I died doing my duty? I've got two brothers, and I expect they will send one on to take my place."

"I will write to them, my lad," the major said, "and tell them all about you." He could give the lad no false hopes, for already a gray shade was stealing over the white face, and the end was close at hand; in a few minutes he ceased to breathe.

Late in the evening the surgeons, having attended to more urgent cases, came round. Vincent's wound was now more carefully examined than before, but the result was the same. Three of the ribs were badly fractured, but there was no serious danger.

"You will want quiet and good nursing for some time, my lad," the principal surgeon said. "There will be a train of wounded going off for Richmond the first thing in the morning, and you shall go by it. You had better get a door, lads," he said to some of the troopers who had come across from the spot where the cavalry were bivouacked to see how their comrades were getting on, "and carry him down and put him in the train. One has just been sent off, and another will be made up at once, so that the wounded can be put in it as they are taken down. Now I will bandage the wound, and it will not want any more attention until you get home."

A wad of lint was placed upon the wound and bandaged tightly round the body.

"Remember you have got to be perfectly quiet, and not attempt to move till the bones have knit. I am afraid that they are badly fractured, and will require some time to heal up again."

A door was fetched from an out-house near, and Vincent and two of his comrades, who were also ordered to be sent to the rear, were one by one carried down to the nearest point on the railway, where a train stood ready to receive them, and they were then laid on the seats.

All night the wounded kept arriving, and by morning the train was packed as full as it would hold, and with two or three surgeons in charge started for Richmond. Dan was permitted to accompany the train, at Vincent's urgent request, in the character of doctor's assistant, and he went about distributing water to the wounded, and assisting the surgeons in moving such as required it.

It was night before the train reached Richmond. A number of people were at the station to receive it; for as soon as the news of the battle had been received, preparations had been made for the reception of the wounded, several public buildings had been converted into hospitals, and numbers of the citizens had come forward with offers to take one or more of the wounded into their houses. The streets were crowded with people, who were wild with joy at the news of the victory which, as they believed, had secured the State from any further fear of invasion. Numbers of willing hands were in readiness to carry the wounded on stretchers to the hospitals, where all the surgeons of the town were already waiting to attend upon them.

Vincent, at his own request, was only laid upon a bed, as he said that he would go home to be nursed the first thing in the morning. This being the case it was needless to put him to the pain and trouble of being undressed. Dan had started as soon as he saw his master carried into the hospital to take the news to the Orangery, being strictly charged by Vincent to make light of his injury, and on no account whatever to alarm them. He was to ask that the carriage should come to fetch him the first thing in the morning.

It was indeed but just daybreak when Mrs. Wingfield drove up to the hospital. Dan had been so severely cross-examined that he had been obliged to give an accurate account of Vincent's injury. There was bustle and movement even at that early hour, for another train of wounded had just arrived. As she entered the hospital she gave an exclamation of pleasure, for at the door were two gentlemen in conversation, one of whom was the doctor who had long attended the family at the Orangery.

"I am glad you are here, Dr. Mapleston; for I want your opinion before I move Vincent. Have you seen him?"

"No, Mrs. Wingfield; I did not know he was here. I have charge of one of the wards, and have not had time to see who are in the others. I sincerely hope Vincent is not seriously hurt."

"That's want I want to find out, doctor. His boy brought us news late last night that he was here. He said the doctors considered that he was not in any danger; but as it seems that he had three ribs broken and a deep flesh wound from the explosion of a shell, it seems to me that it must be serious."

"I will go up and see him at once, Mrs. Wingfield, and find out from the surgeon in charge of his ward exactly what is the matter with him." Dan led the way to the bed upon which Vincent was lying. He was only dozing, and opened his eyes as they came up.

"My poor boy," Mrs. Wingfield said, struggling with her tears at the sight of his pale face, "this is sad indeed."

"It is nothing very bad, mother," Vincent replied cheerfully; "nothing at all to fret about. The wound is nothing to the injuries of most of those here. I suppose, doctor, I can be moved at once?"

Doctor Mapleston felt his pulse.

"You are feverish, my lad; but perhaps the best thing for you would be to get you home while you can be moved. You will do far better there than here. But I must speak to the surgeon in charge of you first, and hear what he says."

"Yes, I think you can move him," the surgeon of the ward said. "He has got a nasty wound, and the ticket with him said that three ribs were badly fractured; but I made no examination, as he said he would be fetched the first thing this morning. I only put on a fresh dressing and bandaged it. The sooner you get him off the better, if he is to be moved. Fever is setting in, and he will probably be wandering by this evening. He will have a much better chance at home, with cool rooms and quiet and careful nursing, than he can have here; though there would be no lack of either comforts or nurses, for half the ladies in the town have volunteered for the work, and we have offers of all the medical comforts that could be required were the list of wounded ten times as large as it is."

A stretcher was brought in, and Vincent was lifted as gently as possible upon it. Then he was carried down-stairs and the stretcher placed in the carriage, which was a large open one, and afforded just sufficient length for it. Mrs. Wingfield took her seat beside him. Dan mounted the box beside the coachman.

"I will be out in an hour, Mrs. Wingfield," Dr. Mapleston said. "I have to go round the ward again, and will then drive out at once. Give him lemonade and cooling drinks; don't let him talk. Cut his clothes off him, and keep the room somewhat dark, but with a free current of air. I will bring out some medicine with me."

The carriage drove slowly to avoid shaking, and when they approached the house Mrs. Wingfield told Dan to jump down and come to the side of her carriage. Then she told him to run on as fast as he could ahead, and to tell her daughters not to meet them upon their arrival, and that all the servants were to be kept out of the way, except three men to carry Vincent upstairs. The lad was consequently got up to his room without any excitement, and was soon lying on his bed with a sheet thrown lightly over him.

"That is comfortable," he said, as his mother bathed his face and hands and smoothed his hair. "Where are the girls, mother?"

"They will come in to see you now, Vincent; but you are to keep quite quiet you know, and not to talk." The girls stole in and said a few words, and left him alone again with Mrs. Wingfield. He did not look to them so ill as they had expected, for there was a flush of fever on his cheeks. Dr. Mapleston arrived in another half-hour, examined and redressed the wound, and comforted Mrs. Wingfield with the assurance that there was nothing in it likely to prove dangerous to life.

"Our trouble will be rather with the effect of the shock than with the wound itself. He is very feverish now, and you must not be alarmed if by this evening he is delirious. You will give him this cooling draught every three hours; he can have anything in the way of cooling drinks he likes. If he begins to wander, put cloths dipped in cold water and wrung out on his head, and sponge his hands with water with a little eau de Cologne in it. If he seems very hot set one of the women to fan him, but don't let her go on if it seems to worry him. I will come round again at half past nine this evening and will make arrangements to pass the night here. We have telegrams saying that surgeons are coming from Charleston and many other places, so I can very well be spared."

When the doctor returned in the evening, he found, as he had anticipated, that Vincent was in a high state of fever. This continued four or five days, and then gradually passed off; and he woke up one morning perfectly conscious. His mother was sitting on a chair at the bedside.

"What o'clock is it, mother?" he asked. "Have I been asleep long?"

"Some time, dear," she answered gently; "but you must not talk. You are to take this draught and to go off to sleep again; when you wake you may ask any questions you like." She lifted the lad's head, gave him the draught and some cold tea, then darkened the room, and in a few minutes he was asleep again.

## CHAPTER VII. THE MERRIMAC AND THE MONITOR.

IT was some weeks before Vincent was able to walk unaided. His convalescence was somewhat slow, for the shock to the system had been a severe one. The long railway journey had been injurious to him, for the bandage had become somewhat loose and the broken pieces of bone had grated upon each other, and were much longer in knitting together than they would have been had he been treated on the spot.

As soon as he could walk he began to be anxious to rejoin his troop, but the doctor said that many weeks must elapse before he would be ready to undergo the hardships of campaign. He was reconciled to some extent to the delay by letters from his friends with the troop and by the perusal of the papers. There was nothing whatever doing in Virginia. The two armies still faced each other, the Northerners protected by the strong fortifications they had thrown up round Washington--fortifications much too formidable to be attacked by the Confederates, held as they were by a force immensely superior to their own, both in numbers and arms.

The Northerners were indeed hard at work, collecting and organizing an army which was to crush out the rebellion. General Scott had been succeeded by McClellan in the supreme command, and the new general was indefatigable in organizing the vast masses of men raised in the North. So great were the efforts that in a few months after the defeat of Bull Run the North had 650,000 men in arms.

But while no move had at present been made against Virginia there was sharp fighting in some of the border states, especially in Missouri and Kentucky, in both of which public opinion was much divided, and regiments were raised on both sides.

Various operations were now undertaken by the Federal fleet at points along the coast, and several important positions were taken and occupied, it being impossible for the Confederates to defend so long a line of sea-coast. The South had lost rather than gained ground in consequence of their victory at Bull Run. For a time they had been unduly elated, and were disposed altogether to underrate their enemies and to believe that the struggle was as good as over. Thus, then, they made no effort at all corresponding to that of the North; but as time went on, and they saw the vastness of the preparations made for their conquest, the people of the Southern States again bestirred themselves.

Owing to the North having the command of the sea, and shutting up all the principal ports, they had to rely upon themselves for everything, while the North could draw arms and ammunition and all the requisites of war from the markets of Europe. Foundries were accordingly established for the manufacture of artillery, and factories for muskets, ammunition, and percussion caps. The South had, in fact, to manufacture everything down to the cloth for her soldiers uniforms and the leather for their shoes; and, as in the past she had relied wholly upon the North for such goods, it was for a time impossible to supply the troops with even the most necessary articles.

The women throughout the States were set to work, spinning and weaving rough cloth, and making uniforms from it. Leather, however, cannot be produced all at once, and indeed with all their efforts the Confederate authorities were never throughout the war able to provide a sufficient supply of boots for the troops, and many a battle was won by soldiers who fought almost barefooted and who reshod themselves for the most part by stripping the boots from their dead foes. Many other articles could not be produced in the Southern States, and the Confederates suffered much from the want of proper medicines and surgical appliances.

For these and many other necessaries they had to depend solely upon the ships which succeeded in making their way through the enemy's cruisers and running the blockade of the ports. Wine, tea, coffee, and other imported articles soon became luxuries beyond the means of all, even the very wealthy. All sorts of substitutes were used; grain roasted and ground being chiefly used as a substitute for coffee. Hitherto the South had been principally occupied in raising cotton and tobacco, depending chiefly upon the North for food; and it was necessary now to abandon the cultivation of products for which they had no sale, and to devote the land to the growth of maize and other crops for food.

By the time that the long period of inaction came to a close, Vincent had completely recovered his strength, and was ready to rejoin the ranks as soon as the order came from Colonel Stuart, who had promised to send for him directly there was a prospect of active service.

One of Vincent's first questions as soon as he became convalescent was whether a letter had been received from Tony. It had come, he was told, among the last batch of letters that crossed the frontier before the outbreak of hostilities, and Mrs. Wingfield, had, as he had requested, opened it. As had been arranged, it had merely contained Tony's address at a village near Montreal; for Vincent had warned him to say nothing in the letter, for there was no saying, in the troubled times which were approaching when Tony left, into whose hands it might fall.

Vincent had before starting told his mother of the share he had taken in getting the negro safely away, and Mrs. Wingfield, brought up as she had been to regard those who assisted runaway slaves to escape in the same light as those who assisted to steal any other kind of property, was at first greatly shocked when she heard that her son had taken part in such an enterprise, however worthy of compassion the slave might be, and however brutal the master from whose hands he had fled. However, as Vincent was on the point of starting for the war to meet danger, and possibly death, in the defense of Virginia, she had said little, and that little was in reference rather to the imprudence of the course he had taken than to what she regarded in her own mind as its folly, and indeed its criminality.

She had, however, promised that as soon as Tony's letter arrived she would, if it was still possible, forward Dinah and the child to him, supplying her with money for the journey, and giving her the papers freeing her from slavery which Vincent had duly signed in the presence of a justice. When the letter came, however, it was already too late. Fighting was on the point of commencing, all intercourse across the border was stopped, the trains were all taken up for the conveyance of troops, and even a man would have had great difficulty in passing northward, while for an unprotected negress with a baby such a journey would have been impossible.

Mrs. Wingfield had therefore written four times at fort-nightly intervals to Tony, saying that it was impossible to send Dinah off at present, but that she should be despatched as soon as the troubles were over, upon receipt of another letter from him saying that his address was unchanged, or giving a new one. These letters were duly posted, and it was probable that one or other of them would in time reach Tony, as mails were sent off to Europe whenever an opportunity offered for them to be taken by a steamer running the blockade from a Southern port. Dinah, therefore, still remained at the Orangery. She was well and happy, for her life there was a delightful one indeed after her toil and hardship at the Jackson's; and although she was anxious to join her husband, the knowledge that he was well and safe from all pursuit, and that sooner or later she would join him with her child, was sufficient to make her perfectly contented.

During Vincent's illness she had been his most constant attendant; for her child now no longer required her care, and passed much of its time down at the nursery, where the young children of the slaves were looked after by two or three aged negresses past active work. She had therefore begged Mrs. Wingfield to be allowed to take her place by the bedside of her young master, and, after giving her a trial, Mrs. Wingfield found her so quiet, gentle, and patient that she installed her there, and was able to obtain the rest she needed, with a feeling of confidence that Vincent would be well attended to in her absence.

When Vincent was well enough to be about again, his sisters were surprised at the change that had taken place in him since he had started a few months before for the war. It was not so much that he had grown, though he had done so considerably, but that he was much older in manner and appearance. He had been doing man's work: work requiring vigilance, activity, and courage, and they could no longer treat him as a boy. As he became stronger he took to riding about the plantation; but not upon Wildfire, for his horse was still with the troop, Colonel Stuart having promised to see that the animal was well cared for, and that no one should ride upon it but himself.

"I hope you like Jonas Pearson better than you used to do, Vincent," Mrs. Wingfield said a day or two before he started to rejoin his troop.

"I can't say I do, mother," he replied shortly. "The man is very civil to me now--too civil, in fact; but I don't like him, and I don't believe he is honest. I don't mean that he would cheat you, though he may do so for anything I know; but he pretends to be a violent Secessionist, which as he comes from Vermont is not natural, and I imagine he would sing a different tune if the blue coats ever get to Richmond. Still

I have nothing particular to say against him, except that I don't like him and I don't trust him. So long as everything goes on well for the Confederacy I don't suppose it matters, but if we should ever get the worst of it you will see that fellow will be mischievous.

"However, I hear that he has obeyed your orders, and that there has been no flogging on the estate since I went away. In fact, as far as I can see, he does not keep anything like such a sharp hand over the slaves as he used to do; and in some of the fields the work seems to be done in a very slovenly way. What his game is I don't know; but I have no doubt whatever that he has some game in his mind."

"You are a most prejudiced boy," Mrs. Wingfield said, laughing. "First of all the man is too strict, and you were furious about it; now you think he's too lenient, and you at once suspect he has what you call a game of some sort or other on. You are hard to please indeed."

Vincent smiled. "Well, as I told you once before, we shall see. I hope I am wrong, and that Pearson is all that you believe him to be. I own that I may be prejudiced against him; but nothing will persuade me that it was not from him that Jackson learned that Dinah was here, and it was to that we owe the visit of the sheriff and the searching the plantation for Tony. However, whatever the man is at heart, he can, as far as I see, do you no injury as long as things go on as they are, and I sincerely trust he will never have an opportunity of doing so."

During the winter Vincent had made the acquaintance of many of the Southern leaders. The town was the center of the movement, the heart of the Confederacy. It was against it, as the capital of the Southern States, that the efforts of the Northerns were principally directed, and to it flocked the leading men from all parts of the country. Although every Virginian family had some of its members at the front, and a feeling of anxiety reigned everywhere, a semblance of gaiety was kept up. The theater was opened, and parties and balls given, in order to keep up the spirits of the people by the example of those of higher rank.

These balls differed widely in appearance from those of eighteen months before. The gentlemen were almost all in uniform, and already calicoes and other cheap fabrics were worn by many of the ladies, as foreign dress materials could no longer be purchased. Mrs. Wingfield made a point of always attending with her daughters at these entertainments, which to the young people afforded a cheerful break in the dullness and monotony of their usual life; for, owing to the absence of almost all the young men with the army, there had been a long cessation of the pleasant interchange of visits, impromptu parties, and social gatherings that had formed a feature in the life in Virginia.

The balls would have been but dull affairs had only the residents of Richmond been present; but leave was granted as much as possible to officers stationed with regiments within a railway run of the town, and as these eagerly availed themselves of the change from the monotony of camp life, the girls had no reason to complain of want of partners. Here and at the receptions given by President Davis, Vincent met all the leaders of the Confederacy, civil and military. Many of them had been personal friends of the Wingfields before the Secession movement began, and among them was General Magruder, who commanded the troops round Richmond.

Early in the winter the general had called at the Orangery. "We are going to make a call upon the patriotism of the planters of this neighborhood, Mrs. Wingfield," he said during lunch time. "You see, our armies are facing those of the Federals opposite Washington, and can offer a firm front to any foe marching down from the North; but, unfortunately they have the command of the sea, and there is nothing to prevent their embarking an army on board ship and landing it in either the James or the York Rivers, and in that case they might make a rush upon Richmond before there would be time to bring down troops to our aid. I am therefore proposing to erect a chain of works between the two rivers, so as to be able to keep even a large army at bay until reinforcements arrive; but to do this a large number of hands will be required, and we are going to ask the proprietors of plantations to place as many negroes as they can spare at our disposal."

"There can be no doubt as to the response your question will meet with, general. At present we have scarce enough work for our slaves to do. I intend to grow no tobacco next year, for it will only rot in the warehouse, and a comparatively small number of hands are required to raise corn crops. I have about a hundred and seventy working hands on the Orangery, and shall be happy to place a hundred at your disposal for as long a time as you may require them. If you want fifty more you can of course have them. Everything else must at present give way to the good of the cause."

"I thank you much, Mrs. Wingfield, for your offers, and will put your name down the first on the list of contributors."

"You seem quite to have recovered now," he said to Vincent a few minutes afterward.

"Yes; I am quite ashamed of staying here so long, general. But I feel some pain at times; and as there is nothing doing at the front, and my doctor says that it is of importance I should have rest as long as possible, I have stayed on. Major Ashley has promised to recall me as soon as there is a prospect of active work."

"I think it is quite likely that there will be active work here as soon as anywhere else," the general said. "We know pretty well what is doing at Washington, and though nothing has been decided upon, there is a party in favor of a landing in force here; and if so, we shall have hot work. What do you say? If you like I will get you a commission and appoint you one of my aides-de-camp. Your knowledge of the country will make you useful, and as Ashley has specially mentioned your name in one of his despatches, you can have your commission by asking for it.

"If there is to be fighting round here, it will be of more interest to you defending your own home than in taking part in general engagements for the safety of the State. It will, too, enable you to be a good deal at home; and although so far the slaves have behaved extremely well, there is no saying exactly what may happen if the Northerners come among us. You can rejoin your own corps afterward, you know, if nothing comes of this."

Vincent was at first inclined to decline the offer, but his mother and sisters were so pleased at having him near them that he finally accepted with thanks, being principally influenced by the general's last argument, that possibly there might be trouble with the slaves in the event of a landing in the James Peninsula by the Northerners. A few days later there came an official intimation that he had received a commission in the cavalry, and had at General Magruder's request been appointed to his staff, and he at once entered upon his new duties.

The fortress of Monroe, at the entrance of Hampton Roads, was still in the hands of the Federals, and a large Federal fleet was assembled here, and was only prevented from sailing up the James River by the Merrimac, a steamer which the Confederates had plated with railway iron. They had also constructed batteries upon some high bluffs on each side of the river. In a short time 5,000 negroes were set to work erecting batteries upon the York River at Yorktown and Gloucester

Point, and upon a line of works extending from Warwick upon the James River to Ship Point on the York, through a line of wooded and swampy country intersected by streams emptying themselves into one or other of the rivers.

This line was some thirty miles in length, and would require 25,000 men to guard it; but Magruder hoped that there would be sufficient warning of an attack to enable reinforcements to arrive in time to raise his own command of about 10,000 men to that strength. The negroes worked cheerfully, for they received a certain amount of pay from the State; but the work was heavy and difficult, and different altogether to that which they were accustomed to perform. The batteries by the sides of the rivers made fair progress, but the advance of the long line of works across the peninsula was but slow. Vincent had, upon receiving his appointment, written at once to Major Ashley, sending his letter by Dan, who was ordered to bring back Wildfire. Vincent stated that had he consulted his personal feeling he should have preferred remaining in the ranks of his old corps; but that as the fighting might be close to his home, and there was no saying what might be the behavior of the slave population in the event of a Northern invasion, he had, for the sake of his mother and sisters, accepted the appointment, but as soon as the danger was over he hoped to rejoin the corps and serve under his former commander.

Dan, on his return with Wildfire, brought a letter from the major saying that although he should have been glad to have had him with him, he quite agreed with the decision at which he had, under the circumstances, arrived. Vincent now took up his quarters at the camp formed a short distance from the city, and much of his time was spent in riding to and from the peninsula, seeing that the works were being carried out according to the plan of the general, and reporting upon the manner in which the contractors for the supply of food to the negroes at work there performed their duties. Sometimes he was away for two or three days upon this work; but he generally managed once or twice a week to get home for a few hours.

The inhabitants of Richmond and its neighborhood were naturally greatly interested in the progress of the works for their defense, and parties were often organized to ride or drive to Yorktown, or to the batteries on the James River, to watch the progress made. Upon one occasion Vincent accompanied his mother and sisters, and a party of ladies and gentlemen from the neighboring plantations, to Drury's Bluff, where an entrenched position named Fort Darling had been erected, and preparations made to sink vessels across the river, and close it against the advance of the enemy's fleet should any misfortune happen to the Merrimac.

Several other parties had been made up, and each brought provisions with them. General Magruder and some of his officers received them upon their arrival, and conducted them over the works. After this the whole party sat down to a picnic meal on the ground, and no stranger could have guessed that the merry party formed part of a population threatened with invasion by a powerful foe. There were speeches and toasts, all of a patriotic character, and General Magruder raised the enthusiasm to the highest point by informing them that in a few days--the exact day was a secret, but it would be very shortly--the Merrimac, or, as she had been re-christened, the Virginia, would put out from Norfolk Harbor, and see what she could do to clear Hampton Roads of the fleet that now threatened them. As they were riding back to Richmond the general said to Vincent:

"I will tell you a little more than I told the others, Wingfield. I believe the Merrimac will go out the day after to-morrow. I wish I could get away myself to see the affair; but, unfortunately, I cannot do so. However, if you like to be present, I will give you three days' leave, as you have been working very hard lately. You can start early to-morrow, and can get down by train to Norfolk in the evening. I should advise you to take your horse with you, and then you can ride in the morning to some spot from which you will get a fair view of the Roads, and be able to see what is going on."

"Thank you very much, sir," Vincent said. "I should like it immensely."

The next day Vincent went down to Norfolk. Arriving there, he found that although there was a general expectation that the Merrimac would shortly go out to try her strength with the enemy, nothing was known of the fact that the next morning had been fixed for the encounter, the secret being kept to the last lest some spy or adherent of the North might take the news to the fleet. After putting up his horse Vincent went down to the navy yard, off which the Merrimac was lying.

This ship had been sunk by the Federals when at the commencement of hostilities they had evacuated Norfolk. Having been raised by the Confederates, the ship was cut down, and a sort of roof covered with iron was built over it, so that the vessel presented the appearance of a huge sunken house. A ram was fixed to her bow, and she was armed with ten guns. Her steam-power was very insufficient for her size, and she could only move through the water at the rate of five knots an hour.

"She is an ugly-looking thing," a man observed to Vincent as he gazed at the ship.

"Frightfully ugly," Vincent agreed. "She may be a formidable machine in the way of fighting, but one can scarcely call her a ship."

"She is a floating-battery, and if they tried their best to turn out the ugliest thing that ever floated they could not have succeeded better. She is just like a Noah's ark sunk down to the eaves of her roof."

"Yes, she is a good deal like that," Vincent agreed. "The very look of her ought to be enough to frighten the Federals, even if she did nothing else."

"I expect it will not be long before she gives them a taste of her quality," the man said. "She has got her coal and ammunition on board, and there's nothing to prevent her going out this evening if she wants to."

"It will be worth seeing when she does go out to fight the Northerners," Vincent said. "It will be a new experiment in warfare, and, if she turns out a success, I suppose all the navies in the world will be taking to cover themselves up with iron."

The next morning, which was the 8th of March--a date forever memorable in naval annals--smoke was seen pouring out from the funnels of the Merrimac, and there were signs of activity on board the Patrick Henry, of six guns, and the Jamestown, Raleigh, Beaufort, and Teazer, little craft carrying one gun each, and at eleven o'clock they all moved down the inlet on which Norfolk is situated. The news that the Merrimac was going out to attack the enemy had now spread, and the whole population of Norfolk turned out and hastened down toward the mouth of the inlet on horseback, in vehicles, or on foot, while Vincent rode to the batteries on Sewell's Point, nearly facing Fort Monroe.

He left his horse at a farmhouse a quarter of a mile from the battery; for Wildfire was always restless under fire, and it was probable that the batteries would take a share in the affair. At one o'clock some of the small Federal lookout launches were seen to be at work signaling, a bustle could be observed prevailing among the large ships over by the fortress, and it was evident that the Merrimac was visible to them as she came down the inlet. The Cumberland and Congress men-of-war moved out in that direction, and the Minnesota and the St. Lawrence, which were at anchor, got under weigh, assisted by steam-tugs.

The Merrimac and the fleet of little gunboats were now visible from the battery, advancing against the Cumberland and Congress. The former opened fire upon her at a distance of a mile with her heavy pivot guns, but the Merrimac, without replying, continued her slow and steady course toward them. She first approached the Congress, and as she did so a puff of smoke burst from the forward end of her pent-house, and the water round the Congress was churned up by a hail of grape-shot. As they passed each other both vessels fired a broadside. The officers in the fort, provided with glasses, could see the effect of the Merrimac's fire in the light patches that showed on the side of the Congress, but the Merrimac appeared entirely uninjured. She now approached the Cumberland, which poured several broadsides into her, but altogether without effect. The Merrimac, without replying, steamed straight on and struck the Cumberland with great force, knocking a large hole in her side, near the water-line. Then backing off she opened fire upon her.

For half an hour the crew of the Cumberland fought with great bravery. The ships lay about three hundred yards apart, and every shot from the Merrimac told on the wooden vessel. The water was pouring in through the breach. The shells of the Merrimac crushed through her side, and at one time set her on fire; but the crew worked their guns until the vessel sank beneath their feet. Some men succeeded in swimming to land, which was not far distant, others were saved by small boats from the shore, but nearly half of the crew of 400 men were either killed in action or drowned.

The Merrimac now turned her attention to the Congress, which was left to fight the battle alone, as the Minnesota had got aground, and the Roanoake and St. Lawrence could not approach near enough to render them assistance from their draught of water. The Merrimac poured broadside after broadside into her, until the officer in command and many of the crew were killed. The lieutenant who succeeded to the command, seeing there was no prospect of help, and that resistance was hopeless, hauled down the flag. A gunboat was sent alongside, with orders that the crew should leave the Congress and come on board, as the ship was to be burned. But the troops and artillery lining the shore now opened fire on the little gunboat, which consequently hauled off. The Merrimac, after firing several more shells into the Congress, moved away to attack the Minnesota, and the survivors of the 200 men who composed the crew of the Congress were conveyed to shore in small boats. The vessel was set on fire either by her own crew or the shells of the Merrimac, and by midnight blew up.

Owing to the shallowness of the water the Merrimac could not get near enough to the Minnesota to use her own small guns to advantage, and the gunboat was driven off by the heavy ten-inch gun of the Federal frigate, and therefore at seven o'clock the Merrimac and her consorts returned to Norfolk. The greatest delight was felt on shore at the success of the engagement, and on riding back to Norfolk Vincent learned that the ram would go out again next morning to engage the rest of the Federal fleet.

She herself had suffered somewhat in the fight. Her loss in men was only two killed and eight wounded; but two of her guns had the muzzles shot off, the armor was damaged in some places, and most serious of all she had badly twisted her ram in running into the Cumberland. Still it appeared that she was more than a match for the rest of the Federal fleet, and that these must either fly or be destroyed.

As the general had given him three days' leave, Vincent was able to stay to see the close of the affair, and early next morning again rode down to Sewell's Point, as the Merrimac was to start at daybreak. At six o'clock the ironclad came out from the river and made for the Minnesota, which was still aground. The latter was seen to run up a signal, and the spectators saw an object which they had not before perceived coming out as if to meet the ram. The glasses were directed toward it, and a general exclamation of surprise was heard.

"What is the thing? It looks like a raft with two round turrets upon it, and a funnel." A moment's consideration, and the truth burst upon them. It was the ship they had heard of as building at New York, and which had been launched six weeks before. It was indeed the Monitor, which had arrived during the night, just in time to save the rest of the Federal fleet. She was the first regular ironclad ever built. She was a turret ship, carrying two very heavy guns, and showing only between two and three feet above the water.

The excitement upon both shores as these adversaries approached each other was intense. They moved slowly, and not until they were within a hundred yards distance did the Monitor open fire, the Merrimac replying at once. The fire for a time was heavy and rapid, the distance between the combatants varying from fifty to two hundred yards. The Monitor had by far the greatest speed, and was much more easily turned than the Confederate ram, and her guns were very much heavier, and the Merrimac while still keeping up the fight made toward the mouth of the river.

Suddenly she turned and steamed directly at the Monitor, and before the latter could get out of her way struck her on the side; but the ram was bent and her weak engines were insufficient to propel her with the necessary force. Consequently she inflicted no damage on the Monitor, and the action continued, the turret-ship directing her fire at the iron roof of the ram, while the latter pointed her guns especially at the turret and pilot-house of the Monitor. At length, after a battle which had lasted six hours, the Monitor withdrew, one of the plates of her pilot-house being seriously damaged and her commander injured in the eyes.

When her foe drew off the Merrimac steamed back to Norfolk. There were no men killed in either battle, and each side claimed a victory; the Federals upon the ground that they had driven off the Merrimac, the Confederates because the Monitor had retreated from the fight. Each vessel however held the strength of the other in respect, the Monitor remaining as sentinel over the ships and transports at Fortress Monroe, while the Merrimac at Norfolk continued to guard the entrance into the James River.

As soon as the fight was over Vincent Wingfield, greatly pleased that he had witnessed so strange and interesting a combat, rode back to Norfolk, and the same evening reached Richmond, where his description of the fight was received with the greatest interest and excitement.

## CHAPTER VIII. McCLELLAN'S ADVANCE.

IT WAS not until three weeks after the fight between the ironclads that the great army under General McClellan arrived off Fortress Monroe, the greater portion of the troops coming down the Potomac in steam transports. Vast quantities of stores had been accumulated in and around the fortress. Guns of a size never before used in war were lying on the wharfs in readiness to be placed in batteries, while Hampton Roads were crowded with transports and store vessels watched over by the Monitor and the other war ships. McClellan's army was a large one, but not so strong a force as he had intended to have taken with him, and as soon as he arrived at Fortress Monroe he learned that he would not be able to expect much assistance from the fleet. The Merrimac completely closed the James River; and were the more powerful vessels of the fleet to move up the York River, she would be able to sally out and destroy the rest of the fleet and the transports.

As it was most important to clear the peninsula between the two rivers before Magruder should receive strong reinforcements, a portion of the troops were at once landed, and on the 4th of April 56,000 men and 100 guns disembarked and started on their march against Yorktown. As soon as the news of the arrival of the Northern army at Fortress Monroe reached Richmond fresh steps were taken for the defense of the city. Magruder soon found that it would be impossible with the force at his command to hold the line he had proposed, and a large body of negroes and troops were set to work to throw up defenses between Yorktown and a point on the Warwick River thirteen and a half miles away.

A portion of this line was covered by the Warwick Creek, which he dammed up to make it unfordable, and erected batteries to guard the dams. Across the intervening ground a weak earthwork with trenches was constructed, there being no time to raise stronger works; but Magruder relied chiefly upon the swampy and difficult nature of the country, and the concealment afforded by the forest, which rendered it difficult for the enemy to discover the weakness of the defenders.

He posted 6,000 men at Yorktown and Gloucester Point, and the remaining 5,000 troops under his command were scattered along the line of works to the Warwick River. He knew that if McClellan pushed forward with all his force he must be successful; but he knew also that if the enemy could but be held in check for a few days assistance would reach him from General Johnston's army.

Fortunately for the Confederates, the weather, which had been fine and clear during the previous week, changed on the very day that McClellan started. The rain came down in torrents, and the roads became almost impassable. The columns struggled on along the deep and muddy tracks all day, and bivouacked for the night in the forests. The next morning they resumed their march, and on reaching the first line of intrenchments formed by the Confederates found them deserted, and it was not until they approached the Warwick Creek that they encountered serious opposition. Had they pushed forward at once they would have unquestionably captured Richmond. But McClellan's fault was over-caution, and he believed himself opposed by a very much larger force than that under the command of Magruder; consequently, instead of making an attack at once he began regular siege operations against the works on Warwick Creek and those at Yorktown.

The delay saved Richmond. Every day reinforcements arrived, and by the time that McClellan's army, over 100,000 strong, had erected their batteries and got their heavy guns into position, Magruder had been reinforced by some 10,000 men under General Johnston, who now assumed the command, while other divisions were hurrying up from Northern and Western Virginia. Upon the very night before the batteries were ready to open, the Confederates evacuated their positions and fell back, carrying with them all their guns and stores to the Chickahominy River, which ran almost across the peninsula at a distance of six miles only from Richmond.

The Confederates crossed and broke down the bridges, and prepared to make another stand. The disappointment of the Federals was great. After ten days of incessant labor and hardship they had only gained possession of the village of Yorktown and a tract of low swampy country. The divisions in front pressed forward rapidly after the Confederates; but these had managed their plan so well that all were safely across the stream before they were overtaken.

The dismay in Richmond had for a few days been great. Many people left the town for the interior, taking their valuables with them, and all was prepared for the removal of the state papers and documents. But as the Federals went on with their fortifications, and the reinforcements began to arrive, confidence was restored, and all went on as before.

The great Federal army was so scattered through the forests, and the discipline of some of the divisions was so lax that it was some days before McClellan had them ranged in order on the Chickahominy. Another week elapsed before he was in a position to undertake fresh operations; but General Johnston had now four divisions on the spot, and he was too enterprising a general to await the attack. Consequently he crossed the Chickahominy, fell upon one of the Federal divisions and almost destroyed it, and drove back the whole of their left wing. The next morning the battle was renewed, and lasted for five hours.

It was fortunate indeed for the Confederates that the right wing of the Northern army did not, while the action was going on, cross the river and march straight upon Richmond; but communication was difficult from one part of the army to another, owing to the thick forests and the swampy state of the ground, and being without orders they remained inactive all day. The loss on their side had been 7,000 men, while the Confederates had lost 4,500; and General Johnston being seriously wounded, the chief command was given to General Lee, by far the ablest soldier the war produced. Satisfied with the success they had gained, the Confederates fell back across the river again.

On the 4th of June, General Stuart--for he had now been promoted-- started with 1,200 cavalry and two guns, and in forty-eight hours made one of the most adventurous reconnaissances ever undertaken. First the force rode out to Hanover Courthouse, where they encountered and defeated, first, a small body of cavalry, and afterward a whole regiment. Then, after destroying the stores there they rode round to the Pamunkey, burned two vessels and a large quantity of stores, captured a train of forty wagons, and burned a railway bridge.

Then they passed right round the Federal rear, crossed the river, and re-entered the city with 165 prisoners and 200 horses, having effected the destruction of vast quantities of stores, besides breaking up the railways and burning bridges.

Toward the end of June McClellan learned that Stonewall Jackson, having struck heavy blows at the two greatly superior armies which were operating against him in the valley of the Shenandoah, had succeeded in evading them, and was marching toward Richmond.

He had just completed several bridges across the river, and was about to move forward to fight a great battle when the news reached him. Believing that he should be opposed by an army of 200,000 men, although, in fact, the Confederate army, after Jackson and all the available reinforcements came up, was still somewhat inferior in strength to his own, he determined to abandon for the present the attempt upon Richmond, and to fall back upon the James River.

Here his ships had already landed stores for his supply, for the river was now open as far as the Confederate defenses at Fort Darling. Norfolk Navy Yard had been captured by the 10,000 men who formed the garrison of Fortress Monroe. No resistance had been offered, as all the Confederate troops had been concentrated for the defense of Richmond. When Norfolk was captured the Merrimac steamed out to make her way out of the river; but the water was low, and the pilot declared that she could not be taken up. Consequently she was set on fire and burned to the water's edge, and thus the main obstacle to the advance of the Federal fleet was removed.

They had advanced as far as Fort Darling and the ironclad gunboats had engaged the batteries there. Their shot, however, did little damage to the defenders upon the lofty bluffs, while the shot from the batteries so injured the gunboats that the attempt to force the passage was abandoned. While falling back to a place called Harrison's Landing on the James River, the Federals were attacked by the Confederates, but after desperate fighting on both sides, lasting for five days, they succeeded in drawing off from the Chickahominy with a loss of fifty guns, thousands of small arms, and the loss of the greater part of their stores.

All idea of a further advance against Richmond was for the present abandoned. President Lincoln had always been opposed to the plan, and a considerable portion of the army was moved round to join the force under General Pope, which was now to march upon Richmond from the north.

From the commencement of the Federal advance to the time when, beaten and dispirited, they regained the James River, Vincent Wingfield had seen little of his family. The Federal lines had at one time been within a mile of the Orangery. The slaves had some days before been all sent into the interior, and Mrs. Wingfield and her daughters had moved into Richmond, where they joined in the work, to which the whole of the ladies of the town and neighborhood devoted themselves, of attending to the wounded, of whom, while the fighting was going on, long trains arrived every day at the city.

Vincent himself had taken no active part in the fighting. Magruder's division had not been engaged in the first attack upon McClellan's force; and although it had taken a share in the subsequent severe fighting, Vincent had been occupied in carrying messages from the general to the leaders of the other divisions, and had only once or twice come under the storm of fire to which the Confederates were exposed as they plunged through the morasses to attack the enemy. As soon as it was certain that the attack was finally abandoned, and that McClellan's troops were being withdrawn to strengthen Pope's army, Vincent resigned his appointment as aide-de-camp, and was appointed to the 7th Virginian Cavalry, stationed at Orange, where it was facing the Federal cavalry. Major Ashley had fallen while protecting the passage of Jackson's division when hard pressed by one of the Federal armies in Western Virginia.

No action in the war had been more brilliant than the manner in which Stonewall Jackson had baffled the two armies--each greatly superior in force to his own-- that had been specially appointed to destroy him if possible, or at any rate to prevent his withdrawing from the Shenandoah Valley and marching to aid in the defense of the Confederate capital. His troops had marched almost day and night, without food, and depending entirely upon such supplies as they could obtain from the scattered farmhouses they passed.

Although Richmond was for the present safe, the prospect of the Confederates was by no means bright. New Orleans had been captured; the blockade of the other ports was now so strict that it was difficult in the extreme for a vessel to make her way in or out; and the Northerners had placed flotillas of gunboats on the rivers, and by the aid of these were gradually making their way into the heart of several of the States.

"Are you thinking of going out to the Orangery again soon, mother?" Vincent asked on the evening before setting out on the march north.

"I think not, Vincent. There is so much to do in the hospitals here that I cannot leave. I should be ashamed to be living in luxury at the Orangery with the girls while other women are giving up their whole time nursing the wounded. Besides, although I do not anticipate that after the way they have been hurled back the Northerners will try again for some time, now they are in possession of Harrison's Landing they can at any moment advance. Besides, it is not pleasant being obliged to turn out of one's house and leave everything to their mercy. I wrote yesterday to Pearson to bring the slaves back at once and take up the work, and I shall go over occasionally to see that everything is in order; but at any rate for a time we will stop here."

"I think that is best, mother. Certainly I should feel more comfortable knowing that you are all at Richmond than alone out there."

"We should be no worse off than thousands of ladies all over the State, Vincent There are whole districts where every white capable of using a gun has gone to the war, leaving nothing but women and slaves behind, and we have not heard of a single case in which there has been trouble."

"Certainly there is no chance of trouble with your slaves, mother; but in some of the other plantations it may not be so. At any rate the quiet conduct of the slaves everywhere is the very best answer that could be given to the accusations that have been made as to their cruel treatment. At present the whole of the property of the slave-owners throughout the Southern States is at their mercy, and they might burn, kill, and destroy; and yet in no single instance have they risen against what are called their oppressors, even when the Federals have been close at hand.

"Please keep your eye on Dinah, mother. I distrust; that fellow Jackson so thoroughly that I believe him capable of having her carried off and smuggled away somewhere down south, and sold there if he saw a chance. I wish, instead of sending her to the Orangery, you would keep her as one of your servants here."

"I will if you wish it, Vincent; but I cannot believe for a moment that this Jackson or any one else would venture to meddle with any of my slaves."

"Perhaps not, mother; but it is best to be on the safe side. Anyhow, I shall be glad to know that she is with you. Young Jackson will be away, for I know he is in one of Stuart's troops of horse, though I have never happened to run against him since the war began."

The firing had hardly ceased before Harrison's Landing, when General Jackson, with a force of about 15,000 men, composed of his own division, now commanded by General Winder, General Ewell's division, and a portion of that of General Hill, started for the Rapidan to check General Pope, who, plundering and wasting the country as he advanced, was marching south, his object being to reach Gordonsville, where he would cut the line of railway connecting Richmond with Western Virginia. Vincent was glad that the regiment to which he had been appointed would be under Jackson's command, and that he would be campaigning again with his old division, which consisted largely of Virginian troops and contained so many of his old friends.

With Jackson, too, he was certain to be engaged in stirring service, for that general ever kept his troops upon the march, striking blows where least expected, and traversing such an extent of country by rapid marches that he and his division seemed to the enemy to be almost ubiquitous.

It was but a few hours after he received his appointment that Vincent took train from Richmond to Gordonsville, Dan being in the horse-box with Wildfire in the rear of the train. His regiment was encamped a mile or two away, and he at once rode on and reported himself to Colonel Jones, who commanded it.

"I am glad to have you with me, sir," the colonel said. "I had the pleasure of knowing your father, and am an old friend of your mother's family. As you were in Ashley's horse and have been serving on Magruder's staff, you are well up in your duties; and it is a comfort to me that the vacancy has been filled up by one who knows his work instead of a raw hand. We have had a brush or two already with the enemy; but at present we are watching each other, waiting on both sides till the generals have got their infantry to the front in readiness for an advance. Jackson is waiting for Hill's division to come up, and I believe Pope is expecting great reinforcements from McClellan."

A few days later Colonel Jones was ordered to take charge of the pickets posted on the Rapidan, but before reaching Orange a gentleman rode up at full speed and informed them that the enemy were in possession of that town. Colonel Jones divided his regiment into two parts, and with one charged the Federal cavalry in the main street of Orange, while the other portion of the regiment, under Major Marshall, attacked them on the flank. After a sharp fight the enemy were driven from the place; but they brought up large reinforcements, and, pouring in a heavy fire, attacked the town on both sides, and the Confederates had to fall back. But they made another stand a little way out of the town, and drove back the Federal cavalry who were pressing them.

Although the fight had been but a short one the losses in the cavalry ranks had been serious. Colonel Jones, while charging at the head of his men, had received a saber-wound, and Major Marshall was taken prisoner.

Five days later, on the 7th of August, Jackson received certain intelligence that General Burnside, with a considerable portion of McClellan's force, had embarked, and was on the way to join Pope. He determined to strike a blow at once, and marched with his entire force from Gordonsville for Barnett Ford on the Rapidan.

At daybreak next morning the cavalry crossed the river and attacked and routed a body of Federal cavalry on the road to Culpepper Courthouse. On the following day Jackson came up with his infantry to a point about eight miles from Culpepper, where Pope's army, 32,000 strong, were stationed upon the crest of a hill. General Ewell's division, which was the only one then up, at once advanced, and, after a severe artillery fight, gained a point on a hill where his guns could command the enemy's position.

Jackson's division now came up, and as it was moving into position General Winder was killed by a shell. For some hours Jackson did not attempt to advance, as Hill's division had not come up. Encouraged by this delay, the enemy at five o'clock in the afternoon took the offensive and advanced through some cornfields lying between the two armies and attacked Ewell's division on the Confederate right; while shortly afterward they fell with overwhelming strength on Jackson's left, and, attacking it in front, flank, and rear, drove it back, and pressed upon it with such force that the day appeared lost.

At this moment Jackson himself rode down among the confused and wavering troops, and by his voice and example rallied them. At the same moment the old Stonewall Brigade came up at a run and poured their fire into the advancing enemy. Jackson led the troops he had rallied forward. The Stonewall Brigade fell upon the enemy's flank and drove them back with terrible slaughter. Other brigades came up, and there was a general charge along the whole Confederate line, and the Federals were driven back a mile beyond the position they had occupied at the commencement of the fight to the shelter of some thick woods. Four hundred prisoners were taken and over 5,000 small-arms.

The battle was known as Cedar Run, and it completely checked Pope's advance upon Richmond. The troops were too much exhausted to follow up their victory, but Jackson urged them to press forward. They moved a mile and a half in advance, and then found themselves so strongly opposed that Jackson, believing that the enemy must have received reinforcements, halted his men. Colonel Jones was sent forward to reconnoiter, and discovered that a large force had joined the enemy.

For two days Jackson remained on the field he had won; his troops had been busy in burying the dead, in collecting the wounded and sending them to the rear, and in gathering the arms thrown away by the enemy in their flight. Being assured that the enemy were now too strong to be attacked by the force under his command, Jackson fell back to Orange Courthouse. There was now a few days' delay, while masses of troops were on both sides moving toward the new field of action. McClellan marched his troops across the James Peninsula from Harrison's Landing to Yorktown, and there the greater portion were embarked in transports and taken up the Rappahannock to Aquia Creek, landed there, and marched to Fredericksburg.

Lee, instead of attacking McClellan on his march across the peninsula, determined to take his army north at once to join Jackson and attack Pope before he was joined by McClellan's army. But Pope, although already largely reinforced, retired hastily and took up a new position so strongly fortified that he could not be attacked. General Stuart had come up with Lee, and was in command of all the cavalry.

"We shall see some work now," was the remark round the fires of the 7th Virginian Cavalry. Hitherto, although they had been several times engaged with the Federals, they had been forced to remain for the most part inactive owing to the vast superiority in force of the enemy's cavalry; but now that Stuart had come up they felt certain that, whatever the disparity of numbers, there would soon be some dashing work to be done.

Except when upon actual duty the strict lines of military discipline were much relaxed among the cavalry, the troopers being almost all the sons of farmers and planters and of equal social rank with their officers, many of whom were their personal friends or relatives. Several of Vincent's schoolfellows were in the ranks; two or three of them were fellow officers, and these often gathered together round a camp fire and chatted over old schooldays and mutual friends.

Many of these had already fallen, for the Virginian regiments of Stonewall Jackson's brigade had been terribly thinned; but the loss of so many friends and the knowledge that their own turn might come next did not suffice to lessen the high spirits of the young fellows. The hard work, the rough life, the exposure and hardship, had braced and invigorated them all, and they were attaining a far more vigorous manhood than they would ever have possessed had they grown up in the somewhat sluggish and enervating life led by young planters.

Many of these young men had, until the campaign began, never done half an hour's hard work in their lives. They had been waited upon by slaves, and their only exercise had been riding. For months now they had almost lived in the saddle, had slept in the open air, and had thought themselves lucky if they could obtain a sufficient meal of the roughest food to satisfy their hunger once a day. In this respect, however, the cavalry were better off than their comrades of the infantry, for scouting as they did in small parties over a wide extent of country, they were sure of a meal and a hearty welcome whenever they could spare time to stop for half an hour at the house of a farmer.

"It's a glorious life, Wingfield! When we chatted over the future at school we never dreamed of such a life as this, though some of us did talk of entering the army; but even then an occasional skirmish with Indians was the limit of our ideas."

"Yes, it is a glorious life!" Vincent agreed. "I cannot imagine anything more exciting. Of course, there is the risk of being shot, but somehow one never seems to think of that. There is always something to do and to think about; from the time one starts on a scout at daybreak to that when one lies down at night one's senses are on the stretch. Besides, we are fighting in defense of our country and not merely as a profession, though I don't suppose, after all, that makes much difference when one is once in for it. As far as I have read all soldiers enjoy campaigning, and it does not seem to make any difference to them who are the foe or what they are fighting about. But I should like to feel a little more sure that we shall win in the long run."

There was a chorus of indignant protests against there being any possible doubts as to the issue.

"Why, we have thrashed them every time we have met them, Wingfield."

"That is all very well," Vincent said. "Here in Virginia we have held our own, and more than held it. We have beat back Scott and McClellan, and now we have thrashed Pope; and Stonewall Jackson has won a dozen battles in Western Virginia. But you must remember that in other parts they are gradually closing in; all the ports not already taken are closely blockaded; they are pushing all along the lines of the great rivers; and worst of all, they can fill up their vacancies with Irishmen and Germans, and as fast as one army disappears another takes its place. I believe we shall beat them again and again, and shall prove, as we have proved before, that one Southerner fighting for home and liberty is more than a match for two hired Germans or Irishmen, even with a good large sprinkling of Yankees among them. But in the long run I am not sure that we shall win, for they can go on putting big armies into the field, while some day we must get used up.

"Of course it is possible that we may some day capture Washington, and that the North may get weary of the tremendous drain of money and men caused by their attempt to conquer us. I hope it may be so, for I should like to think that we should win in the long run. I never feel any doubt about our winning a battle when we begin. My only fear is that we may get used up before the North are tired of it."

"I did not expect to hear you talk so, Wingfield, for you always seem to be in capital spirits."

"I am in capital spirits," Vincent replied, "and ready to fight again and again, and always confident we shall lick the Yankees; the fact that I have a doubt whether in the long run we shall outlast them does not interfere in the slightest degree with my comfort at present. I am very sorry though that this fellow Pope is carrying on the war so brutally instead of in the manner in which General McClellan and the other commanders have waged it. His proclamation that the army must subsist upon the country it passes through gives a direct invitation to the soldiers to pillage, and his order that all farmers who refuse to take the oath to the Union are to be driven from their homes and sent down south means ruin to all the peaceful inhabitants, for there is scarcely a man in this part of Virginia who is not heartily with us."

"I hear," one of the other officers said, "that a prisoner who was captured this morning says that Pope already sees that he has made a mistake, and that he yesterday issued a fresh order saying that the proclamation was not meant to authorize pillage. He finds that the inhabitants who before, whatever their private sentiments were, maintained a sort of neutrality, are now hostile, that they drive off their cattle into the woods, and even set fire to their stacks, to prevent anything from being carried off by the Yanks; and his troops find the roads broken up and bridges destroyed and all sorts of difficulties thrown in their way."

"It does not always pay--even in war--to be brutal. I am glad to see he has found out his mistake so soon," another officer said. "McClellan waged war like a gentleman; and if blackguards are to be allowed to carry fire and sword through the land they will soon find it is a game that two can play at, and matters will become horribly embittered."

"We shall never do that," Vincent said. "Our generals are all gentlemen, and Lee and Jackson and many others are true Christians as well as true soldiers, and I am sure they will never countenance that on our side whatever the Northerners may do. We are ready to fight the hordes of Yankees and Germans and Irishmen as often as they advance against us, but I am sure that none of us would fire a homestead or ill-treat defenseless men and women. It is a scandal that such brutalities are committed by the ruffians who call themselves Southerners. The guerrillas in Missouri and Tennessee are equally bad whether on our side or the other, and if I were the president I would send down a couple of regiments, and hunt down the fellows who bring dishonor on our cause. If the South cannot free herself without the aid of ruffians of this kind she had better lay down her arms at once."

"Bravo, Wingfield! spoken like a knight of chivalry!" one of the others laughed. "But many of these bands have done good nevertheless. They have kept the enemy busy there, and occupied the attention of a very large force who might otherwise have been in the woods yonder with Pope. I agree with you, it would be better if the whole thing were fought out with large armies, but there is a good deal to be said for these bands you are so severe upon. They are composed of men who have been made desperate by seeing their farms harried and their buildings burned by the enemy. They have been denounced as traitors by their neighbors on the other side, and if they retaliate I don't know that they are to be altogether blamed. I know that if my place at home were burned down and my people insulted and ill-treated I should be inclined to set off to avenge it."

"So would I," Vincent agreed, "but it should be upon those who did the wrong, not upon innocent people."

"That is all very well, but if the other side destroy your people's farms, it is only by showing them that two can play at the game that you can make them observe the laws of war. I grant it would be very much better that no such thing should take place; but if the Northerners begin this sort of work they may be sure that there will be retaliation. Anyhow, I am glad that I am an officer in the 7th Virginians and not a guerrilla leader in Missouri. Well, all this talking is dry work. Has no one got a full canteen?"

"I have," Vincent said. "Dan managed to buy a gallon of rum at a farmhouse yesterday. I think the farmer was afraid that the enemy might be paying him a visit before many days, and thought it best to get rid of his spirits. Anyhow, Dan got the keg at ordinary city prices, as well as that couple of fine turkeys he is just bringing along for our supper. So you had better each get your ration of bread and fall to."

There was a cheer as Dan placed the turkeys down in the center of the group, and soon the whole party, using their bread as plates, fell to upon them, and afterward joined in many a merry song, while Dan handed round the jar of spirits.

## CHAPTER IX. A PRISONER.

THE party round the fire were just about to disperse when the captain of Vincent's troop approached. He took the horn of spirits and water that Vincent held up to him and tossed it off.

"That is a stirrup-cup, Wingfield."

"What! are we for duty, captain?" Vincent asked as he rose to his feet.

"Yes; our troop and Harper's are to muster. Get the men together quietly. I think it is a serious business; each of the regiments furnish other troops, and I believe Stuart himself takes the command."

"That sounds like work, indeed," Vincent said. "I will get the troop together, sir."

"There are to be no trumpet calls, Wingfield; we are to get off as quietly as possible."

Most of the men were already fast asleep, but as soon as they learned that there was a prospect of active work all were full of life and animation. The girths of the saddles were tightened, swords buckled on, and revolvers carefully examined before being placed in the holsters. Many of the men carried repeating rifles, and the magazines were filled before these were slung across the riders' shoulders.

In a few minutes the three troops were mounted and in readiness for a start, and almost directly afterward Colonel Jones himself rode up and took the command. A thrill of satisfaction ran through the men as he did so, for it was certain that he would not himself be going in command of the detachment unless the occasion was an important one. For a few minutes no move was made.

"I suppose the others are going to join us here," Vincent said to the officer next him.

"I suppose so," he replied. "We lie in the middle of the cavalry brigade with two regiments each side of us, so it is likely enough this is the gathering place. Yes, I can hear the tramping of horses."

"And I felt a spot of rain," Vincent said. "It has been lightning for some time. I fear we are in for a wet ride."

The contingent from the other regiments soon arrived, and just as the last came up General Stuart himself appeared and took his place at the head of the party, now some 500 strong. Short as the time had been since Vincent felt the first drop, the rain was now coming down in torrents. One by one the bright flames of the fires died down, and the darkness became so intense that Vincent could scarcely see the officer on his right hand.

"I hope the man who rode up with the general, and is no doubt to be our guide, knows the country well. It is no joke finding our way through a forest on such a night as this."

"I believe Stuart's got eyes like a cat," the officer said. "Sometimes on a dark night he has come galloping up to a post where I was in command, when one could scarcely see one's hand before one. It never seems to make any difference to him; day or night he rides about at a gallop."

"He trusts his horse," Vincent said. "That's the only way in the dark. They can see a lot better than we can, and if men would but let them go their own way instead of trying to guide them they would seldom run against anything. The only thing is to lie well down on the horse's neck, otherwise one might get swept out of the saddle by a bough. It's a question of nerve, I think not many of us would do as Stuart does, and trust himself entirely to his horse's instinct."

The word was now passed down the line that perfect silence was to be observed, and that they were to move forward in column, the ranks closing up as much as possible so as not to lose touch of each other. With heads bent down, and blankets wrapped round them as cloaks, the cavalry rode off through the pouring rain. The thunder was clashing overhead, and the flashes of the lightning enabled them to keep their places in close column. They went at a rapid trot, and even those who were ready to charge a body of the enemy, however numerous, without a moment's hesitation, experienced a feeling of nervousness as they rode on in the darkness through the thick forest on their unknown errand. That they were going northward they knew, and knew also, after a short time, that they must be entering the lines of the enemy. They saw no signs of watch-fires, for these would long since have been quenched by the downpour. After half an hour's brisk riding all knew by the sharp sound of the beat of the horses' hoofs that they had left the soft track through the forest and were now upon a regular road.

"Thank goodness for that!" Vincent said in a low tone to his next neighbor. "I don't mind a brush with the enemy, but I own I don't like the idea that at any moment my brains may be knocked out by the branch of a tree."

"I quite agree with you," the other replied; "and I fancy every man felt the same."

There was no doubt as to this. Hitherto no sound had been heard save the jingling of accouterments and the dull heavy sound of the horses' tread; but now there could be heard mingled with these the buzz of voices, and occasionally a low laugh. They were so accustomed to wet that the soaking scarce inconvenienced them. They were out of the forest now, and felt sure of their guide; and as to the enemy, they only longed to discover them.

For another hour the rapid advance continued, and all felt sure that they must now have penetrated through the enemy's lines and be well in his rear. At last they heard a challenge of sentry. Then Stuart's voice shouted, "Charge!" and at full gallop they rode into the village at Catlet's Station on the Orange and Alexandria railroad, where General Pope had his headquarters. Another minute and they were in the midst of the enemy's camp, where the wildest confusion reigned. The Federal officers rushed from their teats and made off in the darkness; but the soldiers, who were lying on the line of railroad, leaped to their feet and opened a heavy fire upon their invisible foes. Against this the cavalry, broken up in the camp, with its tents, its animals, and its piles of baggage, could do little, for it was impossible to form them up in the broken and unknown ground.

The quarters of Pope were soon discovered; he himself had escaped, leaving his coat and hat behind. Many of his officers were captured, and in his quarters were found a box of official papers which were invaluable, as among them were copies of his letters asking for reinforcements, lists giving the strength and position of his troops, and other particulars of the greatest value to the Confederates. No time was lost, as the firing would set the whole Federal army on the alert, and they might find their retreat cut off. Therefore placing their prisoners in the center, and taking the box of papers with them, the cavalry were called off from the camp, and without delay started on their return ride.

They did not take the road by which they had come, but made a long detour, and just as daylight was breaking re-entered the Confederate lines without having encountered a foe from the time of their leaving Catlet's Station. Short as their stay in the camp had been, few of the men had returned empty handed. The Northern army was supplied with an abundance of excellent food of all descriptions, forming the strongest possible contrast to the insufficient rations upon which the Confederate troops existed, and the troopers had helped themselves to whatever they could lay hands upon in the darkness and confusion.

Some rode in with a ham slung on each side of their saddle, others had secured a bottle or two of wine or spirits. Some had been fortunate enough to lay hands on some tins of coffee or a canister of tea, luxuries which for months had been unknown to them save when they were captured from the enemy. The only article captured of no possible utility was General Pope's coat, which was sent to Richmond, where it was hung up for public inspection; a wag sticking up a paper beside it, "This is the coat in which General Pope was going to ride in triumph into Richmond. The coat is here, but the general has not yet arrived."

The Confederates had lost but two or three men from the fire of the Federal infantry, and they were in high spirits at the success of their raid. No sooner had General Lee informed himself of the contents of the papers and the position of the enemy's forces than he determined to strike a heavy blow at him; and General Jackson, who had been sharply engaged with the enemy near Warrenton, was ordered to make a long detour, to cross the Blue Ridge mountains through Thoroughfare Gap, to fall upon Pope's rear and cut his communications with Washington, and if possible to destroy the vast depot of stores collected at Manassas.

The cavalry, under Stuart, were to accompany him. The march would be a tremendous one, the danger of thus venturing into the heart of the enemy's country immense, but the results of such an expedition would, if successful, be great; for Lee himself was to advance with his army on Pope's flank, and there was therefore a possibility of the utter defeat of that general before he could be joined by the army marching to reinforce him from Fredericksburg.

It was on Monday the 25th of August that Jackson started on his march, ascending the banks of the Rappahannock, and crossed the river at a ford, dragging his artillery with difficulty up the narrow and rocky road beyond. There was not a moment to be lost, for if the news reached the enemy the gorge known as Thoroughfare Gap would be occupied, and the whole object of the movement be defeated. Onward the force pushed, pressing on through fields and lanes without a single halt, until at night, hungry and weary but full of spirit, they marched into the little town of Salem, twenty miles from their starting-place. They had neither wagons nor provisions with them, and had nothing to eat but some ears of corn and green apples plucked on the road.

It was midnight when they reached Salem, and the inhabitants turned out in blank amazement at the sight of Confederate troops in that region, and welcomed the weary soldiers with the warmest manifestations. At daylight they were again upon the march, with Stuart's cavalry, as before, out upon each flank. Thoroughfare Gap was reached, and found undefended, and after thirty miles' marching the exhausted troops reached the neighborhood of Manassas. The men were faint from want of food, and many of them limped along barefooted; but they were full of enthusiasm.

Just at sunset, Stuart, riding on ahead, captured Bristoe, a station on the Orange and Alexandria Railroad four miles from Manassas. As they reached it a train came along at full speed. It was fired at, but did not stop, and got safely through to Manassas. Two trains that followed were captured; but by this time the alarm had spread, and no more trains arrived. Jackson had gained his point. He had placed himself on the line of communication of the enemy, but his position was a dangerous one indeed. Lee, who was following him, was still far away. An army was marching from Fredericksburg against him, another would be despatched from Washington as soon as the news of his presence was known, and Pope might turn and crush him before Lee could arrive to his assistance.

Worn out as the troops were, it was necessary at once to gain possession of Manassas, and the 21st North Carolina and 21st Georgia volunteered for the service, and, joined by Stuart with a portion of his cavalry, marched against it. After a brief contest the place was taken, the enemy stationed there being all taken prisoners. The amount of arms and stores captured was prodigious: Eight pieces of artillery, 250 horses, 3 locomotives, and tens of thousands of barrels of beef, pork, and flour, with an enormous quantity of public stores and the contents of innumerable sutlers' shops.

The sight of this vast abundance to starving men was tantalizing in the extreme. It was impossible to carry any of it away and all that could be done was to have at least one good meal. The troops therefore were marched in and each helped himself to as much as he could consume, and the ragged and barefooted men feasted upon tinned salmon and lobsters, champagne and dainties of every description forwarded for the use of officers. Then they set to work to pile the enormous mass of stores together and to set it on fire. While they were engaged at this a brigade of New Jersey troops which had come out from Washington to save Manassas was attacked and utterly routed. Ewell's division had remained at Bristoe, while those of Hill and Jackson moved to Manassas, and in the course of the afternoon Ewell saw the whole of Pope's army marching against him.

He held them in check for some hours, and thus gave the troops at Manassas time to destroy completely the vast accumulation of stores, and when Stuart's cavalry, covering the retreat, fell back at nightfall through Manassas, nothing but blackened cinders remained where the Federal depots had been situated. The blow to the Northerners was as heavy as it was unexpected. Pope had no longer either provisions for his men or forage for his cattle, and there was nothing left for him but to force his way past Jackson and retire upon Washington.

Jackson had now the option of falling back and allowing the enemy to pass, or of withstanding the whole Federal army with his own little force until Lee came up to the rescue. He chose the latter course, and took up a strong position. The sound of firing at Thoroughfare Gap was audible, and he knew that Longstreet's division of Lee's army was hotly engaged with a force which, now that it was too late, had been sent to hold the gorge. It was nearly sunset before Pope brought up his men to the attack. Jackson did not stand on the defensive, but rushed down and attacked the enemy--whose object had been to pass the position and press on--with such vigor that at nine o'clock they fell back.

An hour later a horseman rode up with the news that Longstreet had passed the Gap and was pressing on at full speed, and in the morning his forces were seen approaching, the line they were taking bringing them up at an angle to Jackson's position. Thus their formation as they arrived was that of an open V, and it was through the angle of this V that Pope had to force his way. Before Longstreet could arrive, however, the enemy hurled themselves upon Jackson, and for hours the Confederates held their own against the vast Federal army, Longstreet's force being too far away to lend them a hand. Ammunition failed, and the soldiers fought with piles of stones, but night fell without any impression being made upon these veterans. General Lee now came up with General Hood's division, and hurled this against the Federals and drove them back. In the evening Longstreet's force took up the position General Lee had assigned to it, and in the morning all the Confederate army had arrived, and the battle recommenced.

The struggle was long and terrible; but by nightfall every attack had been repulsed, and the Confederates, advancing on all sides, drove the Northerners, a broken and confused crowd, before them, the darkness alone saving them from utter destruction. Had there been but one hour more of daylight the defeat would have been as complete as was that in the battle of Bull Run, which had been fought on precisely the same ground. However, under cover of the darkness the Federals retreated to Centreville, whence they were driven on the following day.

In the tremendous fighting in which Jackson's command had for three long days been engaged, the cavalry bore a comparatively small part. The Federal artillery was too powerful to permit the employment of large bodies of cavalry and although from time to time charges were made when an opportunity seemed to offer itself, the battle was fought out by the infantry and artillery. When the end came Jackson's command was for a time hors de combat. During the long two days' march they had at least gathered corn and apples to sustain life; but during these three days' fighting they had had no food whatever, and many were so weak that they could no longer march.

They had done all that was possible for men to do; had for two days withstood the attack of an enemy of five times their numbers, and had on the final day borne their full share in the great struggle, but now the greater part could do no more, thousands of men were unable to drag themselves a step further, and Lee's army was reduced in strength for the time by nearly 20,000 men. All these afterward rejoined it; some as soon as they recovered limped away to take their places in the ranks again, others made their way to the depot at Warrenton, where Lee had ordered that all unable to accompany his force should rendezvous until he returned and they were able to rejoin their regiments.

Jackson marched away and laid siege to Harper's Ferry, an important depot garrisoned by 11,000 men, who were forced to surrender just as McClellan with a fresh army, 100,000 strong, which was pressing forward to its succor, arrived within a day's march. As soon as Jackson had taken the place he hurried away with his troops to join Lee, who was facing the enemy at the Antietam river. Here upon the following day another terrible battle was fought; the Confederates, though but 39,000 strong, repulsing every attack by the Federals, and driving them with terrible slaughter back across the river.

Their own loss, however, had been very heavy, and Lee, knowing that he could expect no assistance, while the enemy were constantly receiving reinforcements, waited for a day to collect his wounded, bury his dead, and send his stores and artillery to the rear, and then retired unpursued across the Rappahannock. Thus the hard-fought campaign came to an end.

Vincent Wingfield was not with the army that retired across the Rappahannock. A portion of the cavalry had followed the broken Federals to the very edge of the stream, and just as they reined in their horses a round shot from one of the Federal batteries carried away his cap, and he fell as if dead from his horse. During the night some of the Northerners crossed the stream to collect and bring back their own wounded who had fallen near it, and coming across Vincent, and finding that he still breathed, and was apparently without a wound, they carried him back with them across the river as a prisoner.

Vincent had indeed escaped without a wound, having been only stunned by the passage of the shot that had carried away his cap, and missed him but by the fraction of an inch. He had begun to recover consciousness just as his captors came up, and the action of carrying him completely restored him. That he had fallen into the hands of the Northerners he was well aware; but he was unable to imagine how this had happened. He remembered that the Confederates had been, up to the moment when he fell, completely successful, and he could only imagine that in a subsequent attack the Federals had turned the tables upon them.

How he himself had fallen, or what had happened to him, he had no idea. Beyond a strange feeling of numbness in the head he was conscious of no injury, and he could only imagine that his horse had been shot under him, and that he must have fallen upon his head. The thought that his favorite horse was killed afflicted him almost as much as his own capture. As soon as his captors perceived that their prisoner's consciousness had returned they at once reported that an officer of Stuart's cavalry had been taken, and at daybreak next morning General McClellan on rising was acquainted with the fact, and Vincent was conducted to his tent.

"You are unwounded, sir?" the general said in some surprise.

"I am, general," Vincent replied. "I do not know how it happened, but I believe that my horse must have been shot under me, and that I must have been thrown and stunned; however, I remember nothing from the moment when I heard the word halt, just as we reached the side of the stream, to that when I found myself being carried here."

"You belong to the cavalry?"

"Yes, sir."

"Was Lee's force all engaged yesterday?"

"I do not know," Vincent said. "I only came up with Jackson's division from Harper's Ferry the evening before."

"I need not have questioned you," McClellan said. "I know that Lee's whole army, 100,000 strong, opposed me yesterday."

Vincent was silent. He was glad to see that the Federal general, as usual, enormously overrated the strength of the force opposed to him.

"I hear that the whole of the garrison of Harper's Ferry were released on parole not to serve again during the war. If you are ready to give me your promise to the same effect I will allow you to return to your friends; if not, you must remain a prisoner until you are regularly exchanged."

"I must do so, then, general," Vincent said quietly. "I could not return home and remain inactive while every man in the South is fighting for the defense of his country, so I will take my chance of being exchanged."

"I am sorry you choose that alternative," McClellan said. "I hate to see brave men imprisoned if only for a day; and braver men than those across yonder stream are not to be found. My officers and men are astonished. They seem so thin and worn as to be scarce able to lift a musket, their clothes are fit only for a scarecrow, they are indeed pitiful objects to look at; but the way in which they fight is wonderful. I could not have believed had I not seen it, that men could have charged as they did again and again across ground swept by a tremendous artillery and musketry fire; it was wonderful! I can tell you, young sir, that even though you beat us we are proud of you as our countrymen; and I believe that if your General Jackson were to ride through our camp he would be cheered as lustily and heartily by our men as he is by his own."

Some fifty or sixty other prisoners had been taken; they had been captured in the hand-to-hand struggle that had taken place on some parts of the field, having got separated from their corps and mixed up with the enemy, and carried off the field with them as they retired. These for the most part accepted the offered parole; but some fifteen, like Vincent, preferred a Northern prison to promising to abstain from fighting in defense of their country, and in the middle of the day they were placed together in a tent under a guard at the rear of the camp.

The next morning came the news that Lee had fallen back. There was exultation among the Federals, not unmingled with a strong sense of relief; for the heavy losses inflicted in the previous fighting had taken all the ardor of attack out of McClellan's army, and they were glad indeed that they were not to be called upon to make another attempt to drive the Confederates from their position. Vincent was no less pleased at the news. He knew how thin were the ranks of the Confederate fighting men, and how greatly they were worn and exhausted by fatigue and want of food, and that, although they had the day before repulsed the attacks of the masses of well-fed Northerners, such tremendous exertions could not often be repeated, and a defeat, with the river in their rear, approachable only by one rough and narrow road, would have meant a total destruction of the army.

The next morning Vincent and his companions were put into the train and sent to Alexandria. They had no reason to complain of their treatment upon the way. They were well fed, and after their starvation diet for the last six weeks their rations seemed to them actually luxurious. The Federal troops in Alexandria, who were for the most part young recruits who had just arrived from the north and west, looked with astonishment upon these thin and ragged men, several of whom were barefooted. Was it possible that such scarecrows as these could in every battle have driven back the well-fed and cared-for Northern soldiers!

"Are they all like this?" one burly young soldier from a western state asked their guard.

"That's them, sir," the sergeant in charge of the party replied. "Not much to look at, are they? But, by gosh, you should see them fight! You wouldn't think of their looks then."

"If that's soldiering," the young farmer said solemnly, "the sooner I am back home again the better. But it don't seem to me altogether strange as they should fight so hard, because I should say they must look upon it as a comfort to be killed rather than to live like that."

A shout of laughter from the prisoners showed the young rustic that the objects of his pity did not consider life to be altogether intolerable even under such circumstances, and he moved away meditating on the discomforts of war, and upon the remarks that would be made were he to return home in so sorrowful a plight as that of these Confederate prisoners.

"I bargained to fight," he said, "and though I don't expect I shall like it, I sha'n't draw back when the time comes; but as to being starved till you are nigh a skeleton, and going about barefooted and in such rags as a tramp wouldn't look at, it ain't reasonable." And yet, had he known it, among those fifteen prisoners more than half were possessors of wide estates, and had been brought up from their childhood in the midst of luxuries such as the young farmer never dreamed of.

Among many of the soldiers sympathy took a more active form, and men pressed forward and gave packets of tobacco, cigars, and other little presents to them, while two or three pressed rolls of dollar notes into their hands, with words of rough kindness.

"There ain't no ill feeling in us, Rebs. You have done your work like men and no doubt you thinks your cause is right, just as we does; but it's all over now, and maybe our turn will come next to see the inside of one of your prisons down south. So we are just soldiers together, and can feel for each other."

Discipline in small matters was never strictly enforced in the American armies, and the sergeant in charge offered no opposition to the soldiers mingling with the prisoners as they walked along.

Two days later they were sent by railway to the great prison at Elmira, a town in the southwest of the State of New York. When they reached the jail the prisoners were separated, Vincent, who was the only officer, being assigned quarters with some twenty others of the same rank. The prisoners crowded round him as he entered, eager to hear the last news from the front, for they heard from their guards only news of constant victories won by the Northerners; for every defeat was transformed by the Northern papers into a brilliant victory, and it was only when the shattered remains of the various armies returned to Alexandria to be re-formed that the truth gradually leaked out. Thus Antietam had been claimed as a great Northern victory, for although McClellan's troops had in the battle been hurled back shattered and broken across the river, two days afterward Lee had retired.

One of the prisoners, who was also dressed in cavalry uniform, hung back from the rest, and going to the window looked out while Vincent was chatting with the others. Presently he turned round, and Vincent recognized with surprise his old opponent Jackson. After a moment's hesitation he walked across the room to him.

"Jackson," he said, "we have not been friends lately, but I don't see why we should keep up our quarrel any longer; we got on all right at school together; and now we are prisoners together here it would be foolish to continue our quarrel. Perhaps we were both somewhat to blame in that affair. I am quite willing to allow I was, for one, but I think we might well put it all aside now."

Jackson hesitated, and then took the hand Vincent held out to him.

"That's right, young fellows," one of the other officers said. "Now that every Southern gentleman is fighting and giving his life, if need be, for his country, no one has a right to have private quarrels of his own. Life is short enough as it is, certainly too short to indulge in private animosities. A few weeks ago we were fighting side by side, and facing death together; to-day we are prisoners; a week hence we may be exchanged, and soon take our places in the ranks again. It's the duty of all Southerners to stand shoulder to shoulder, and there ought to be no such thing as ill-feeling among ourselves."

Vincent was not previously aware that Jackson had obtained a commission. He now learned that he had been chosen by his comrades to fill a vacancy caused by the death of an officer in a skirmish just before Pope fell back from the Rappahannock, and that he had been made prisoner a few days afterward in a charge against a greatly superior body of Federal cavalry.

The great majority of the officers on both sides were at the commencement of the war chosen by their comrades, the elections at first taking place once a year. This, however, was found to act very badly. In some cases the best men in the regiment were chosen; but too often men who had the command of money, and could afford to stand treat and get in supplies of food and spirits, were elected. The evils of the system were found so great, indeed, that it was gradually abandoned; but in cases of vacancies occurring in the field, and there being a necessity for at once filling them up, the colonels of the regiments had power to make appointments, and if the choice of the men was considered to be satisfactory their nominee would be generally chosen.

In the case of Jackson, the colonel had hesitated in confirming the choice of the men. He did not for a moment suspect him to be wanting in courage; but he regarded him as one who shirked his work, and who won the votes of the men rather by a fluent tongue and by the violence of his expressions of hatred against the North than by any soldierly qualities.

Some of the officers had been months in prison, and they were highly indignant at the delays that had occurred in effecting their exchange. The South, indeed, would have been only too glad to get rid of some of their numerous prisoners, who were simply an expense and trouble to them, and to get their own men back into their ranks. They could ill spare the soldiers required to guard so large a number of prisoners, and a supply of food was in itself a serious matter.

Thus it was that at Harper's Ferry and upon a good many other occasions they released vast numbers of prisoners on their simple paroles not to serve again. The North, however, were in no hurry to make exchange; and moreover, their hands were so full with their enormous preparations that they put aside all matters which had not the claim of urgency.

## CHAPTER X. THE ESCAPE.

THE discipline in the prison at Elmira was not rigorous. The prisoners had to clean up the cells, halls, and yard, but the rest of their time they could spend as they liked. Some of those whose friends had money were able to live in comparative luxury, and to assist those who had no such resources; for throughout the war there was never any great difficulty in passing letters to and from the South. The line of frontier was enormous, and it was only at certain points that hostilities, were actively carried on; consequently letters and newspapers were freely passed, and money could be sent in the same way from one part of the country to another.

At certain hours of the day hawkers and vendors of such articles as were in most demand by the prisoners were allowed to enter the yard and to sell their wares to the Confederates. Spirits were not allowed to be carried in, but tobacco and all kinds of food were permitted to pass. Vincent had at Alexandria written a letter to his mother, and had given it to a man who represented that he made it his business to forward letters to an agent at Richmond, being paid for each letter the sum of a dollar on its delivery. Vincent therefore felt confident that the anxiety that would be felt at home when they learned that he was among the missing at the battle of Antietam would be relieved.

He was fairly supplied with money. He had, indeed, had several hundred dollars with him at the time he was captured; but these were entirely in Confederate notes, for which he got but half their value in Northern paper at Alexandria. He himself found the rations supplied in the prison ample, and was able to aid any of his fellow-prisoners in purchasing clothes to replace the rags they wore when captured.

One day Vincent strolled down as usual toward the gate, where, under the eye of the guard, a row of men and women, principally negroes and negresses, were sitting on the ground with their baskets in front of them containing tobacco, pipes, fruit, cakes, needles and thread, buttons, and a variety of other articles in demand, while a number of prisoners were bargaining and joking with them. Presently his eye fell upon a negro before whom was a great pile of watermelons. He started as he did so, for he at once recognized the well-known face of Dan. As soon as the negro saw that his master's eye had fallen upon him he began loudly praising the quality of his fruit.

"Here, massa officer, here berry fine melyons, ripe and sweet; no green trash; dis un good right through. Five cents each, sah. Berry cheap dese."

"I expect they cost you nothing, Sambo," one of the Confederate soldiers said as he bought a melon. "Got a neighbor's patch handy, eh?"

Dan grinned at the joke, and then selecting another from the bottom of his pile in the basket, offered it to Vincent.

"Dis fine fruit, sah. Me sure you please with him!"

Vincent took the melon and handed Dan five cents. A momentary glance was exchanged, and then he walked away and sat down in a quiet corner of the yard and cut open the melon. As he expected, he found a note rolled up in the center. A small piece of the rind had been cut out and the pulp removed for its reception. The bit of rind had then been carefully replaced so that the cut would not be noticed without close inspection. It was from one of his fellow-officers, and was dated the day after his capture. He read as follows:

"My Dear Wingfield.-We are all delighted this afternoon to hear that instead, as we had believed, of your being knocked on the head you are a prisoner among the Yanks. Several of us noticed you fall just as we halted at the river, and we all thought that from the way in which you fell you had been shot through the head or heart. However, there was no time to inquire in that terrific storm of shot and shell. In the morning when the burying parties went down we could find no signs of you, although we knew almost to a foot where you had fallen.

"We could only conclude at last that you had been carried off in the night by the Yanks, and as they would hardly take the trouble of carrying off a dead body, it occurred to us that you might after all be alive. So the colonel went to Lee, who at once sent a trumpeter with a flag down to the river to inquire, and we were all mightily pleased, as you may imagine, when he came back with the news that you were not only a prisoner, but unwounded, having been only stunned in some way. From the way you fell we suppose a round shot must have grazed your head; at least that is the only way we can account for it.

"Your horse came back unhurt to the troop, and will be well cared for until you rejoin us, which we hope will not be long. Your boy kept the camp awake last night with his howlings, and is at present almost out of his mind with delight. He tells me he has made up his mind to slip across the lines and make his way as a runaway to Alexandria, where you will, of course, be taken in the first place. He says he's got some money of yours; but I have insisted on his taking another fifty dollars, which you can repay me when we next meet. As he will not have to ask for work, he may escape the usual lot of runaways, who are generally pounced upon and set to work on the fortifications of Alexandria and Washington.

"He intends to find out what prison you are taken to, and to follow you, with some vague idea of being able to aid you to escape. As he cannot write, he has asked me to write this letter to you, telling you what his idea is. He will give it to you when he finds an opportunity, and he wishes you to give him an answer, making any suggestion that may occur to you as to the best way of his setting about it. He says that he shall make acquaintances among the negroes North, and will find some one who will read your note to him and write you an answer. I have told him that if he is caught at the game he is likely to be inside a prison a bit longer than you are, even if worse doesn't befall him. However, he makes light of this, and is bent upon carrying out his plans, and I can only hope he will succeed.

"I have just heard that we shall fall back across the Rappahannock to-morrow, and I imagine there will not be much hard fighting again until spring, long before which I hope you will be in your place among us again. We lost twenty-three men and two officers (Ketler and Sumner) yesterday. Good-by, old fellow! I need not say keep up your spirits, for that you are pretty sure to do.

"Yours truly,
"James Sinclair."

After the first start at seeing Dan, Vincent was scarcely surprised, for he had often thought over what the boy would do, and had fancied that while, if he supposed him dead, he would go straight back to the Orangery, it was quite possible that, should he hear that he was a prisoner, Dan might take it into his head to endeavor to join him. As to his making his escape, that did not appear to be a very difficult undertaking now that he had a friend outside. The watch kept up was not a very vigilant one, for such numbers of prisoners were taken on both sides that they were not regarded as of very great importance, and, indeed, the difficulty lay rather in making across the country to the Southern border than in escaping from prison; for with a friend outside, with a disguise in readiness, that matter was comparatively easy. All that was required for the adventure was a long rope, a sharp file, and a dark night.

The chief difficulty that occurred to Vincent arose from the fact that there were some twenty other prisoners in the same ward. He could hardly file through the bars of the window unnoticed by them, and they would naturally wish to share in his flight; but where one person might succeed in evading the vigilance of the guard, it was unlikely in the extreme that twenty would do so, and the alarm once given all would be recaptured. He was spared the trouble of making up his mind as to his plans, for by the time he had finished his letter the hour that the hucksters were allowed to sell their goods was passed, and the gates were shut and all was quiet.

After some thought he came to the conclusion that the only plan would be to conceal himself somewhere in the prison just before the hour at which they were locked up in their wards. The alarm would be given, for the list of names was called over before lock-up, and a search would of course be made. Still, if he could find a good place for concealment, it might succeed, since the search after dark would not be so close and minute as that which would be made next morning. The only disadvantage would be that the sentries would be especially on the alert, as, unless the fugitive had succeeded in some way in passing out of the gates in disguise, he must still be within the walls, and might attempt to scale them through the night. This certainty largely increased the danger, and Vincent went to bed that night without finally determining what had better be done.

The next morning while walking in the grounds he quite determined as to the place he would choose for his concealment if he adopted the plan he had thought of the evening before. The lower rooms upon one side of the building were inhabited by the governor and officers of the prison, and if he were to spring through an open window unnoticed just as it became dusk, and hide himself in a cupboard or under a bed there he would be safe for a time, as, however close the search might be in other parts of the building, it would be scarcely suspected, at any rate on the first alarm, that he had concealed himself in the officers' quarters. There would, of course, be the chance of his being detected as he got out of the window again at night, but this would not be a great risk. It was the vigilance of the sentries that he most feared, and the possibility that, as soon as the fact of his being missing was known, a cordon of guards might be stationed outside the wall in addition to those in the yard. The danger appeared to him to be so great that he was half inclined to abandon the enterprise. It would certainly be weary work to be shut up there for perhaps a year while his friends were fighting the battles of his country; but it would be better after all to put up with that than to run any extreme risk of being shot.

When he had arrived at this conclusion he went upstairs to his room to write a line to Dan. The day was a fine one, and he found that the whole of the occupants of the room had gone below. This was an unexpected bit of good fortune, and he at once went to the window and examined the bars. They were thick and of new iron, but had been hastily put up. The building had originally been a large warehouse, and when it had been converted into a prison for the Confederate prisoners the bars had been added to the windows. Instead, therefore, of being built into solid stone and fastened in by lead, they were merely screwed on to the wooden framework of the windows, and by a strong turn-screw a bar could be removed in five minutes. This altogether altered the position. He had only to wait until the rest of the occupants of the room were asleep and then to remove the bar and let himself down.

He at once wrote:

"I want twenty yards of strong string, and the same length of rope that will bear my weight; also a strong turn-screw. When I have got this I will let you know night and hour. Shall want disguise ready to put on."

He folded the note up into a small compass, and at the hour at which Dan would be about to enter he sauntered down to the gate. In a short time the vendors entered, and were soon busy selling their wares. Dan had, as before, a basket of melons. Vincent made his way up to him.

"I want another melon," he said, "as good as that you me last night."

"Dey all de same, sah. First-rate melyons dose; just melt away in your mouf like honey."

He held up one of the melons, and Vincent placed in his hands the coppers in payment. Between two of them he had placed the little note. Dan's hands closed quickly on the coins, and dropping them into his pocket he addressed the next customer, while Vincent sauntered away again. This time the melon was a whole one, and Vincent divided it with a couple of other prisoners for the fruit was too large for one person to consume, being quite as large as a man's head.

The next day another melon was bought, but this time Vincent did not open it in public. Examining it closely, he perceived that it had been cut through the middle, and no doubt contained a portion of the rope. He hesitated as to his next step. If he took the melon up to his room he would be sure to find some men there, and would be naturally called upon to divide the fruit; and yet there was nowhere else he could hide it. For a long time he sat with his back to the wall and the melon beside him, abusing himself for his folly in not having told Dan to send the rope in small lengths that he could hide about him. The place where he had sat down was one of the quietest in the yard, but men were constantly strolling up and down. He determined at last that the only possible plan was in the first place to throw his coat over his melon, to tuck it up underneath it, then to get hold of one end of the ball of rope that it doubtless contained and to endeavor to wind it round his body without being observed. It was a risky business, and he would gladly have tossed the melon over the wall had he dared to do so; for if he were detected, not only would he be punished with much more severe imprisonment, but Dan might be arrested and punished most severely.

Unfortunately the weather was by no means hot, and it would look strange to take off his coat, besides, if he did so, how could he coil the rope round him without being observed? So that idea was abandoned. He got up and walked to an angle in the wall, and there sat down again, concealing the melon as well as he could between him and the wall when any one happened to come near him. He pulled the halves apart and found, as he had suspected, it was but a shell, the whole of the fruit having been scooped out. But he gave an exclamation of pleasure on seeing that instead, as he feared, of a large ball of rope being inside, the interior was filled with neatly-made hanks, each containing several yards of thin but strong rope, together with a hank of strong string.

Unbuttoning his coat, he thrust them in; then he took the melon rind and broke it into very small pieces and threw them about. He then went up to his room and thrust the hanks, unobserved, one by one among the straw which, covered by an army blanket, constituted his bed. To-morrow, no doubt, Dan would supply him somehow with a turn-screw. On going down to the gate next day he found that the negro had changed his commodity, and that this time his basket contained very large and fine cucumbers. These were selling briskly, and Vincent saw that Dan was looking round anxiously, and that an expression of relief came over his face as he perceived him. He had, indeed, but eight or ten cucumbers left.

"Cucumbers to-day, sah? Berry fine cucumbers--first-rate cucumbers dese."

"They look rather over-ripe," Vincent said.

"Not a bit, sah; dey just ripe. Dis berry fine one-ten cents dis."

"You are putting up your prices, darkey, and are making a fortune out of us," Vincent said as he took the cucumber, which was a very large and straight one. He had no difficulty with this, as with the melon; a sharp twist broke it in two as he reached the corner he had used the day previously. It had been cut in half, one end had been scooped out for the reception of the handle of the turn-screw, and the metal been driven in to the head in the other half. Hiding it under his jacket, he felt that he was now prepared for escape.

He now asked himself whether he should go alone or take one or more of his comrades into his confidence, and finally determined to give a young Virginian officer named Geary, with whom he had been specially friendly during his imprisonment, and Jackson, a chance of escape. He did not like the latter, but he thought that after the reconciliation that had taken place between them it was only right to take him rather than a stranger. Drawing them aside, then, he told them that he had arranged a mode of escape; it was impossible that all could avail themselves of it, but that they were welcome to accompany him. They thanked him heartily for the offer, and, when he explained the manner in which he intended to make off, agreed to try their fortune with him.

"I propose," he said, "as soon as we are fairly beyond the prison, we separate, and each try to gain the frontier as best he can. The fact that three prisoners have escaped will soon be known all over the country, and there would be no chance whatever for us if we kept together. I will tell my boy to have three disguises ready; and when we once put aside our uniforms I see no reason why, traveling separately, suspicion should fall upon us; we ought to have no difficulty until at any rate we arrive near the border, and there must be plenty of points where we can cross without going anywhere near the Federal camps." The others at once agreed that the chances of making their way separately were much greater than if together. This being arranged, Vincent passed a note next day to Dan, telling him to have three disguises in readiness, and to be at the foot of the western wall, halfway along, at twelve o'clock on the first wet night. A string would be thrown over, with a knife fastened to it. He was to pull on the string till the rope came into his hand, and to hold that tight until they were over. Vincent chose this spot because it was equally removed from the sentry-boxes at the corners of the yard, and because there was a stone seat in the yard to which one end of the rope could be attached.

That night was fine, but the next was thick and misty. At nine o'clock all were in bed, and he lay listening to the clocks in the distance. Ten struck, and eleven, and when he thought it was approaching twelve he got up and crept to the window. He was joined immediately by the others; the turn-screw was set to work; and, as he expected, Vincent found no trouble whatever with the screws, which were not yet rusted in the wood, and turned immediately when the powerful screw-driver was applied to them. When all were out the bar was carefully lifted from its place and laid upon the floor.

The rope was then put round one of the other bars and drawn through it until the two ends came together. These were then dropped to the ground below. Geary went first, Jackson followed, and Vincent was soon standing beside them. Taking one end of the rope, he pulled it until the other passed round the bar and fell at their feet. All three were barefooted, and they stole noiselessly across the yard to the seat, which was nearly opposite their window. Vincent had already fastened his clasp-knife to the end of the string, and he now threw it over the wall, which was about twenty feet high.

He had tied a knot at forty feet from the end, and, standing close to the wall, he drew in the string until the knot was in his hand. Another two yards, and he knew that the knife was hanging a yard from the ground against the wall. He now drew it up and down, hoping that the slight noise the knife made against the wall might aid Dan in finding it. In two or three minutes he felt a jerk, and knew that Dan had got it. He fastened the end of the string to the rope and waited. The rope was gradually drawn up; when it neared the end he fastened it to the stone seat.

"Now," he said, "up you go, Geary."

The order in which they were to ascend had been settled by lot, as Geary insisted that Vincent, who had contrived the whole affair, should be the first to escape; but Vincent declined to accept the advantage, and the three had accordingly tossed up for precedence.

Geary was quickly over, and lowered himself on the opposite side. The others followed safely, but not without a good deal of scraping against the wall, for the smallness of the rope added to the difficulty of climbing it. However, the noise was so slight that they had little fear of attracting attention, especially as the sentries would be standing in their boxes, for the rain was now coming down pretty briskly. As soon as they were down Vincent seized Dan by the hand.

"My brave lad," he said, "I owe you my freedom, and I sha'n't forget it. Now, where are the clothes?"

"Here day are, sah. One is a rough suit, like a workingman's; another is a black-and-white sort of suit--a check-suit; de oder one is for you--a clargy's suit, sir. You make very nice young minister, for sure."

"All right, Dan!" Vincent said laughing; "give me the minister's suit."

"Then I will be the countryman," Geary said.

There was a little suppressed laughter as they changed their clothes in the dark; and then, leaving their uniforms by the wall, they shook hands and started at once in different directions, lest they might come across some one who would, when the escape was known, remember four men having passed him in the dark.

"Now, Dan, what is the next move?" Vincent asked as they walked off. "Have you fixed upon any plan?"

"No special plan, sah, but I have brought a bag; you see I have him in my hand."

"I suppose that's what you carried the clothes in?"

"No, sir; I carried dem in a bundle. Dis bag has got linen, and boots, and oder tings for you, sah. What I tink am de best way is dis. Dar am a train pass trou here at two o'clock and stop at dis station. Some people always get out. Dar is an hotel just opposite the station, and some of de passengers most always go there. I thought the best way for you would be to go outside the station. Just when the train come in we walk across de road wid the others and go to hotel. You say you want bedroom for yo'self, and that your sarvant can sleep in de hall. Den in de morning you get up and breakfast, and go off by de fust train."

"But then they may send down to look at the passengers starting, and I should be taken at once."

"De train go out at seven o'clock, sah. I don't expect dey find dat you have got away before dat."

"No, Dan. We all turn out at seven, and I shall be missed then; but it will be some little time before the alarm is given, and they find out how we got away, and send out search-parties. If the train is anything like punctual we shall be off long before they get to the station."

"Besides, sah, dar are not many people knows your face, and it not likely de bery man dat know you come to the station. Lots of oder places to search, and dey most sure to tink you go right away--not tink you venture to stop in town till the morning."

"That is so, Dan; and I think your plan is a capital one."

Dan's suggestion was carried out, and at seven o'clock next morning they were standing on the platform among a number of other parsons waiting for the train. Just as the locomotive's whistle was heard the sound of a cannon boomed out from the direction of the prison.

"That means some of the prisoners have escaped," one of the porters on the platform said. "There have been five or six of them got away in the last two months, but most of them have been caught again before they have gone far. You see, to have a chance at all, they have got to get rid of their uniforms, and as we are all Unionists about here that ain't an easy job for 'em to manage."

Every one on the platform joined in the conversation, asking which way the fugitive would be likely to go, whether there were any cavalry to send after him, what would be done to him if he were captured, and other questions of the same kind, Vincent joining in the talk. It was a relief to him when the train drew up, and he and Dan took their place in it, traveling, however, in different cars. Once fairly away, Vincent had no fear whatever of being detected, and could travel where he liked, for outside the prison there were not ten people who knew his face throughout the Northern States. It would be difficult for him to make his way down into

Virginia from the North as the whole line of frontier there was occupied by troops, and patrols were on the watch night and day to prevent persons from going through the lines. He therefore determined to go west to St. Louis, and from there work his way down through Missouri. After two days' railway traveling they reached St. Louis, a city having a large trade with the South, and containing many sympathizers with the Confederate cause. Vincent, having now no fear of detection, went at once to an hotel, and taking up the newspaper, one of the first paragraphs that met his eye was headed:

"Escape of three Confederate officers from Elmira. Great excitement was caused on Wednesday at Elmira by the discovery that three Confederate officers had, during the night, effected their escape from prison. One of the bars of the window of the ward on the first floor in which they were, with fifteen other Confederate officers, confined, had been removed; the screws having been taken out by a large screw-driver which they left behind them. They had lowered themselves to the yard, and climbed over the wall by means of a rope which was found in position in the morning. The rest of the prisoners professed an entire ignorance of the affair, and declare that until they found the beds unoccupied in the morning they knew nothing of the occurrence.

"This is as it may be, but it is certain they must have been aided by traitors outside the prison, for the rope hung loose on the outside of the wall, and must have been held by some one there as they climbed it. The inside end was fastened to a stone seat, and they were thus enabled to slide down it on the other side. Their uniforms were found lying at the foot of the wall, and their accomplice had doubtless disguises ready for them. The authorities of the prison are unable to account for the manner in which the turn-screw and rope were passed in to them, or how they communicated with their friends outside."

Then followed the personal description of each of the fugitives, and a request that all loyal citizens would be on the look-out for them, and would at once arrest any suspicious character unable to give a satisfactory account of himself. As Vincent sat smoking in the hall of the hotel he heard several present discussing the escape of the prisoners.

"It does not matter about them one way or the other," one of the speakers said. "They seem to be mere lads, and whether they escape or not will not make any difference to any one. The serious thing is that there must be some traitors among the prison officials, and that next time, perhaps two or three generals may escape, and that would be a really serious misfortune."

"We need not reckon that out at present," another smoker said. "We haven't got three of the rebel generals yet, and as far as things seem to be going on, we may have to wait some time before we have. They are pretty well able to take care of themselves, I reckon."

"They are good men, some of them, I don't deny," the first speaker said; "but they might as well give up the game. In the spring we shall have an army big enough to eat them up."

"So I have heard two or three times before. Scott was going to eat them up, McClellan was going to eat them up, then Pope was going to make an end of 'em altogether. Now McClellan is having a try again, but somehow or other the eating up hasn't come off yet. It looks to me rather the other way."

There was an angry growl from two or three of those sitting round, while others uttered a cordial "That's so."

"It seems to me, by the way you put it, that you don't wish to see this business come to an end."

"That's where you are wrong now. I do wish to see it come to an end. I don't want to see tens of thousands of men losing their lives because one portion of these States wants to ride roughshod over the other. The sooner the North looks this affair squarely in the face and sees that it has taken up a bigger job than it can carry through, and agrees to let those who wish to leave it go if they like, the better for all parties. That's what I think about it."

"I don't call that Union talk," the other said angrily.

"Union or not Union, I mean to talk it, and I want to know who is going to prevent me?"

The two men rose simultaneously from their chairs, and in a second the crack of two revolvers sounded. As if they had only been waiting for the signal, a score of other men leaped up and sprang at each other. They had, as the altercation grew hotter, joined in with exclamations of anger or approval, and Vincent saw that although the Unionists were the majority the party of sympathizers with the South was a strong one. Having neither arms nor inclination to join in a broil of this kind he made his escape into the street the instant hostilities began, and hurried away from the sound of shouts, oaths, the sharp cracks of pistols, and the breaking of glass. Ten minutes later he returned. The hotel was shut up, but an angry mob were assembled round the door shouting, "Down with the rebels! down with the Secessionists!" and were keeping up a loud knocking at the door. Presently a window upstairs opened, and the proprietor put out his head.

"Gentlemen," he said, "I can assure you that the persons who were the cause of this disturbance all left the hotel by the back way as soon as the affair was over. I have sent for the police commissioner, and upon his arrival he will be free to search the house, and to arrest any one concerned in this affair."

The crowd were not satisfied, and renewed their knocking at the door; but two or three minutes later an officer, with a strong body of police, arrived on the spot. In a few words he told the crowd to disperse, promising that the parties concerned in the affair would be taken in and duly deal with. He then entered the house with four of his men, leaving the rest to wait. Vincent entered with the constables, saying that he was staying at the house. The fumes of gunpowder were still floating about the hall, three bodies were lying on the floor, and several men were binding up their wounds. The police-officer inquired into the origin of the broil, and all present concurred in saying that it arose from some Secessionists speaking insultingly of the army of the Union.

Search was then made in the hotel, and it was found that eight persons were missing. One of the killed was a well-known citizen of the town; he was the speaker on the Union side of the argument. The other two were strangers, and no one could say which side they espoused. All those present declared that they themselves were Union men, and it was supposed that the eight who were missing were the party who had taken the other side of the question. The evidence of each was taken down by the police- officer. Vincent was not questioned, as, having entered with the constables, it was supposed he was not present at the affair.

In the morning Vincent read in the local paper a highly colored account of the fray. After giving a large number of wholly fictitious details of the fray, it went on to say: "The victims were Cyrus D. Jenkins, a much-esteemed citizen and a prominent Unionist; the other two were guests at the hotel; one had registered as P. J. Moore of Vermont, the other James Harvey of Tennessee. Nothing is as yet known as to the persons whose rooms were unoccupied, and who had doubtless made their escape as soon as the affray was over; but the examination of their effects, which will be made by the police in the morning, will doubtless furnish a clew by which they will be brought to justice."

Having read this, Vincent looked for the news as to the escape from Elmira, being anxious to know whether his companions had been as fortunate as himself in getting clear away. He was startled by reading the following paragraph: "We are enabled to state that the police have received a letter stating that one of the officers who escaped from Elmira prison has adopted the disguise of a minister, and is traveling through the country with a black servant. At present the authorities are not disposed to attach much credit to this letter, and are inclined to believe that it has been sent in order to put them on a wrong scent. However a watch will doubtless be kept by the police throughout the country for a person answering to this description."

Accustomed to rise early, Vincent was taking his breakfast almost alone, only two or three of the other guests having made their appearance. He finished his meal hastily, and went out to Dan, who was lounging in front of the hotel.

"Dan, go upstairs at once, pack the bag, bring it down and get out with it immediately. I will pay the bill. Don't stop to ask questions now."

Vincent then walked up to the desk at the end of the hall, at which a clerk was sitting reading the paper. Sincerely hoping that the man's eye had not fallen on this paragraph, he asked if his account was made out. As he had fortunately mentioned on the preceding evening that he should be leaving in the morning, the bill was ready; and the clerk, scarce looking up from the paper, handed it to him. Vincent paid him the amount, saying carelessly, "I think I have plenty of time to catch the train for the east?"

The clerk glanced at the clock.

"Yes, it goes at 8, and you have twenty minutes. It's only five minutes' walk to the station."

## CHAPTER XI. FUGITIVES.

ON leaving the hotel Vincent walked a short distance, and then stopped until Dan came up to him.

"Anyting de matter, sah?"

"Yes, Dan. There is a notice in the paper that the police have obtained information that I am traveling disguised as a minister, and have a negro servant with me.."

"Who told dem dat?" Dan asked in surprise.

"We can talk about that presently, Dan; the great thing at present is to get away from here. The train for the south starts at ten. Give me the bag, and follow me at a distance. I will get you a ticket for Nashville, and as you pass me in the station I will hand it to you. It must not be noticed that we are traveling together. That is the only clew they have got."

Dan obeyed his instructions. The journey was a long one. The train was slow and stopped frequently; passengers got in and out at every station. The morning's news from the various points at which the respective forces were facing each other was the general topic of conversation, and Vincent was interested in seeing how the tone gradually changed as the passengers from St. Louis one by one left the train and their places were taken by those of the more southern districts. At first the sentiment expressed had been violently Northern, and there was no dissent from the general chorus of hope and expectation that the South were on their last legs and that the rebellion would shortly be stamped out; but gradually, as the train approached the State of Tennessee, the Unionist opinion, although expressed with even greater force and violence, was by no means universal. Many man read their papers in silence and took no part whatever in the conversation, but Vincent could see from the angry glances which they shot at the speakers that the sentiments uttered were distasteful to them. He himself had scarcely spoken during the whole journey. He had for some time devoted himself to the newspaper, and had then purchased a book from the newsboy who perambulated the cars. Presently a rough-looking man who had been among the wildest and most violent in his denunciation of the South said, looking at Vincent:

"I see by the papers to-day that one of the cursed rebel officers who gave them the slip at Elmira is traveling in the disguise of a minister. I guess it's mighty unpleasant to know that even if you meet a parson in a train like as not he is a rebel in disguise. Now, mister, may I ask where you have come from and where you are going to?"

"You may ask what you like," Vincent said quietly; "but I am certainly not going to answer impertinent questions."

A hum of approval was heard from several of the passengers.

"If you hadn't got that black coat on," the man said angrily, "I would put you off the car in no time."

"Black coat or no black coat," Vincent said, "you may find it more difficult than you think. My profession is a peaceful one; but even a peaceful man, if assaulted, may defend himself. You say it's unpleasant to know that if you travel with a man in a black coat he may be a traitor. It's quite as unpleasant to me to know that if I travel with a man in a brown one he may be a notorious ruffian, and may as likely as not have just served his time in a penitentiary."

Two or three of the passengers laughed loudly. The man, starting up, crossed the car to where Vincent was sitting and laid his hand roughly on his shoulder.

"You have got to get out!" he said. "No man insults Jim Mullens twice."

"Take your hand off my shoulder," Vincent said quietly, "or you will be sorry for it."

The man shifted his hold to the collar of Vincent's coat amid cries of shame from some of the passengers, while the others were silent, even those of his own party objecting to an assault upon a minister. It was only the fact that the fellow was a notorious local ruffian that prevented their expressing open disapproval of the act. As the man grasped Vincent's collar with his right hand Vincent saw his left go under his coat toward the pocket in the back of the trousers where revolvers were always carried. In an instant he sprang to his feet, and before the man, who was taken by surprise at the suddenness of the movement, could steady himself, he struck him a tremendous blow between the eyes, and at the same moment, springing at his throat, threw him backward on to the floor of the carriage. As he fell the man drew out his revolver, but Vincent grasped his arm and with a sharp twist wrenched the revolver from his grasp, and leaping up, threw it out of the open window. The ruffian rose to his feat, for a moment half dazed by the violence with which he had fallen, and poured out a string of imprecations upon Vincent. The latter stood calmly awaiting a fresh attack. For a moment the ruffian hesitated, and then, goaded to fury by the taunting laughter of the lookers-on, was about to spring upon him when he was seized by two or three of the passengers.

"I reckon you have made a fool enough of yourself already," one of them said; "and we are not going to see a minister ill-treated, not if we know it."

"You need not hold him," Vincent said. "It is not because one wears a black coat and is adverse to fighting that one is not able to defend one's self. We all learn the same things at college whether we are going into the church or any other profession. You can let him alone if he really wants any more, which I do not believe. I should be ashamed of myself if I could not punish a ruffian of his kind."

"Let me get at him!" yelled Mullens; and the men who held him, taking Vincent at his word, released him. He rushed forward, but was received with another tremendous blow on the mouth. He paused a moment in his rush, and Vincent, springing forward, administered another blow upon the same spot, knocking him off his legs on to the floor. On getting up he gave no sign of a desire to renew the conflict. His lips were badly cut and the blood was streaming from his mouth, and he looked at Vincent with an air of absolute bewilderment. The latter, seeing that the conflict was over, quietly resumed his seat; while several of the passengers came up to him, and, shaking him warmly by the hand, congratulated him upon having punished his assailant.

"I wish we had a few more ministers of your sort down this way," one said. "That's the sort of preaching fellows like this understand. It was well you got his six-shooter out of his hand, for he would have used it as sure as fate. He ought to have been lynched long ago, but since the troubles began these fellows have had all their own way. But look to yourself when he gets out; he belongs to a hand who call themselves Unionists, but who are nothing but plunderers and robbers. If you take my advice, when you get to the end of your journey you will not leave the station, but take a ticket straight back north. I tell you your life won't be safe five minutes when you once get outside the town. They daren't do anything there, for though folks have had to put up with a good deal they wouldn't stand the shooting of a minister; still, outside the town I would not answer for your life for an hour."

"I have my duties to perform," Vincent said, "and I shall certainly carry them through; but I am obliged to you for your advice I can quite understand that ruffian," and he looked at Mullens, who, with his handkerchief to his mouth, was sitting alone in a corner--for the rest had all drawn away from him in disgust--and glaring ferociously at him, "will revenge himself if he has the opportunity. However as far as possible I shall be on my guard."

"At any rate," the man said, "I should advise you when you get to Nashville to charge him with assault. We can all testify that he laid hands on you first. That way he will get locked up for some days anyhow, and you can go away about your business, and he won't know where to find you when he gets out."

"Thank you--that would be a very good plan; but I might lose a day or two in having to appear against him; I am pressed for time and have some important business on hand and I have no doubt I shall be able to throw him off my track, finish my business, and be off again before he can come across me."

"Well, I hope no harm will come of it," the other said. "I like you, and I never saw any one hit so quickly and so hard. It's a downright pity you are a preacher. My name's John Morrison, and my farm is ten miles from Nashville, on the Cumberland River. If you should be going in that direction I should be right glad if you would drop in on me."

The real reason that decided Vincent against following the advice to give his assailant in charge was that he feared he himself might be questioned as to the object of his journey and his destination. The fellow would not improbably say that he believed he was the Confederate officer who was trying to escape in the disguise of a clergyman and that he had therefore tried to arrest him. He could of course give no grounds for the accusation, still questions might be asked which would be impossible for him to answer; and, however plausible a story he might invent, the lawyer whom the fellow would doubtless employ to defend him might suggest that the truth of his statements might be easily tested by the despatch of a telegram, in which case he would be placed in a most awkward situation. It was better to run the risk of trouble with the fellow and his gang than to do anything which might lead to inquiries as to his identity.

When the train reached Nashville, Vincent proceeded to an hotel. It was already late in the afternoon, for the journey had occupied more than thirty hours. As soon as it was dark he went out again and joined Dan, whom he had ordered to follow him at a distance and to be at the corner of the first turning to the right of the hotel as soon as it became dark. Dan was at the point agreed upon, and he followed Vincent until the latter stopped in a quiet and badly lighted street.

"Things are going badly, Dan. I had a row with a ruffian in the train, and he has got friends here, and this will add greatly to our danger in getting to our lines. I must get another disguise. What money have you left?"

"Not a cent, sah. I had only a five-cent piece left when we left St. Louis, and I spent him on bread on de journey."

"That is bad, Dan. I did not think your stock was so nearly expended."

"I had to keep myself, sah, and to pay for de railroad, and to buy dem tree suits of clothes, and to make de nigger I lodged with a present to keep him mouth shut."

"Oh, I know you have had lots of expenses, Dan, and I am sure that you have not wasted your money; but I had not thought about it. I have only got ten dollars left, and we may have a hundred and fifty miles to travel before we are safe. Anyhow, you must get another disguise, and trust to luck for the rest. We have tramped a hundred and fifty miles before now without having anything beyond what we could pick up on the road. Here's the money. Get a rough suit of workingman's clothes, and join me here again in an hour's time. Let us find out the name of the street before we separate, for we may miss our way and not be able to meet again."

Passing up into the busy streets, Vincent presently stopped and purchased a paper of a newsboy who was running along shouting, "News from the war. Defeat of the rebels. Fight in a railway car near Nashville; a minister punishes a border ruffian."

"Confound those newspaper fellows!" Vincent muttered to himself as he walked away. "They pick up every scrap of news. I suppose a reporter got hold of some one who was in the car." Turning down a quiet street, he opened the paper and by the light of the lamp read a graphic and minute account of the struggle in the train.

"I won't go back to the hotel," he said to himself. "I shall be having reporters to interview me. I shall be expected to give them a history of my whole life; where I was born, and where I went to school, and whether I prefer beef to mutton, and whether I drink beer, and a thousand other things. No; the sooner I am away the better. As to the hotel, I have only had one meal, and they have got the bag with what clothes there are; that will pay them well." Accordingly when he rejoined Dan he told him that they would start at once.

"It is the best way, anyhow," he said. "To-morrow, no doubt, the fellow I had the row with will be watching the hotel to see which way I go off, but after once seeing me go to the hotel he will not guess that I shall be starting this evening. What have you got left, Dan?"

"I got two dollars, sah."

"That makes us quite rich men. We will stop at the first shop we come to and lay in a stock of bread and a pound or two of ham."

"And a bottle of rum, sah. Berry wet and cold sleeping out of doors now, sah. Want a little comfort anyhow."

"Very well, Dan; I think we can afford that."

"Get one for half a dollar, massa. Could not lay out half a dollar better."

Half an hour later they had left Nashville behind them, and were tramping along the road toward the east, Dan carrying a bundle in which the provisions were wrapped, and the neck of the bottle of rum sticking out of his pocket. As soon as they were well in the country Vincent changed his clothes for those Dan had just bought him, and making the others up into a bundle continued his way.

"Why you not leave dem black clothes behind, sah? What good take dem wid you?"

"I am not going to carry them far, Dan. The first wood or thick clump of bushes we come to I shall hide them away; but if you were to leave them here they would be found the first thing in the morning, and perhaps be carried into the town and handed over to the police, and they might put that and the fact of my not having returned to the hotel--which is sure to be talked about--together, and come to the conclusion that either Mullens was right and that I was an escaped Confederate, or that I had been murdered by Mullens. In either case they might get up a search, and perhaps send telegrams to the troops in the towns beyond us. Anyhow, it's best the clothes should not be found."

All night they tramped along, pausing only for half an hour about midnight, when Dan suggested that as he had only had some bread to eat--and not too much of that--during the last forty-eight hours, he thought that he could do with some supper. Accordingly the bundle was opened, and they sat down and partook of a hearty meal. Dan had wisely taken the precaution of having the cork drawn from the bottle when he bought it, replacing it so that it could be easily extracted when required, and Vincent acknowledged that the spirit was a not unwelcome addition to the meal. When morning broke they had reached Duck's River, a broad stream crossing the road.

Here they drew aside into a thick grove, and determined to get a few hours' sleep before proceeding. It was nearly midday before they woke and proceeded to the edge of the trees. Vincent reconnoitered the position.

"It is just as well we did not try to cross, Dan. I see the tents of at least a regiment on the other bank. No doubt they are stationed there to guard the road and railway bridge. This part of the country is pretty equally divided in opinion, though more of the people are for the South than for the North; but I know there are guerrilla parties on both sides moving about, and if a Confederate band was to pounce down on these bridges and destroy them it would cut the communication with their army in front, and put them in a very ugly position if they were defeated. No doubt that's why they have stationed that regiment there. Anyhow, it makes it awkward for us. We should be sure to be questioned where we are going, and as I know nothing whatever of the geography of the place we should find it very difficult to satisfy them. We must cross the river somewhere else. There are sure to be some boats somewhere along the banks; at any rate, the first thing to do is to move further away from the road."

They walked for two or three miles across the country. The fields for the most part were deserted, and although here and there they saw cultivated patches, it was evident that most of the inhabitants had quitted that part of the country, which had been the scene of almost continued fighting from the commencement of the war; the sufferings of the inhabitants being greatly heightened by the bands of marauders who moved about plundering and destroying under the pretense of punishing those whom they considered hostile to the cause in whose favor--nominally, at least--they had enrolled themselves. The sight of ruined farms and burned houses roused Vincent's indignation; for in Virginia private property had, up to the time of Pope's assuming command of the army, been respected, and this phase of civil war was new and very painful to him.

"It would be a good thing," he said to Dan, "if the generals on both sides in this district would agree to a month's truce, and join each other in hunting down and hanging these marauding scoundrels. On our side Mosby and a few other leaders of bands composed almost entirely of gentlemen, have never been accused of practices of this kind; but, with these exceptions, there is little to choose between them."

After walking for four or five miles they again sat down till evening, and then going down to the river endeavored to find a boat by which they could cross, but to their disappointment no craft of any kind was visible, although in many places there were stages by the riverside, evidently used by farmers for unloading their produce into boats. Vincent concluded at last that at some period of the struggle all the boats must have been collected and either sunk or carried away by one of the parties to prevent the other crossing the river.

Hitherto they had carefully avoided all the farmhouses that appeared to be inhabited; but Vincent now determined to approach one of them and endeavor to gain some information as to the distance from the next bridge, and whether it was guarded by troops, and to find out if possible the position in which the Northern forces in Tennessee were at present posted--all of which points he was at present ignorant of. He passed two or three large farmhouses without entering, for although the greater part of the male population were away with one or other of the armies, he might still find two or three hands in such buildings. Besides, it was now late, and whatever the politics of the inmates they would be suspicious of such late arrivals, and would probably altogether refuse them admittance. Accordingly another night was spent in the wood.

The next morning, after walking a mile or two, they saw a house at which Vincent determined to try their fortune. It was small, but seemed to have belonged to people above the class of farmer. It stood in a little plantation, and was surrounded by a veranda. Most of the blinds were down, and Vincent judged that the inmates could not be numerous.

"You remain here, Dan, and I will go and knock at the door. It is better that we should not be seen together." Vincent accordingly went forward and knocked at the door. An old negress opened it.

"We have nothing for tramps," she said. "De house am pretty well cleared out ob eberyting." She was about to shut the door when Vincent put his foot forward and prevented it closing. "Massa Charles," the negress called out, "bring yo' shot-gun quick; here am tief want to break into the house."

"I am neither a thief nor a tramp," Vincent said; "and I do not want anything, except that I should be glad to buy a loaf of bread if you have one that you could spare. I have lost my way, and I want to ask directions."

"Dat am pretty likely story," the old woman said. "Bring up dat shot-gun quick, Massa Charles."

"What is it, Chloe?" another female voice asked.

"Here am a man pretend he hab lost his way and wants to buy a loaf. You stand back, Miss Lucy, and let your broder shoot de villain dead."

"I can assure you that I am not a robber, madam," Vincent said through the partly opened door. "I am alone, and only beg some information, which I doubt not you can give me."

"Open the door, Chloe," the second voice said inside; "that is not the voice of a robber."

The old woman reluctantly obeyed the order and opened the door, and Vincent saw in the passage a young girl of some sixteen years old. He took off his hat.

"I am very sorry to disturb you," he said; "but I am an entire stranger here, and am most desirous of crossing the river, but can find no boat with which to do so."

"Why did you not cross by the bridge?" the girl asked. "How did you miss the straight road?"

"Frankly, because there were Northern troops there," Vincent said, "and I wish to avoid them if possible."

"You are a Confederate?" the girl asked, when the old negress interrupted her:

"Hush! Miss Lucy, don't you talk about dem tings; der plenty of mischief done already. What hab you to do wid one side or do oder?"

The girl paid no attention to her words, but stood awaiting Vincent's answer. He did not hesitate. There was something in her face that told him that, friend or foe, she was not likely to betray a fugitive, and he answered:

"I am a Confederate officer, madam. I have made my escape from Elmira prison, and am trying to find my way back into our lines."

"Come in, sir," the girl said, holding out her hand. "We are Secessionists, heart and soul. My father and my brother are with our troops--that is, if they are both alive. I have little to offer you, for the Yankee bands have been here several times, have driven off our cattle, emptied our barns, and even robbed our hen-nests, and taken everything in the house they thought worth carrying away. But whatever there is, sir, you are heartily welcome to. I had a paper yesterday--it is not often I get one--and I saw there that three of our officers had escaped from Elmira. Are you one of them?"

"Yes, madam. I am Lieutenant Wingfield."

"Ah! then you are in the cavalry. You have fought under Stuart," the girl said. "The paper said so. Oh, how I wish we had Stuart and Stonewall Jackson on this side! we should soon drive the Yankees out of Tennessee."

"They would try to, anyhow," Vincent said, smiling, "and if it were possible they would assuredly do it. I was in Ashley's horse with the Stonewall division through the first campaign in the Shenandoah Valley and up to Bull Run, and after that under Stuart. But is not your brother here? Your servant called to him."

"There is no one here but ourselves," the girl replied. "That was a fiction of Chloe's, and it has succeeded sometimes when we have had rough visitors. And now what can I do for you, sir? You said you wanted to buy a loaf of bread, and therefore, I suppose, you are hungry. Chloe, put the bacon and bread on the table, and make some coffee. I am afraid that is all we can do, sir, but such as it is you are heartily welcome to it."

"I thank you greatly," Vincent replied, "and will, if you will allow me, take half my breakfast out to my boy who is waiting over there."

"Why did you not bring him in?" the girl asked. "Of course he will be welcome too."

"I did not bring him in before because two men in these days are likely to alarm a lonely household; and I would rather not bring him in now, because, if by any possibility the searchers, who are no doubt after me, should call and ask you whether two men, one a white and the other a negro, had been here, you could answer no."

"But they cannot be troubling much about prisoners," the girl said. "Why, in the fighting here and in Missouri they have taken many thousands of prisoners, and you have taken still more of them in Virginia; surely they cannot trouble themselves much about one getting away."

"I am not afraid of a search of that kind," Vincent said; "but, unfortunately, on my way down I had a row in the train with a ruffian named Mullens, who is, I understand, connected with one of these bands of brigands, and I feel sure that he will hunt me down if he can."

The girl turned pale.

"Oh!" she said, "I saw that in the paper too, but it said that it was a minister. And it was you who beat that man and threw his revolver out of the window? Oh, then, you are in danger indeed, sir. He is one of the worst ruffians in the State, and is the leader of the party who stripped this house and threatened to burn it to the ground. Luckily I was not at home, having gone away to spend the night with a neighbor. His band have committed murders all over the country, hanging up defenseless people on pretense that they were Secessionists. They will show you no mercy if they catch you."

"No. I should not expect any great mercy if I fell into their hands, Miss Lucy. I don't know your other name."

"My name is Kingston. I ought to have introduced myself to you at once."

"Now you understand, Miss Kingston, how anxious I am to get across the river, and that brings me to the question of the information I want you to give me. How far is it from the next bridge on the south, and are there any Federal troops there?"

"It is about seven miles to the bridge at William sport, we are just halfway between that and the railway bridge at Columbus. Yes, there are certainly troops there--"

"Then I see no way for it but to make a small raft to carry us across, Miss Kingston. I am a good swimmer, but the river is full and of considerable width; still, I think I can get across. But my boy cannot swim a stroke."

"I know where there is a boat hid in the wood near the river," the girl said. "It belongs to a neighbor of ours, and when the Yankees seized the boats he had his hauled up and hidden in the woods. He was a Southerner, heart and soul, and thought that he might be able sometimes to take useful information across the river to our people; but a few weeks afterward his house was attacked by one of these bands--it was always said it was that of Mullens--and he was killed defending it to the last. He killed several of the band before he fell, and they were so enraged that after plundering it they set it on fire and fastened the door, and his wife and two maid-servants were burned to death."

"I wish instead of throwing his pistol out of the window I had blown his brains out with it," Vincent said; "and I would have done so if I had known what sort of fellow he was. However, as to the boat, can you give me instructions where to find it, and is it light enough for two men to carry?"

"Not to carry, perhaps, but to push along. It is a light boat he had for pleasure. He had a large one, but that was carried away with the others. I cannot give you directions, but I can lead you to the place."

"I should not like you to do that," Vincent said. "We might be caught, and your share in the affair might be suspected."

"Oh! there is no fear of that," the girl said; "besides, I am not afraid of danger."

"I don't think it is right, Miss Kingston, for a young lady like you to be living here alone with an old servant in such times as these. You ought to go into a town until it's all over."

"I have no one to go to," the girl said simply. "My father bought this place and moved here from Georgia only six years ago, and all my friends are in that State. Except our neighbors round here I do not know a soul in Tennessee. Besides, what can I do in a town? We can manage here, because we have a few fowls, and some of our neighbors last spring plowed an acre or two of ground and planted corn for us, and I have a little money left for buying other things; but it would not last us a month if we went into a town. No, I have nothing to do but to stay here until you drive the Yankees back. I will willingly take you down to the boat to-night. Chloe can come with us and keep me company on the way back. Of course it would not be safe to cross in the daytime."

"I thank you greatly, Miss Kingston, and shall always remember your kindness. Now, when I finish my meal I will go out and join my boy, and will come for you at eight o'clock; it will be quite dark then."

"Why should you not stay here till then, Mr. Wingfield? It is very unlikely that any one will come along."

"It is unlikely, but it is quite possible," Vincent replied, "and were I caught here by Mullens, the consequence would be very serious to you as well as to myself. No, I could not think of doing that. I will go out, and come back at eight o'clock. I shall not be far away; but if any one should come and inquire, you can honestly say that you do not know where I am."

"I have two revolvers here, sir; in fact I have three. I always keep one loaded, for there is never any saying whether it may not be wanted; the other two I picked up last spring. There was a fight about a quarter of a mile from here and after it was over and they had moved away, for the Confederates won that time and chased them back toward Nashville, I went out with Chloe with some water and bandages to see if we could do anything for the wounded. We were at work there till evening, and I think we did some good. As we were coming back I saw something in a low bush, and going there found a Yankee officer and his horse both lying dead; they had been killed by a shell, I should think. Stooping over to see if he was quite dead I saw a revolver in his belt and another in the holster of his saddle, so I took them out and brought them home, thinking I might give them to some of our men, for we were then, as we have always been, very short of arms; but I never had an opportunity of giving them away, and I am very glad now that I have not. Here they are, sir, and two packets of cartridges, for they are of the same size as those of the pistol my father gave me when he went away. You are heartily welcome to them."

"Thank you extremely," Vincent said, as he took the pistols and placed the packets of ammunition in his pocket. "We cut two heavy sticks the night we left Nashville so as to be able to make something of a fight; but with these weapons we shall feel a match for any small parties we may meet. Then at eight o'clock I will come back again."

"I shall be ready," the girl said; "but I wish you would have stopped, there are so many things I want to ask you about, and these Yankee papers, which are all we see now, are full of lies."

"They exaggerate their successes and to some extent conceal their defeats," Vincent said; "but I do not think it is the fault of the newspapers, whose correspondents do seem to me to try and tell the truth to their readers, but of the official despatches of the generals. The newspapers tone matters down, no doubt, because they consider it necessary to keep up the public spirit; but at times they speak out pretty strongly too. I am quite as sorry to leave as you can be that I should go, Miss Kingston, but I am quite sure that it is very much the wisest thing for me to do. By the way, if I should not be here by half-past eight I shall not come at all, and you will know that something has occurred to alter our plans. I trust there is no chance of anything doing so, but it is as well to arrange so that you should not sit up expecting me. Should I not come back you will know that I shall be always grateful to you for your kindness, and that when this war is over, if I am alive, I will come back and thank you personally."

"Good-by till this evening!" the girl said. "I will not even let myself think that anything can occur to prevent your return."

"Golly, Massa Vincent, what a time you hab been!" Dan said when Vincent rejoined him. "Dis child began to tink dat somefing had gone wrong, and was going in anoder five minutes to knock at do door to ask what dey had done to you."

"It is all right, Dan, I have had breakfast, and have brought some for you; here is some bread and bacon and a bottle of coffee."

"Dat good, massa; my teeth go chatter chatter wid sleeping in dese damp woods; dat coffee do me good, sah. After dat I shall feel fit for anyting."

## CHAPTER XII. THE BUSHWHACKERS.

"By the way, Dan," Vincent said when the negro had finished his meal, "we have not talked over that matter of my clothes. I can't imagine how that letter saying that one of us was disguised as a minister and would have a negro servant came to be written. Did you ever tell the people you lodged with anything about the disguise?"

"No, sah, neber said one word to dem about it; dey know nothing whatsoeber. De way me do wid your letter was dis. Me go outside town and wait for long time. At last saw black fellow coming along. Me say to him, 'Can you read?' and he said as he could. I said 'I got a letter, I want to read him, I gib you a quarter to read him to me;' so he said yes, and he read de letter. He a long time of making it out, because he read print but not read writing well. He spell it out word by word, but I don't tink he understand dat it come from prison, only dat it come from some one who wanted some rope and a turn-screw. Me do just de same way wid de second letter. As for de clothes, me buy dem dat day, make dem up in bundle, and not go back to lodging at all. Me not know how any one could know dat I buy dat minister clothes for you, sah. Me told de storekeeper dat dey was for cousin of mine, who preach to de colored folk, and dat I send him suit as present. Onless dat man follow me and watch me all de time till we go off together, sah, me no see how de debbil he guess about it."

"That's quite impossible, Dan; it never could have been that way. It is very strange, for it would really seem that no one but you and I and the other two officers could possibly know about it."

"Perhaps one of dem want to do you bad turn, massa, and write so as to get you caught and shut up again."

Vincent started at the suggestion. Was it possible that Jackson could have done him this bad turn after his having aided him to make his escape It would be a villainous trick; but then he had always thought him capable of villainous tricks, and it was only the fact that they were thrown together in prison that had induced him to make up his quarrel with him; but though Jackson had accepted his advances, it was probable enough that he had retained his bad feeling against him, and had determined, if possible, to have his revenge on the first opportunity.

"The scoundrel," he said to himself, "after my getting him free, to inform against me! Of course I have no proof of it, but I have not the least doubt that it was him. If we ever meet again, Mr. Jackson, I will have it out with you."

"You got two pistols, sah," Dan said presently. "How you get dem?"

"The lady of that house gave them to me, Dan; they are one for you and one for me."

"Dis chile no want him, sah; not know what to do wid him. Go off and shoot myself, for sure."

"Well, I don't suppose you would do much good with it, Dan. As I am a good shot, perhaps I had better keep them both. You might load them for me as I fire them."

"Berry well, sah; you show me how to load, me load."

Vincent showed Dan how to extricate the discharged cartridge-cases and to put in fresh ones, and after a quarter of an hour's practice Dan was able to do this with some speed.

"When we going on, sah?" he said as, having learned the lesson, he handed the pistol back to Vincent.

"We are not going on until the evening, Dan. When it gets dark the lady is going to take us to a place where there is a boat hidden, and we shall then be able to cross the river."

"Den I will hab a sleep, sah. Noting like sleeping when there is a chance."

"I believe you could sleep three-quarters of your time, Dan. However, you may as well sleep now if you can, for there will be nothing to do till night."

Vincent went back to the edge of the wood, and sat down where he could command a view of the cottage. The country was for the most part covered with wood, for it was but thinly inhabited except in the neighborhood of the main roads. Few of the farmers had cleared more than half their ground; many only a few acres. The patch, in which the house with its little clump of trees stood nearly in the center, was of some forty or fifty acres in extent, and though now rank with weeds, had evidently been carefully cultivated, for all the stumps had been removed, and the fence round it was of a stronger and neater character than that which most of the cultivators deemed sufficient.

Presently he heard the sound of horses' feet in the forest behind him, and he made his way back to a road which ran along a hundred yards from the edge of the wood. He reached it before the horsemen came up, and lay down in the underwood a few yards back. In a short time two horsemen came along at a walking pace.

"I call this a fool's errand altogether," one of them said in a grumbling tone. "We don't know that they have headed this way; and if they have, we might search these woods for a month without finding them."

"That's so," the other said; "but Mullens has set his heart on it, and we must try for another day or two. My idea is that when the fellow heard what sort of a chap Mullens was, he took the hack train that night and went up north again."

Vincent heard no more, but it was enough to show him that a sharp hunt was being kept up for him; and although he had no fear of being caught in the woods, he was well pleased at the thought that he would soon be across the water and beyond the reach of his enemy. He went back again to the edge of the clearing and resumed his watch. It was just getting dusk, and he was about to join Dan when he saw a party of twelve men ride out from the other side of the wood and make toward the house. Filled with a vague alarm that possibly some one might have caught sight of him and his follower on the previous day, and might, on being questioned by the searchers, have given them a clew as to the direction in which they were going, Vincent hurried to the spot where he left Dan. The negro jumped up as he approached.

"Me awake long time, sah. Began to wonder where you had got to."

"Take your stick and come along, Dan, as fast as you can."

Without another word Vincent led the way along the edge of the wood to the point where the clump of trees at the back of the house hid it from his view.

"Now, Dan, stoop low and get across to those trees."

Greatly astonished at what was happening, but having implicit faith in his master, Dan followed without a question.

It was but ten minutes since Vincent had seen the horsemen, but the darkness had closed in rapidly, and he had little fear of his approach being seen. He made his way through the trees, and crept up to the house, and then kept close along it until he reached the front. There stood the horses, with the bridles thrown over their neck. The riders were all inside the house.

"Look here, Dan," he whispered, "you keep here perfectly quiet until I join you again or you hear a pistol-shot. If you do hear a shot, rush at the horses with your stick and drive them off at full gallop. Drive them right into the woods if you can and then lie quiet there till you hear me whistle for you. If you don't hear my whistle you will know that something has happened to me, and then you must make your way home as well as you can."

"Oh, Master Vincent," Dan began; but Vincent stopped him.

"It's no use talking, Dan; you must do as I order you. I hope all will be well; but it must be done anyhow."

"Let me come and load your pistol and fight with you, sah."

"You can do more good by stampeding the horses, Dan. Perhaps, after all, there will be no trouble."

So saying, leaving Dan with the tears running down his cheeks, Vincent went to the back of the house and tried the door there. It was fastened. Then he went to the other side; and here, the light streaming through the window, which was open, and the sound of loud voices, showed him the room where the party were. He crept cautiously up and looked in. Mullens was standing facing Lucy Kingston; the rest of the men were standing behind him. The girl was as pale as death, but was quiet and composed.

"Now," Mullens said, "I ask you for the last time. You have admitted that a man has been here to-day, and that you gave him food. You say he is not in the house; and as we have searched it pretty thoroughly, we know that's right enough. You say you don't know where he is, and that may be true enough in a sense; but I have asked you whether he is coming back again, and you won't answer me. I just give you three seconds;" and he held out his arm with a pistol in it. "One!" As the word "Two" left his lips, a pistol cracked, and Mullens fell back with a bullet in his forehead.

At the same time Vincent shouted at the top of his voice, "Come on, lads; wipe 'em out altogether. Don't let one of them escape." As he spoke he discharged his pistol rapidly into the midst of the men, who were for the moment too taken by surprise to move, and every shot took effect upon them. At the same moment there was a great shouting outside, and the trampling of horses' feet. One or two of the men hastily returned Vincent's fire, but the rest made a violent rush to the door. Several fell over the bodies of their comrades, and Vincent had emptied one of his revolvers and fired three shots with the second before the last of those able to escape did so. Five bodies remained on the floor. As they were still seven to one against him, Vincent ran to the corner of the house, prepared to shoot them as they came round; but the ruffians were too scared to think of anything but escape, and they could be heard running and shouting across the fields.

Vincent ran into the house. He had seen Lucy Kingston fall prostrate at the same instant as the ruffian facing her. Strung up to the highest tension, and expecting in another second to be shot, the crack of Vincent's pistol had brought her down as surely as the bullet of Mullens would have done. Even in the excitement of firing, Vincent felt thankful when he saw her fall, and knew that she was safe from the bullets flying about. When he entered the room he found the old negress lying beside her, and thought at first that she had fallen in the fray. He found that she was not only alive, but unhurt, having, the instant she saw her young mistress fall, thrown herself upon her to protect her from harm.

"Am dey all gone, sah?" she asked, as Vincent somewhat roughly pulled her off the girl's body.

"They have all gone, Chloe; but I do not know how soon they may be back again. Get your mistress round as soon as you can. I am sure that she has only fainted, for she fell the instant I fired, before another pistol had gone off."

Leaving the old woman to bring Miss Kingston round, he reloaded his pistols and went to the door. In a few minutes the sound of horses galloping was heard.

"Halt, or I fire!" he shouted.

"Don't shoot, sah! Don't shoot! It am me!" and Dan rode up, holding a second horse by the bridle. "I thought I might as well get two ob dem, so I jump on de back ob one and get hold ob anoder bridle while I was waiting to hear your pistol fire. Den de moment I heard dat I set de oders off, and chased dem to de corner where de gate was where dey came in at, and along de road for half a mile; dey so frightened dey not stop for a long time to come. Den I turn into de wood and went through de trees, so as not to meet dem fellows, and lifted two of de bars of the fence, and here I am. You are not hurt, massa?"

"My left arm is broken, I think, Dan; but that is of no consequence. I have shot five of these fellows--their leader among them--and I expect three of the others have got a bullet somewhere or other in them. There was such a crowd round the door that I don't think one shot missed. It was well I thought of stampeding the horses; that gave them a greater fright than my pistols. No doubt they thought that there was a party of our bushwhackers upon them. Now, Dan, you keep watch, and let me know if you see any signs of their returning. I think they are too shaken up to want any more fighting; but as there are seven of them, and they may guess there are only two or three of us, it is possible they may try again."

"Me don't tink dey try any more, sah. Anyhow, I look out sharp." So saying, Dan, fastening up one of the horses, rode the other in a circle round and round the house and little plantation, so that it would not be possible for any one to cross the clearing without being seen. Vincent returned to the house, and found Miss Kingston just recovering consciousness. She sat upon the ground in a confused way.

"What has happened, nurse?"

"Never mind at present, dearie. Juss you keep yourself quiet, and drink a little water."

The girl mechanically obeyed. The minute she put down the glass her eye fell upon Vincent, who was standing near the door.

"Oh! I remember now!" she said, starting up. "Those men were here and they were going to shoot me. One--two--and then he fired, and it seemed that I fell dead. Am I not wounded?"

"He never fired at all, Miss Kingston; he will never fire again. I shot him as he said 'two,' and no doubt the shock of the sudden shot caused you to faint dead away. You fell the same instant that he did."

"But where are the others?" the girl said with a shudder. "How imprudent of you to come here! I hoped you had seen them coming toward the house."

"I did see them, Miss Kingston, and that was the reason I came. I was afraid they might try rough measures to learn from you where I was hidden. I arrived at the window just as the scoundrel was pointing his pistol toward you, and then there was no time to give myself up, and I had nothing to do for it but to put a bullet through his head in order to save you. Then I opened fire upon the rest, and my boy drove off their horses. They were seized with a panic and bolted, thinking they were surrounded. Of course I kept up my fire, and there are four of them in the next room besides their captain. And now, if you please, I will get you, in the first place, to bind my arm tightly across my chest, for one of their bullets hit me in the left shoulder, and has, I fancy, broken it."

The girl gave an exclamation of dismay.

"Do not be alarmed, Miss Kingston; a broken shoulder is not a very serious matter, only I would rather it had not happened just at the present moment; there are more important affairs in hand. The question is, What is to become of you? It is quite impossible that you should stay here after what has happened. Those scoundrels are sure to come back again."

"What am I to do, Chloe?" the girl asked in perplexity. "I am sure we cannot stay here. We must find our way through the woods to Nashville, and I must try and get something to do there."

"There is another way, Miss Kingston, if you like to try it," Vincent said. "Of course it would be toilsome and unpleasant, but I do not think it would be dangerous, for even if we got caught there would be no fear of your receiving any injury from the Federal troops. My proposal is that you and Chloe should go with us. If we get safely through the Federal lines I will escort you to Georgia and place you with your friends there."

The girl looked doubtful for a moment, and then she shook her head.

"I could not think of that, sir. It would be difficult enough for you to get through the enemy by yourselves It would add terribly to your danger to have us with you."

"I do not think so," Vincent replied. "Two men would be sure to be questioned and suspected, but a party like ours would be far less likely to excite suspicion. Every foot we get south we shall find ourselves more and more among people who are friendly to us, and although they might be afraid to give shelter to men, they would not refuse to take women in. I really think, Miss Kingston, that this plan is the best. In the first place it would be a dangerous journey for you through the woods to Nashville and if you fall into the hands of any of those ruffians who have been here you may expect no mercy. At Nashville you will have great difficulty in obtaining employment of any kind and even suppose you went further north your position as a friendless girl would be a most painful one. As to your staying here that is plainly out of the question. I think that there is no time to lose in making a decision. Those fellows may go to the camp at the bridge, give their account of the affair, declare they have been attacked by a party of Confederate sympathizers, and return here with a troop of horse."

"What do you say, Chloe?" Lucy asked.

"I'se ready to go wid you whereber you like, Miss Lucy; but I do tink dat in times like dis dat a young gal is best wid her own folk. It may be hard work getting across, but as to danger dar can't be much more danger than dar has been in stopping along here, so it seems to me best to do as dis young officer says."

"Very well, then, I will, sir. We will go under your protection, and will give you as little trouble as we can. We will be ready in five minutes. Now, Chloe, let us put a few things together. The fewer the better. Just a small bundle which we can carry in our hands."

In a few minutes they returned to the room, Chloe carrying a large basket, and looking somewhat ruffled.

"Chloe is a little upset," the girl said, smiling, "because I won't put my best things on; and the leaving her Sunday gown behind is a sore trouble to her."

"No wonder, sah," Chloe said, "why dey say dat thar am no pretty dresses in de 'Federacy, and dat blue gown wid red spots is just as good as new, and it am downright awful to tink dat dose fellows will come back and take it."

"Never mind, Chloe," Vincent said, smiling. "No doubt we are short of pretty dresses in the South, but I dare say we shall be able to find you something that will be almost as good. But we must not stand talking. You are sure you have got everything of value, Miss Kingston?"

"I have got my purse," she said, "and Chloe has got some food. I don't think there is anything else worth taking in the house."

"Very well, we will be off," Vincent said, leading the way to the door.

A minute later Dan rode past, and Vincent called him and told him they were going to start.

"Shall we take de horses, sah?"

"No, Dan. We are going to carry out our original plan of crossing the river in a boat, and I think the horses would be rather in our way than not. But you had better not leave them here. Take them to the farther side of the clearing and get them through the fence into the forest, then strike across as quickly as you can and join us where we were stopping to-day. Miss Kingston and her servant are going with us. They cannot stay here after what has taken place."

Dan at once rode off with the two horses, and the others walked across to the edge of the clearing and waited until he rejoined them.

"Now, Miss Kingston, you must be our guide at present."

"We must cross the road first," the girl said. "Nearly opposite to where we are there is a little path through the wood leading straight down to the river. The boat lies only a short distance from it."

The path was a narrow one, and it was very dark under the trees.

"Mind how you go," Vincent said as the girl stepped lightly on ahead. "You might get a heavy fall if you caught your foot on a root."

She instantly moderated her pace. "I know the path well, but it was thoughtless of me to walk so fast. I forgot you did not know it, and if you were to stumble you might hurt your arm terribly. How does it feel now?"

"It certainly hurts a bit," Vincent replied in a cheerful tone; "but now it is strapped tightly to me it cannot move much. Please do not worry about me."

"Ah!" she said, "I cannot forget how you got it--how you attacked twelve men to save me!"

"Still less can I forget, Miss Kingston, how you, a young girl, confronted death rather than say a word that would place me in their power."

"That was quite different, Mr. Wingfield. My own honor was pledged not to betray you, who had trusted me."

"Well, we will cry quits for the present, Miss Kingston; or, rather, we will be content to remain for the present in each other's debt."

A quarter of an hour's walking brought them to the river.

"Now," Lucy said, "we must make our way about ten yards through these bushes to the right."

With some difficulty they passed through the thick screen of bushes, the girl still leading the way.

"Here it is," she said; "I have my hand upon it." Vincent was soon beside her, and the negroes quickly joined them.

"There are no oars in the boat," Vincent said, feeling along the seat.

"Oh! I forgot! They are stowed away behind the bushes on the right; they were taken out, so that if the Yankees found the boat it would be of no use to them."

Dan made his way through the bushes, and soon found the oars. Then uniting their strength they pushed the boat through the high rushes that screened it from the river.

"It is afloat," Vincent said. "Now, Dan, take your place in the bow."

"I will row, Mr. Wingfield. I am a very good hand at it. So please take your seat with Chloe in the stern."

"Dan can take one oar, anyhow," Vincent replied; "but I will let you row instead of me. I am afraid I should make a poor hand of it with only one arm."

The boat pushed quietly out. The river was about a hundred yards wide at this point. They had taken but a few strokes when Vincent said:

"You must row hard, Miss Kingston, or we shall have to swim for it. The water is coming through the seams fast."

The girl and Dan exerted themselves to the utmost; but, short as was the passage, the boat was full almost to the gunwale before they reached the opposite bank, the heat of the sun having caused the planks to open during the months it had been lying ashore.

"This is a wet beginning," Lucy Kingston said laugh as she tried to wring the water out of the lower part of her dress. "Here, Chloe; you wring me and I will wring you."

"Now, Dan, get hold of that head-rope," Vincent said; "haul her up little by little as the water runs out over the stern."

"I should not trouble about the boat, Mr. Wingfield; it is not likely we shall ever want it again."

"I was not thinking of the boat; I was thinking of ourselves. If it should happen to be noticed at the next bridge as it drifted down, it would at once suggest to any one on the lookout for us that we had crossed the river; whereas, if we get it among the bushes here, they will believe that we are hidden in the woods or have headed back to the north, and we shall be a long way across the line, I hope, before they give up searching for us in the woods on the other side."

"Yes; I didn't think of that. We will help you with the rope."

The boat was very heavy, now that it was full of water. Inch by inch it was pulled up, until the water was all out except near the stern. Dan and Vincent then turned it bottom upward, and it was soon hauled up among the bushes.

"Now, Miss Kingston, which do you think is our best course? I know nothing whatever of the geography here."

"The next town is Mount Pleasant; that is where the Williamsport road passes the railway. If we keep south we shall strike the railway, and that will take us to Mount Pleasant. After that the road goes on to Florence, on the Tennessee River. The only place that I know of on the road is Lawrenceburg. That is about forty miles from here, and I have heard that the Yankees are on the line from there right and left. I believe our troops are at Florence; but I am not sure about that, because both parties are constantly shifting their position, and I hear very little, as you may suppose, of what is being done. Anyhow, I think we cannot do better than go on until we strike the railway, keep along by that till we get within a short distance of Mount Pleasant, and then cross it. After that we can decide whether we will travel by the road or keep on through the woods. But we cannot find our way through the woods at night; we should lose ourselves before we had gone twenty yards."

"I am afraid we should, Miss Kingston."

"Please call me Lucy," the girl interrupted. "I am never called anything else, and I am sure this is not a time for ceremony."

"I think that it will be better; and will you please call me Vin. It is much shorter and pleasanter using our first names; and as we must pass for brother and sister if we get among the Yankees, it is better to get accustomed to it. I quite agree with you that it will be too dark to find our way through the woods unless we can discover a path.

"Dan and I will see if we can find one. If we can, I think it will be better to go on a little way at any rate, so as to get our feet warm and let our clothes dry a little."

"They will not dry to-night," Lucy said. "It is so damp in the woods that even if our clothes were dry now they would be wet before morning."

"I did not think of that. Yes, in that case I do not see that we should gain anything by going farther; we will push on for two or three hundred yards, if we can, and then we can light a fire without there being any chance of it being seen from the other side."

"That would be comfortable, Mr.--I mean Vin," the girl agreed. "That is, if you are quite sure that it would be safe. I would rather be wet all night than that we should run any risks."

"I am sure if we can get a couple of hundred yards into this thick wood the fire would not be seen through it," Vincent said; "of course I do not mean to make a great bonfire which would light up the forest."

For half an hour they forced their way through the bushes, and then Vincent said he was sure that they had come far enough. Finding a small open space, Dan, and Lucy, and the negress set to work collecting leaves and dry sticks. Vincent had still in his pocket the newspaper he had bought in the streets of Nashville, and he always carried lights. A piece of the paper was crumpled up and lighted, a few of the driest leaves they could find dropped upon it, then a few twigs, until at last a good fire was burning.

"I think that is enough for the present," Vincent said. "We will keep on adding wood as fast as it burns down, so as to get a great pile of embers, and keep two or three good big logs burning all night."

He then gave directions to Dan, who cut a long stick and fastened it to two saplings, one of which grew just in front of the fire. Then he set to work and cut off branches, and laid them sloping against it, and soon had an arbor constructed of sufficient thickness to keep off the night dews.

"I think you will be snug in there," Vincent said when he had finished. "The heat of the fire will keep you dry and warm, and if you lie with your heads the other way I think your things will be dry by the morning. Dan and I will lie down by the other side of the fire. We are both accustomed to sleep in the open air, and have done so for months."

"Thank you very much," she said. "Our things are drying already, and I am as warm as a toast; but, indeed, you need not trouble about us. We brought these warm shawls with us on purpose for night-work in the forest. Now, I think we will try the contents of the basket Dan has been carrying."

The basket, which was a good-sized one, was opened. Chloe had before starting put all the provisions in the house into it, and it contained three loaves, five or six pounds of bacon, a canister of tea and loaf-sugar, a small kettle, and two pint mugs, besides a number of odds and ends. The kettle Dan had, by Chloe's direction, filled with water before leaving the river, and this was soon placed among the glowing embers.

"But you have brought no teapot, Chloe."

"Dar was not no room for it, Miss Lucy. We can make tea berry well in de kettle."

"So we can. I forgot that. We shall do capitally."

The kettle was not long in boiling. Chloe produced some spoons and knives and forks from the basket.

"Spoons and forks are luxuries, Chloe," Vincent said laughing. "We could have managed without them."

"Yes, sah; but me not going to leave massa's silver for dose villains to find."

Lucy laughed. "At any rate, Chloe, we can turn the silver into money if we run short. Now the kettle is boiling."

It was taken off the fire, and Lucy poured some tea into it from the canister, and then proceeded to cut up the bread. A number of slices of bacon had already been cut off, and a stick thrust through them, and Dan, who was squatted at the other side of the fire holding it over the flames, now pronounced them to be ready. The bread served as plates, and the party were soon engaged upon their meal, laughing and talking over it as if it had been an ordinary picnic in the woods, though at times Vincent's face contracted from the sharp twitching of pain in his shoulder. Vincent and Lucy first drank their tea, and the mugs were then handed to Dan and Chloe.

"This is great fun," Lucy said. "If it goes on like it all through our journey we shall have no need to grumble. Shall we Chloe?"

"If you don't grumble, Miss Lucy, you may be quite sure dat Chloe will not. But we hab not begun our journey at present; and I spec dat we shall find it pretty hard work before we get to de end. But neber mind dat; anyting is better dan being all by ourselves in dat house. Terrible sponsibility dat."

"It was lonely," the girl said, "and I am glad we are away from it whatever happens. What a day this has been. Who could have dreamed when I got up in the morning that all this would take place before night. It seems almost like a dream, and I can hardly believe"--and here she stopped with a little shiver as she thought of the scene she had passed through with the band of bushwhackers.

"I would not think anything at all about it," Vincent said. "And now I should recommend your turning in, and getting to sleep as soon as you can. We will be off at daybreak, and it is just twelve o'clock now."

Five minutes later Lucy and her old nurse were snugly ensconced in their little bower, while Vincent and Dan stretched themselves at full length on the other side of the fire. In spite of the pain in his shoulder Vincent dozed off occasionally, but he was heartily glad when he saw the first gleam of light in the sky. He woke Dan.

"Dan, do you take the kettle down to the river and fill it. We had better have some breakfast before we make our start. If you can't find your way back, whistle and I will answer you."

Dan, however, had no occasion to give the signal. It took him little more than five minutes to traverse the distance that had occupied them half an hour in the thick darkness, and Vincent was quite surprised when he reappeared again with the kettle. Not until it was boiling, and the bacon was ready, did Vincent raise his voice and call Lucy and the nurse.

"This is reversing the order of things altogether," the girl said as she came out and saw breakfast already prepared. "I shall not allow it another time, I can tell you."

"We are old campaigners, you see," Vincent said, "and accustomed to early movements. Now please let us waste no time, as the sooner we are off the better."

In a quarter of an hour breakfast was eaten and the basket packed, and they were on their way. Now the bright, glowing light in the east was sufficient guide to them as to the direction they should take, and setting their face to the south they started through the forest. In a quarter of an hour they came upon a little stream running through the wood, and here Vincent suggested that Lucy might like a wash, a suggestion which was gratefully accepted. He and Dan went a short distance down the streamlet, and Vincent bathed his face and head.

"Dan, I will get you to undo this bandage and get off my coat; then I will make a pad of my handkerchief and dip it in the water and you can lay it on my shoulder, and then help me on again with my coat. My arm is getting horribly painful."

Vincent's right arm was accordingly drawn through the sleeve and the coat turned down so as to enable Dan to lay the wet pad on the shoulder.

"It has not bled much," Vincent said, looking down at it.

"No, sah, not much blood on de shirt."

"Pull the coat down as far as the elbow, Dan, and bathe it for a bit."

Using his cap as a bailer, Dan bathed the arm for ten minutes, then the wet pad was placed in position, and with some difficulty the coat got on again. The arm was then bandaged across the chest, and they returned to the women, who were beginning to wonder at the delay.

## CHAPTER XIII. LAID UP.

"You must see a surgeon whatever the risk," Lucy said when the others joined them, for now that it was light she could see by the paleness of Vincent's face, and the drawn expression of the mouth, how much he had suffered.

"You have made so light of your wound that we have not thought of it half as much as we ought to do, and you must have thought me terribly heartless to be laughing and talking when you were in such pain. But it will never do to go on like this; it is quite impossible for you to be traveling so far without having your shoulder properly attended to."

"I should certainly be glad to have it looked to," Vincent replied. "I don't know whether the bullet's there or if it has made its way out, and if that could be seen to, and some splints or something of that sort put on to keep things in their right place, no doubt I should be easier; but I don't see how it is to be managed. At any rate, for the present we must go on, and I would much rather that you said nothing about it. There it is, and fretting over it won't do it any good, while if you talk of other things I may forget it sometimes."

In two hours they came upon the railway, whose course lay diagonally across that they were taking. They followed it until they caught sight of the houses of Mount Pleasant, some two miles away, and then crossed it. After walking some distance farther they came upon a small clearing with a log-hut, containing apparently three or four rooms, in the center.

"We had better skirt round this," Vincent suggested.

"No," Lucy said in a determined voice. "I have made up my mind I would go to the first place we came to and see whether anything can be done for you. I can see you are in such pain you can hardly walk, and it will be quite impossible for you to go much further. They are sure to be Confederates at heart here, and even if they will not take us in, there is no fear of their betraying us; at any rate we must risk it."

Vincent began to remonstrate, but without paying any attention to him the girl left the shelter of the trees and walked straight toward the house. The others followed her. Vincent had opposed her suggestion, but he had for some time acknowledged to himself that he could not go much further. He had been trying to think what had best be done, and had concluded that it would be safest to arrange with some farmer to board Lucy and her nurse for a time, while he himself with Dan went a bit further; and then, if they could get no one to take them in, would camp up in the woods and rest. He decided that in a day or two if no improvement took place in his wound he would give himself up to the Federals at Mount Pleasant, as he would there be able to get his wound attended to.

"I don't think there is any one in the house," Lucy said, looking back over her shoulder; "there is no smoke coming from the chimney, and the shutters are closed, and besides the whole place looks neglected."

Upon reaching the door of the house it was evident that it had been deserted. Lucy had now assumed the command.

"Dan," she said, "there is no shutter to the window of that upper room. You must manage to climb up there and get in at that window, and then open the door to us."

"All right, missie, me manage dat," Dan said cheerfully. Looking about he soon found a long pole which would answer his purpose, placed the end of this against the window, and climbed up. It was not more than twelve feet above the ground. He broke one of the windows, and inserting his hand undid the fastening and climbed in at the window. A minute later they heard a grating sound, and then the lock shot back under the application of his knife, and the door swung open.

"That will do nicely," Lucy said, entering. "We will take possession. If the owners happen to come back we can pay them for the use of the place."

The furniture had been removed with the exception of a few of the heavy articles, and Chloe and Lucy at once set to work, and with bunches of long grass swept out one of the rooms. Dan cut a quantity of grass and piled it upon an old bedstead that stood in the corner, and Lucy smoothed it down.

"Now, sir," she said peremptorily to Vincent, "you will lie down and keep yourself quiet, but first of all I will cut your coat off."

One of the table-knives soon effected the work, and the coat was rolled up as a pillow. Dan removed his boots, and Vincent, who was now beyond even remonstrating, laid himself down on his cool bed.

"Now, Chloe," Miss Kingston said when they had left Vincent's room, "I will leave him to your care. I am sure that you must be thoroughly tired, for I don't suppose you have walked so many miles since you were a girl."

"I is tired, missie; but I am ready to do anyting you want."

"I only want you to attend to him, Chloe. First of all you had better make some tea. You know what is a good thing to give for a fever, and if you can find anything in the garden to make a drink of that sort, do; but I hope he will doze off for some time. When you have done, you had better get this place tidy a little; it is in a terrible litter. Evidently no one has been in since they moved out."

The room, indeed, was strewed with litter of all sorts, rubbish not worth taking away, old newspapers, and odds and ends of every description. Lucy looked about among these for some time, and with an exclamation of satisfaction at last picked up two crumpled envelopes. They were both addressed "William Jenkins, Woodford, near Mount Pleasant."

"That is just what I wanted," she said.

"What am you going to do, Miss Lucy?"

"I am going to Mount Pleasant," she said.

"Lor' a marcy, dearie, you are not going to walk that distance! You must have walked twelve miles already."

"I should if it were twice as far, Chloe. There are some things we must get. Don't look alarmed, I shall take Dan with me. Now, let me see. In the first place there are lemons for making drink and linseed for poultices, some meat for making broth, and some flour, and other things for ourselves; we may have to stay here for some time. Tell me just what you want and I will get it."

Chloe made out a list of necessaries.

"I sha'n't be gone long," the girl said. "If he asks after me or Dan, make out we are looking about the place to see what is useful. Don't let him know I have gone to Mount Pleasant, it might worry him."

Dan at once agreed to accompany the girl to Mount Pleasant when he heard that she was going to get things for his master.

Looking about he found an old basket among the litter, and they started without delay by the one road from the clearing, which led, they had no doubt, to the town. It was about two miles distant, and was really but a large village. A few Federal soldiers from the camp hard by were lounging about the streets but these paid no attention to them. Lucy soon made her purchases, and then went to the house that had been pointed out to her as being inhabited by the doctor who attended to the needs of the people of Mount Pleasant and the surrounding district. Fortunately he was at home. Lucy looked at him closely as he entered the room and took his seat. He was a middle-aged man with a shrewd face, and she at once felt that she might have confidence in it.

"Doctor," she said, "I want you to come out to see some one who is very ill."

"What is the matter with him? Or is it him or her?"

"It is--it's--" and Lucy hesitated, "a hurt he has got."

"A wound, I suppose?" the doctor said quietly. "You may as well tell me at once, as for me to find out when I get there, then I can take whatever is required with me."

"Yes, sir. It is a wound," Lucy said. "His shoulder is broken, I believe, by a pistol bullet."

"Umph!" the doctor said. "It might have been worse. Do not hesitate to tell me all about it, young lady. I have had a vast number of cases on hand since these troubles began. By the way, I do not know your face, and I thought I knew every one within fifteen miles around."

"I come from the other side of the Duck river. But at present he is lying at a place called Woodford, but two miles from here."

"Oh, yes! I know it. But I thought it was empty. Let me see, a man named Jenkins lived there. He was killed at the beginning of the troubles in a fight near Murfreesboro. His widow moved in here; and she has married again and gone five miles on the other side. I know she was trying to sell the old place."

"We have not purchased it, sir; we have just squatted there. My friend was taken so bad that we could go no further. We were trying, doctor, to make our way down south."

"Your friend, whoever he is, did a very foolish thing to bring a young lady like yourself on such a long journey. You are not a pair of runaway lovers, are you?"

"No, indeed," Lucy said, flushing scarlet; "we have no idea of such a thing. I was living alone, and the house was attacked by bushwhackers, the band of a villain named Mullens."

"Oh! I saw all about that in the Nashville paper this morning. They were attacked by a band of Confederate plunderers, it said."

"They were attacked by one man," the girl replied. "They were on the point of murdering me when he arrived. He shot Mullens and four of his band and the rest made off, but he got this wound. And as I knew the villains would return again and burn the house and kill me, I and my old nurse determined to go southward to join my friends in Georgia."

"Well, you can tell me more about it as we go," the doctor said. "I will order my buggy round to the door, and drive you back. I will take my instruments and things with me. It is no business of mine whether a sick man is a Confederate or a Federal; all my business is to heal them."

"Thank you very much, doctor. While the horse is being put in I will go down and tell the negro boy with me to go straight on with a basket of things I have been buying."

"Where is he now?" the doctor asked.

"I think he is sitting down outside the door, sir."

"Then you needn't go down," the doctor said. "He can jump up behind and go with us. He will get there all the quicker."

In five minutes they were driving down the village, with Dan in the back seat. On the way the doctor obtained from Lucy a more detailed account of their adventures.

"So he is one of those Confederate officers who broke prison at Elmira," he said. "I saw yesterday that one of his companions was captured."

"Was he, sir? How was that?"

"It seems that he had made his way down to Washington, and was staying at one of the hotels there as a Mr. James of Baltimore. As he was going through the street he was suddenly attacked by a negro, who assaulted him with such fury that he would have killed him had he not been dragged off by passers-by. The black would have been very roughly treated, but he denounced the man he had attacked as one of the Confederate officers who had escaped from the prison. It seems that the negro had been a slave of his who had been barbarously treated, and finally succeeded in making his escape and reaching England, after which he went to Canada; and now that it is safe for an escaped slave to live in the Northern States without fear of arrest or ill-treatment he had come down to Washington with the intention of engaging as a teamster with one of the Northern armies, in the hope when he made his way to Richmond of being able to gain some news of his wife, whom his master had sold before he ran away from him."

"It served the man right!" Lucy said indignantly. "It's a good thing that the slaves should turn the tables sometimes upon masters who ill-treat them."

"You don't think my patient would ill-treat his slaves?" the doctor asked with a little smile.

"I am sure he wouldn't," the girl said indignantly. "Why, the boy behind you is one of his slaves, and I am sure he would give his life for his master."

Dan had overheard the doctor's story, and now exclaimed:

"No, sah. Massa Vincent de kindest of masters. If all like him, do slaves everywhere contented and happy. What was de name of dat man, sah, you was speaking of?"

"His name was Jackson," the doctor answered.

"I tought so," Dan exclaimed in excitement. "Massa never mentioned de names of de two officers who got out wid him, and it war too dark for me to see their faces, but dat story made me tink it must be him. Berry bad man that; he libs close to us, and Massa Vincent one day pretty nigh kill him because he beat dat bery man who has catched him now on de street of Washington. When dat man sell him wife Massa Vincent buy her so as to prevent her falling into bad hands. She safe now wid his mother at de Orangery--dat's the name of her plantation."

"My patient must be quite an interesting fellow, young lady," the doctor said, with a rather slight twinkle of his eye. "A very knight-errant. But there is the house now; we shall soon see all about him."

Taking with him the case of instruments and medicines he had brought, the doctor entered Vincent's room. Lucy entered first; and although surprised to see a stranger with her, Vincent saw by her face that there was no cause for alarm.

"I have brought you a doctor," she said. "You could not go on as you were, you know. So Dan and I have been to fetch one."

The doctor now advanced and took Vincent's hand.

"Feverish," he said, looking at his cheeks, which were now flushed. "You have been doing too much, I fancy. Now let us look at this wound of yours. Has your servant got any warm water?" he asked Lucy.

Lucy left the room, and returned in a minute with a kettleful of warm water and a basin, which was among the purchases she had made at Mount Pleasant.

"That is right," the doctor said, taking it from her. "Now we will cut open the shirt sleeve. I think, young lady, you had better leave us, unless you are accustomed to the sight of wounds."

"I am not accustomed to them, sir; but as thousands of women have been nursing the wounded in the hospitals, I suppose I can do so now."

Taking a knife from the case, the doctor cut open the shirt from the neck to the elbow. The shoulder was terribly swollen and inflamed, and a little exclamation of pain broke from Lucy.

"That is the effect of walking and inattention," the doctor said. "If I could have taken him in hand within an hour of his being hit the matter would have been simple enough; but I cannot search for the ball, or in fact do anything, till we have reduced the swelling. You must put warm poultices on every half-hour, and by to-morrow I hope the inflammation will have subsided, and I can then see about the ball. It evidently is somewhere there still, for there is no sign of its having made its exit anywhere. In the meantime you must give him two tablespoonfuls of this cooling draught every two hours, and to-night give him this sleeping draught. I will be over to-morrow morning to see him. Do not be uneasy about him; the wound itself is not serious, and when we have got rid of the fever and inflammation I have no doubt we shall pull him round before long."

"I know the wound is nothing," Vincent said; "I have told Miss Kingston so all along. It is nothing at all to one I got at the first battle of Bull Run, where I had three ribs badly broken by a shell. I was laid up a long time over that business. Now I hope in a week I shall be fit to travel."

The doctor shook his head. "Not as soon as that. Still we will hope it may not be long. Now all you have to do is to lie quiet and not worry, and to get to sleep as quick as you can. You must not let your patient talk, Miss Kingston. It will be satisfactory to you, no doubt," he went on turning to Vincent, "to know that there is no fear whatever of your being disturbed here. The road leads nowhere, and is entirely out of the way of traffic. I should say you might be here six months without even a chance of a visitor. Every one knows the house is shut up, and as you have no neighbor within half a mile no one is likely to call in. Even if any one did by accident come here you would be in no danger; we are all one way of thinking about here."

"Shall we make some broth for him?" Lucy asked after they had left the room.

"No; he had best take nothing whatever during the next twenty-four hours except his medicine and cooling drinks. The great thing is to get down the fever. We can soon build him up afterward."

By nightfall the exertions of Dan, Lucy, and Chloe had made the house tidy. Beds of rushes and grass had been made in the room upstairs for the women, and Dan had no occasion for one for himself, as he was going to stop up with his master. He, however, brought a bundle of rushes into the kitchen, and when it became dark threw himself down upon them for a few hours' sleep, Lucy and her old nurse taking their place in Vincent's room, and promising to rouse Dan at twelve o'clock.

During the easy part of the night Vincent was restless and uneasy, but toward morning he became more quiet and dozed off, and had but just awoke when the doctor drove up at ten o'clock. He found the inflammation and swelling so much abated that he was able at once to proceed to search for the ball. Chloe was his assistant. Lucy felt that her nerves would not be equal to it, and Dan's hand shook so that he could not hold the basin. In a quarter of an hour, which seemed to Lucy to be an age, the doctor came out of the room.

"There is the bullet, Miss Kingston."

"And is he much hurt, sir?"

"It is a nasty wound," the doctor replied. "The collarbone is badly broken, and I fancy the head of the bone of the upper arm, to put it in language you will understand, is fractured; but of that I cannot be quite sure. I will examine it again to-morrow, and will then bandage it in its proper position. At present I have only put a bandage round the arm and body to prevent movement. I should bathe it occasionally with warm water, and you can give him a little weak broth to-day. I think, on the whole, he is doing very well. The feeling that you are all for the present safe from detection has had as much to do with the abatement of the fever as my medicine."

The next morning the report was still satisfactory. The fever had almost disappeared, and Vincent was in good spirits. The doctor applied the splints to keep the shoulder up in its proper position, and then tightly bandaged it.

"It depends upon yourself now," he said, "whether your shoulders are both of the same width as before or not. If you will lie quiet, and give the broken bones time to reunite, I think I can promise you that you will be as straight as before; but if not--putting aside the chances of inflammation--that shoulder will be lower than the other, and you will never get your full strength in it again. Quiet and patience are the only medicines you require, and as there can be no particular hurry for you to get south, and as your company here is pleasant and you have two good nurses, there is no excuse for your not being quiet and contented."

"Very well, doctor. I promise that unless there is a risk of our being discovered I will be as patient as you can wish. As you say, I have everything to make me contented and comfortable."

The doctor had a chat with Lucy, and agreed with her that perhaps it would be better to inform the mistress of the house that there were strangers there. Some of the people living along the road might notice him going or coming, or see Dan on his way to market, and might come and ascertain that the house was inhabited, and communicate the fact to their old neighbor.

"I will see her myself, Miss Kingston, and tell her that I have sent a patient of mine to take up his quarters here. I will say he is ready to pay some small sum weekly as long as he occupies the house. I have no doubt she would be willing enough to let you have it without that; for although I shall say nothing actually I shall let her guess from my manner that it is a wounded Confederate, and that will be enough for her. Still, I have no doubt that the idea of getting a few dollars for the rent of an empty house will add to her patriotism. People of her class are generally pretty close-fisted, and she will look upon this as a little pocket-money. Good-by! I shall not call to-morrow, but will be round next day again."

On his next visit the doctor told Lucy that he had arranged the matter with her landlady, and that she was to pay a dollar a week as rent. "I should not tell your patient about this," he said. "It will look to him as if I considered his stay was likely to be a long one, and it might fidget him."

"How long will it be, doctor, do you think?"

"That I cannot say. If all goes well, he ought in a month to be fairly cured; but before starting upon a journey which will tax his strength, I should say at least six weeks."

Ten days later Vincent was up, and able to get about. A pile of grass had been heaped up by the door, so that he could sit down in the sun and enjoy the air. Lucy was in high spirits, and flitted in and out of the house, sometimes helping Chloe, at others talking to Vincent.

"What are you laughing at?" she asked as she came out suddenly on one of these occasions.

"I was just thinking," he said, "that no stranger who dropped in upon us would dream that we were not at home here. There is Dan tidying up the garden; Chloe is quite at her ease in the kitchen, and you and I might pass very well for brother and sister."

"I don't see any likeness between us--not a bit."

"No, there is no personal likeness; but I meant in age and that sort of thing. I think, altogether, we have a very homelike look."

"The illusion would be very quickly dispelled if your stranger put his head inside the door. Did any one ever see such a bare place?"

"Anyhow, it's very comfortable," Vincent said, "though I grant that it would be improved by a little furniture."

"By a great deal of furniture, you mean. Why, there isn't a chair in the house, nor a carpet, nor a curtain, nor a cupboard, nor a bed; in fact all there is is the rough dresser in the kitchen and that plank table, and your bedstead. I really think that's all. Chloe has the kettle and two cooking-pots, and there is the dish and six plates we bought."

"You bought, you mean," Vincent interrupted.

"We bought, sir; this is a joint expedition. Then, there is the basin and a pail. I think that is the total of our belongings."

"Well, you see, it shows how little one can be quite comfortable upon," Vincent said. "I wonder how long it will be before the doctor gives me leave to move. It is all very well for me who am accustomed to campaigning, but it is awfully rough for you."

"Don't you put your impatience down to my account, at any rate until you begin to hear me grumble. It is just your own restlessness, when you are pretending you are comfortable."

"I can assure you that I am not restless, and that I am in no hurry at all to be off on my own account. I am perfectly contented with everything. I never thought I was lazy before, but I feel as if I could do with a great deal of this sort of thing. You will see that you will become impatient for a move before I do."

"We shall see, sir. Anyhow, I am glad you have said that, because now whatever you may feel you will keep your impatience to yourself."

Another four weeks passed by smoothly and pleasantly. Dan went into the village once a week to do the shopping, and the doctor had reduced his visits to the same number. He would have come oftener, for his visits to the lonely cottage amused him; but he feared that his frequent passage in his buggy might attract notice. So far no one else had broken the solitude of their lives. If the doctor's calls had been noticed, the neighbors had not taken the trouble to see who had settled down in Jenkins' old place. His visits were very welcome, for he brought newspapers and books, the former being also purchased by Dan whenever he went into the village, and thus they learned the course of events outside.

Since Antietam nothing had been done in Northern Virginia; but Burnside, who had succeeded McClellan, was preparing another great army, which was to march to Richmond and crush out the rebellion. Lee was standing on the defensive. Along the whole line of the frontier, from New Orleans to Tennessee, desultory fighting was going on, and in these conflicts the Confederates had generally the worse of things, having there no generals such as Lee, Jackson, and Longstreet, who had made the army of Virginia almost invincible.

At the last of these visits the doctor told Vincent that he considered he was nearly sufficiently restored in health to be able to start on their journey.

"It is a much better job than I had expected it would turn out. I was almost afraid that your shoulder would never be quite square again. However, as you can see for yourself it has come out quite right; and although I should not advise you to put any great strain on your left arm, I believe that in a very short time it will be as strong as the other."

"And now, doctor, what am I in debt to you? Your kindness cannot be repaid, but your medical bill I will discharge as soon as I get home. We have not more than twenty dollars left between us, which is little enough for the journey there is before us. You can rely that the instant I get to Richmond I will send you the money. There is no great difficulty in smuggling letters across the frontier."

"I am very pleased to have been able to be of service to you," the doctor said. "I should not think of accepting payment for aid rendered to an officer of our army; but it will give me real pleasure to receive a letter saying you have reached home in safety. It is a duty to do all we can for the brave men fighting for our cause. As I have told you, I am not a very hot partisan, for I see faults on both sides. Still, I believe in the principle of our forefathers, that each State has its own government and is master of its own army, joining with the others for such purposes as it may think fit. If I had been a fighting man I should certainly have joined the army of my State; but as it is, I hope I can do more good by staying and giving such aid and comfort as I can to my countrymen. You will, I am sure, excuse my saying that I think you must let me aid you a little further. I understand you to say that Miss Kingston will go to friends in Georgia, and I suppose you will see her safely there. Then you have a considerable journey to make to Richmond, and the sum that you possess is utterly inadequate for all this. It will give me real pleasure if you will accept the loan of one hundred dollars, which you can repay when you write to me from Richmond. You will need money for the sake of your companions rather than your own. When you have once crossed the line you will then be able to appear in your proper character."

"Thank you greatly, doctor. I will accept your offer as frankly as it is made. I had intended telegraphing for money as soon as I was among our own people, but there would be delay in receiving it, and it will be much more pleasant to push on at once."

"By the way, you cannot cross at Florence, for I hear that Hood has fallen back across the river, the forces advancing against him from this side being too strong to be resisted. But I think that this is no disadvantage to you, for it would have been far more difficult to pass the Federals and get to Florence than to make for some point on the river as far as possible from the contending armies."

"We talked that over the last time you were here, doctor, and you know we agreed it was better to run the risk of falling into the hands of the Yankee troops than into those of one of those partisan bands whose exploits are always performed at a distance from the army. However, if Hood has retreated across the Tennessee there is an end of that plan, and we must take some other route. Which do you advise?"

"The Yankees will be strong all round the great bend of the river to the west of Florence and along the line to the east, which would, of course, be your direct way. The passage, however, is your real difficulty, and I should say that instead of going in that direction you had better bear nearly due south. There is a road from Mount Pleasant that strikes into the main road from Columbia up to Camden. You can cross the river at that point without any question or suspicion, as you would be merely traveling to the west of the State. Once across you could work directly south, crossing into the State of Mississippi, and from there take train through Alabama to Georgia.

"It seems a roundabout way, but I think you would find it far the safest, for there are no armies operating upon that line. The population, at any rate as you get south, are for us, and there are, so far as I have heard, very few of these bushwhacking bands about either on one side or the other. The difficult part of the journey is that up to Camden, but as you will be going away from the seat of war instead of toward it there will be little risk of being questioned."

"I had thought of buying a horse and cart," Vincent said. "Jogging along a road like that we should attract no attention. I gave up the idea because our funds were not sufficient, but, thanks to your kindness, we might manage now to pick up something of the sort."

The doctor was silent for a minute.

"If you will send Dan over to me to-morrow afternoon I will see what can be done," he said. "It would certainly be the safest plan by far; but I must think it over. You will not leave before that, will you?"

"Certainly not, doctor. In any case we should have stayed another day to get a few more things for our journey."

The next afternoon Dan went over to Mount Pleasant. He was away two hours longer than they had expected, and they began to feel quite uneasy about him, when the sound of wheels was heard, and Dan appeared coming along the road driving a cart. Vincent gave a shout of satisfaction, and Lucy and the negress ran out from the house in delight.

"Here am de cart. Me had to go to five miles from de town to get him. Dat what took me so long. Here am a letter, sah, from the doctor. First-rate man dat Good man all ober."

The letter was as follows:

"My Dear Mr. Wingfield: I did not see how you would be able to buy a cart, and I was sure that you could not obtain one with the funds in your possession. As from what you have said I knew that you would not in the least mind the expense, I have taken the matter upon myself, and have bought from your landlady a cart and horse, which will, I think, suit you well. I have paid for them a hundred and fifty dollars, which you can remit me with the hundred I handed you yesterday. Sincerely trusting that you may succeed in carrying out your plans in safety, and with kind regards to yourself and Miss Kingston,

"I remain, yours truly,

"James Spencer."

"That is a noble fellow," Vincent said, "and I trust, for his sake as well as our own, that we shall get safely through. Now, Lucy, I think you had better go into the town the first thing and buy some clothes of good homely fashion. What with the water and the bushes your dress is grievously dilapidated, to say the least of it. Dan can go with you and buy a suit for me--those fitted for a young farmer. We shall look like a young farmer and his sister jogging comfortably along to market; we can stop and buy a stock of goods at some farm on the way."

"That will be capital," the girl said. "I have been greatly ashamed of my old dress, but knowing we were running so short, and that every dollar was of consequence, I made the best of it; now that we are in funds we can afford to be respectable."

Lucy started early the next morning for the town, and the shopping was satisfactorily accomplished. They returned by eleven o'clock. The new purchases were at once donned, and half an hour later they set off in the cart, Vincent sitting on the side driving, Lucy in the corner facing him on a basket turned topsy-turvy, Dan and Chloe on a thick bag of rushes in the bottom of the cart.

## CHAPTER XIV. ACROSS THE BORDER.

DAN on his return with the cart had brought back a message from its late owner to say that if she could in any way be of use to them she should be glad to aid them. Her farm lay on the road they were now following, and they determined therefore to stop there. As the cart drew up at the door the woman came out.

"Glad to see you," she said; "come right in. It's strange now you should have been lodging in my house for more than six weeks and I should never have set eyes on you before. The doctor talked to me a heap about you, but I didn't look to see quite such a young couple."

Lucy colored hotly and was about to explain that they did not stand in the supposed relationship to each other, but Vincent slightly shook his head. It was not worth while to undeceive the woman, and although they had agreed to pass as brother and sister Vincent was determined not to tell an untruth about it unless deceit was absolutely necessary for their safety.

"And you want to get out of the way without questions being asked, I understand?" the woman went on. "There are many such about at present. I don't want to ask no questions; the war has brought trouble enough on me. Now is there anything I can do? If so, say it right out."

"Yes, there is something you can do for us. We want to fill up our cart with the sort of stuff you take to market--apples and pumpkins, and things of that sort. If we had gone to buy them anywhere else there might have been questions asked. From what the doctor said you can let us have some."

"I can do that. The storeroom's chuck full; and it was only a few days ago I said to David it was time we set about getting them off. I will fill your cart, sir; and not overcharge you neither. It will save us the trouble of taking it over to Columbia or Camden, for there's plenty of garden truck round Mount Pleasant, and one cannot get enough to pay for the trouble of taking them there."

The cart was soon filled with apples, pumpkins, and other vegetables, and the price put upon them was very moderate.

"What ought we to ask for these?" Vincent soon inquired. "One does not want to be extra cheap or dear."

The woman informed them of the prices they might expect to get for the produce; and they at once started amid many warm good wishes from her.

Before leaving the farm the woman had given them a letter to her sister who lived a mile from Camden.

"It's always awkward stopping at a strange place," she said, "and farmers don't often put up at hotels when they drive in with garden truck to a town, though they may do so sometimes; besides it's always nice being with friends. I will write a line to Jane and tell her you have been my tenants at Woodford and where you are going, and ask her to take you in for the night and give you a note in the morning to any one she or her husband may know a good bit along that road."

When they reached the house it was dark, but directly Vincent showed the note the farmer and his wife heartily bade them come in.

"Your boy can put up the horse at the stable, and you are heartily welcome. But the house is pretty full, and we can't make you as comfortable as we should wish at night; but still we will do our best."

Vincent and Lucy were soon seated by the fire. Their hostess bustled about preparing supper for them, and the children, of whom the house seemed full, stared shyly at the newcomers. As soon as the meal was over, Chloe's wants were attended to, and a lunch of bread and bacon taken out by the farmer to Dan in the stables. The children were then packed off to bed, and the farmer and his wife joined Vincent and Lucy by the fire.

"As to sleeping," the woman said, "John and I have been talking it over, and the best way we can see is that you should sleep with me, ma'am, and we will make up a bed on the floor here for my husband and yours."

"Thank you--that will do very nicely; though I don't like interfering with your arrangements."

"Not at all, ma'am, not at all, it makes a nice change having some one come in, especially of late, when there is no more pleasure in going about in this country, and people don't go out after dark more than they can help. Ah! it's a bad time. My sister says you are going west, but I see you have got your cart full of garden truck. How you have raised it so soon I don't know; for Liza wrote to me two months since as she hadn't been able to sell her place, and it was just a wilderness. Are you going to get rid of it at Camden to-morrow?"

Vincent had already been assured as to the politics of his present host and hostess, and he therefore did not hesitate to say:

"The fact is, madam, we are anxious to get along without being questioned by any Yankee troops we may fall in with; and we have bought the things you see in the cart from your sister, as, going along with a cart full, any one we met would take us for farmers living close by on their road to the next market-town."

"Oh, oh! that's it!" the farmer said significantly. "Want to get through the lines, eh?"

Vincent nodded.

"Didn't I think so!" the farmer said, rubbing his hands. "I thought directly my eyes hit upon you that you did not look the cut of a granger. Been fighting--eh? and they are after you?"

"I don't think they are after me here," Vincent said. "But I have seen a good deal of fighting with Jackson and Stuart; and I am just getting over a collar-bone which was smashed by a Yankee bullet."

"You don't say!" the farmer exclaimed. "Well, I should have gone out myself if it hadn't been for Jane and the children. But there are such a lot of them that I could not bring myself to run the chance of leaving them all on her hands. Still, I am with them heart and soul."

"Your wife's sister told me that you were on the right side," Vincent said, "and that I could trust you altogether."

"Now, if you tell me which road you want to go, I don't mind if I get on my horse to-morrow and ride with you a stage, and see you put for the night. I know a heap of people, and I am sure to be acquainted with some one whichever road you may go. We are pretty near all the right side about here, though, as you get further on, there are lots of Northern men. Now, what are your ideas as to the roads?"

Vincent told him the route he intended to take.

"You ought to get through there right enough," the farmer said. "There are some

Yankee troops moving about to the west of the river, but not many of them; and even if you fell in with them, with your cargo of stuff they would not suspect you. Anyhow, I expect we can get you passed down so as always to be among friends. So you fought under Jackson and Stuart, did you? Ah, they have done well in Virginia! I only wish we had such men here. What made you take those two darkies along with you? I should have thought you would have got along better by yourself."

"We couldn't very well leave them," Vincent said; "the boy has been with me all through the wars, and is as true as steel. Old Chloe was Lucy's nurse, and would have broken her heart had she been left behind."

"They are faithful creatures when they are well treated. Mighty few of them have run away all this time from their masters, though in the parts the Yankees hold there is nothing to prevent their bolting if they have a mind to it. I haven't got no niggers myself. I tried them, but they want more looking after than they are worth; and I can make a shift with my boys to help me, and hiring a hand in busy times to work the farm. Now, sir, what do you think of the look-out?"

The subject of the war fairly started, his host talked until midnight, long before which hour Lucy and the farmer's wife had gone off to bed.

"We will start as soon as it is light," the farmer said, as he and Vincent stretched themselves upon the heap of straw covered with blankets that was to serve as their bed, Chloe having hours before gone up to share the bed of the negro girl who assisted the farmer's wife in her management of the house and children.

"It's best to get through Camden before people are about. There are Yankee soldiers at the bridge, but it will be all right you driving in, however early, to sell your stuff. Going out you ain't likely to meet with Yankees; but as it would look queer, you taking your garden truck out of the town, it's just as well to be on the road before people are about. Once you get five or six miles the other side you might be going to the next place to sell your stuff."

"That is just what I have been thinking," Vincent said, "and I agree with you the earlier we get through Camden the better."

Accordingly as soon as daylight appeared the horse was put in the cart, the farmer mounting his own animal, and with a hearty good-by from his wife the party started away. The Yankee sentinels at each end of the bridge were passed without questions, for early as it was the carts were coming in with farm produce.

As yet the streets of the town were almost deserted, and the farmer, who before starting had tossed a tarpaulin into the back of the cart, said:

"Now, pull that over all that stuff, and then any one that meets us will think that you are taking out bacon and groceries and such like for some store way off."

This suggestion was carried out, and Camden was soon left behind. A few carts were met as they drove along. The farmer knew some of the drivers and pulled up to say a few words to them. After a twenty-mile drive they stopped at another farm, where their friend's introduction ensured them as cordial a welcome as that upon the preceding evening. So step by step they journeyed on, escorted in almost every case by their host of the night before and meeting with no interruption. Once they passed a strong body of Federal cavalry, but these supposing that the party belonged to the neighborhood asked no questions; and at last, after eight days' traveling, they passed two posts which marked the boundary between Tennessee and Alabama.

For the last two days they had been beyond the point to which the Federal troops had penetrated. They now felt that all risk was at an end. Another day's journey brought them to a railway station, and they learned that the trains were running as usual, although somewhat irregular as to the hours at which they came along or as to the time they took upon their journey. The contents of the cart had been left at the farm at which they stopped the night before, and Vincent had now no difficulty in disposing of the horse and cart, as he did not stand out for price, but took the first offer made. Two hours later a train came along, and the party were soon on their way to the east. After many hours' traveling they reached Rome, in Georgia, and then proceeded by the southern line a few miles to Macon, at which place they alighted and hired a conveyance to take them to Antioch, near which place Lucy's relatives resided.

The latter part of the journey by rail had been a silent one. Lucy felt none of the pleasure that she had expected at finding herself safely through her dangers and upon the point of joining relations who would be delighted to see her, and she sat looking blankly out of the window at the surrounding country. At last Vincent, who had been half an hour without speaking, said:

"Are you sorry our journey is just over, Lucy?"

The girl's lip quivered, but she did not speak for a moment. "Of course it is unpleasant saying good-by when people have been together for some time," she said with an effort.

"I hope it will not be good-by for long," he said. "I shall be back here as soon as this horrible war is over."

"What for?" the girl asked, looking round in surprise. "You live a long way from here, and you told me you knew nobody in these parts."

"I know you," Vincent said, "and that is quite enough. Do you not know that I love you?"

The girl gave a start of surprise, her cheek flushed, but her eyes did not drop as she looked frankly at him.

"No, Vin," she said after a pause, "I never once thought you loved me, never once. You have not been a bit like what I thought people were when they felt like that."

"I hope not, Lucy. I was your protector then, that is to say when you were not mine. Your position has been trying enough, and I should have been a blackguard if I had made it more uncomfortable than it was by showing you that I cared for you. I have tried my best to be what people thought me--your brother; but now that you are just home and among your own people, I think I may speak and tell you how I feel toward you and how I have loved you since the moment I first saw you. And you, Lucy, do you think you could care for me?"

"Not more than I do now, Vin. I love you with all my heart. I have been trying so hard to believe that I didn't, because I thought you did not care for me that way."

For some minutes no further word was spoken. Vincent was the first to speak:

"It is horrid to have to sit here in this stiff, unnatural way, Lucy, when one is inclined to do something outrageous from sheer happiness. These long, open cars, where people can see from end to end what every one is doing, are hateful inventions. It is perfectly absurd, when one finds one's self the happiest fellow living, that one is obliged to look as demure and solemn as if one was in church."

"Then you should have waited, sir," the girl said.

"I meant to have waited, Lucy, until I got to your home, but directly I felt that there was no longer any harm in my speaking, out it came; but it's very hard to have to wait for hours perhaps."

"To wait for what?" Lucy asked demurely.

"You must wait for explanations until we are alone, Lucy. And now I think the train begins to slacken, and it is the next station at which we get out."

"I think, Lucy," Vincent said, when they approached the house of her relatives, "you and Chloe had better get out and go in by yourselves and tell your story. Dan and I will go to the inn, and I will come round in an hour. If we were to walk in together like this it would be next to impossible for you to explain how it all came about."

"I think that would be the best plan. My two aunts are the kindest creatures possible, but no doubt they will be bewildered at seeing me so suddenly. I do think it would be best to let me have a talk with them and tell them all about it before you appear upon the scene."

"Very well, then, in an hour I will come in."

When they arrived at the gate, therefore, Vincent helped Lucy and Chloe to alight, and then jumping into the buggy again told the driver to take him to the inn.

Having engaged a room and indulged in a thorough wash Vincent sallied out into the little town, and was fortunate enough to succeed in purchasing a suit of tweed clothes, which, although they scarcely fitted him as if they had been made for him, were still an immense improvement upon the rough clothes in which he had traveled. Returning to the hotel he put on his new purchases, and then walked to the house of Lucy's aunts, which was a quarter of a mile outside the town.

Lucy had walked up the little path through the garden in front of the house, and turning the handle of the door had entered unannounced and walked straight into the parlor. Two elderly ladies rose with some surprise at the entry of a strange visitor. It was three years since she had paid her last visit there, and for a moment they did not recognize her.

"Don't you know me, aunts?"

"Why, goodness me!" the eldest exclaimed, "if it isn't our little Lucy grown into a woman! My dear child, where have you sprung from?" And the two ladies warmly embraced their niece, who, as soon as they released her from their arms, burst into a fit of crying, and it was some time before she could answer the questions showered upon her.

"It is nothing, aunts," she said at last, wiping her eyes; "but I am so glad to be with you again, and I have gone through so much, and I am so happy, and it is so nice being with you again. Here is Chloe waiting to speak to you, aunts. She has come with me all the way."

The old negress, who had been waiting in the passage, was now called in.

"Why, Chloe, you look no older than when you went away from here six years ago," Miss Kingston said. "But how ever did you both get through the lines? We have been terribly anxious about you. Your brother was here only a fortnight ago, and he and your father were in a great way about you, and reproached themselves bitterly that they did not send you to us before the troubles began, which certainly would have been a wiser step, as I told them. Of course your brother said that when they left you to join the army they had no idea that matters were going so far, or that the Yankees would drive us out of Tennessee, or they would never have dreamed of leaving you alone. However, here you are, so now tell me all about it."

Lucy told the story of the various visits of the Federal bushwhackers to the house, and how they had narrowly escaped death for refusing to betray the Confederate officer who had come to the house for food. Her recital was frequently interrupted by exclamations of indignation and pity from her aunts.

"Well, aunts, after that," she went on, "you see it was impossible for me to stop there any longer. No doubt they came back again a few hours afterward and burned the house, and had I been found there I should have been sure to be burned in it, so Chloe agreed with me that there was nothing to do but to try and get through the lines and come to you. There was no way of my getting my living at Nashville except by going out as a help, and there might have been some difficulties about that."

"Quite right, my dear. It was clearly the best thing for you to come to us-- indeed, the only thing. But how in the world did you two manage to travel alone all that distance and get through the Federal lines?"

"You see, we were not alone, aunts," Lucy said; "the Confederate officer and his servant were coming through, and of course they took care of us. We could never have got through alone, and as Chloe was with me we got on very nicely; but we have been a long time getting through, for in that fight, where he saved my life and killed five of the band, he had his shoulder broken by a pistol bullet, and we had to stop in a farmhouse near Mount Pleasant, and he was very ill for some time, but the doctor who attended him was a true Southerner, and so we were quite safe till he was able to move again."

"And who is this officer, Lucy?" Miss Kingston asked rather anxiously.

"He is a Virginian gentleman, auntie. His mother has large estates near Richmond. He was in the cavalry with Stuart, and was made prisoner while he was lying wounded and insensible, at Antietam; and I think, auntie, that that--" and she hesitated--"some day we are going to be married."

"Oh, that's it, is it?" the old lady said kindly. "Well, I can't say anything about that until I see him, Lucy. Now tell us the whole story, and then we shall be better able to judge about it. I don't think, my dear, that while you were traveling under his protection he ought to have talked to you about such things."

"He didn't, auntie; not until we were half a mile from the station here. I never thought he cared for me the least bit; he was just like a brother to me--just like what Jack would have been if he had been bringing me here."

"That's right, my dear; I am glad to hear it. Now, let us hear all about it."

Lucy told the whole story of her escape and her adventures, and when she had finished her aunts nodded to each other.

"That's all very satisfactory, Lucy. It was a difficult position to be placed in, though I don't see how it was to be avoided, and the young man really seems to have behaved very well. Don't you think so, Ada?" The younger Miss Kingston agreed, and both were prepared to receive Vincent with cordiality when he appeared.

The hour had been considerably exceeded when Vincent came to the door. He felt it rather an awkward moment when he was ushered into the presence of Lucy's aunts, who could scarcely restrain an exclamation of surprise at his youth, for although Lucy had said nothing about his age, they expected to meet an older man, the impression being gained from the recital of his bravery in attacking single-handed twelve men, and by the manner in which he had piloted the party through their dangers.

"We are very glad to see you--my sister Ada and myself," Miss Kingston said, shaking hands cordially with their visitor. "Lucy has been telling us all about you; but we certainly expected from what you had gone through that you were older."

"I am two or three years older than she is, Miss Kingston, and I have gone through so much in the last three years that I feel older than I am. She has told you,

I hope, that she has been good enough to promise to be my wife some day?"

"Yes, she has told us that, Mr. Wingfield; and although we don't know you personally, we feel sure--my sister Ada and I--from what she has told us of your behavior while you have been together that you are an honorable gentleman, and we hope and believe that you will make her happy."

"I will do my best to do so," Vincent said earnestly. "As to my circumstances, I shall in another year come into possession of estates sufficient to keep her in every comfort."

"I have no doubt that that is all satisfactory, Mr. Wingfield, and that her father will give his hearty approval when he hears all the circumstances of the case. Now, if you will go into the next room, Mr. Wingfield, I will call her down"--for Lucy had run upstairs when she heard Vincent knock.

"I dare say you will like a quiet talk together," she added smiling, "for she tells me you have never been alone together since you started."

Lucy required several calls before she came down. A new shyness such as she had never before felt had seized her, and it was with flushed cheeks and timid steps that she at last came downstairs, and it needed an encouraging--"Go in, you silly child, your lover will not eat you," before she turned the handle and went into the room where Vincent was expecting her.

Vincent had telegraphed from the first station at which he arrived within the limits of the Confederacy to his mother, announcing his safe arrival there, and asking her to send money to him at Antioch. Her letter in reply reached him three days after his arrival. It contained notes for the amount he wrote for; and while expressing her own and his sisters' delight at hearing he had safely reached the limits of the Confederacy, she expressed not a little surprise at the out-of-the-way place to which he had requested the money to be sent.

"We have been examining the maps, my dear boy," she said, "and find that it is seventy or eighty miles out of your direct course, and we have puzzled ourselves in vain as to why you should have made your way there. The girls guess that you have gone there to deliver in person some message from one of your late fellow-prisoners to his family. I am not good at guessing, and am content to wait until you return home. We hope that you will leave as soon as you get the remittance. We shall count the hours until we see you. Of course we learned from a Yankee paper smuggled through the lines that you had escaped from prison, and have been terribly anxious about you ever since. We are longing to hear your adventures."

A few hours after the receipt of this letter Vincent was on his way home. It was a long journey. The distance was considerable, and the train service greatly disordered and unpunctual. When within a few hours of Richmond he telegraphed, giving the approximate time at which he might be expected to arrive. The train, however, did not reach Richmond until some hours later. The carriage was waiting at the station, and the negro coachman shouted with pleasure at the sight of his young master.

"Missis and the young ladies come, sah; but de station-master he say de train no arrive for a long time, so dey wait for you at de town house, sah."

Dan jumped up beside the coachman and Vincent leaped into the carriage, and a few minutes later he was locked in the arms of his mother and sisters.

"You grow bigger and bigger, Vincent," his mother said after the first greeting was over. "I thought you must have done when you went away last, but you are two or three inches taller and ever so much wider."

"I think I have nearly done now, mother--anyhow as to height. I am about six feet one."

"You are a dreadful trouble to us, Vincent," Annie said. "We have awful anxiety whenever we hear of a battle being fought, and it was almost a relief to us when we heard that you were in a Yankee prison. We thought at least you were out of danger for some time; but since the news came of your escape it has been worse than ever, and as week passed after week without our hearing anything of you we began to fear that something terrible had happened to you."

"Nothing terrible has happened at all, Annie. The only mishap I had was getting a pistol bullet in my shoulder which laid me up for about six weeks. There was nothing very dreadful about it," he continued, as exclamations of alarm and pity broke from his mother and sister. "I was well looked after and nursed. And now I will tell you my most important piece of news, and then I will give you a full account of my adventures from the time when Dan got me out of prison, for it is entirely to him that I owe my liberty."

"Well, what is the piece of news?" Annie asked.

"Guess!" Vincent replied smiling.

"You have got promoted?" his mother said. He shook his head.

"Is it about a lady?" Annie asked.

Vincent smiled.

"Oh, Vincent, you are not engaged to be married! That would be too ridiculous!" Vincent laughed and nodded.

"Annie is right, mother; I am engaged to be married." Mrs. Wingfield looked grave, Rosie laughed, and Annie threw her arms round his neck and kissed him.

"You dear, silly old boy:" she said. "I am glad, though it seems so ridiculous. Who is she, and what is she like?"

"We needn't ask where she lives," Rosie said. "Of course it is in Antioch, though how in the world you managed it all in the two or three days you were there I can't make out."

Mrs. Wingfield's brow cleared. "At any rate, in that case, Vincent, she is a Southerner. I was afraid at first it was some Yankee woman who had perhaps sheltered you on your way."

"Is she older than you, Vincent?" Annie asked suddenly. "I shouldn't like her to be older than you are."

"She is between sixteen and seventeen," Vincent replied, "and she is a Southern girl, mother, and I am sure you will love her, for she saved my life at the risk of her own, besides nursing me all the time I was ill."

"I have no doubt I shall love her, Vincent, for I think, my boy, that you would not make a rash choice. I think you are young, much too young, to be engaged; still, that is a secondary matter. Now tell us all about it. We expected your story to be exciting, but did not dream that love-making had any share in it."

Vincent accordingly told them the whole story of his adventures from the time of his first meeting Dan in prison. When he related the episode of Lucy's refusal to say whether he would return, although threatened with instant death unless she did so, his narrative was broken by the exclamations of his hearers.

"You need not say another word in praise of her," his mother said. "She is indeed a noble girl, and I shall be proud of such a daughter."

"She must be a darling!" Annie exclaimed. "Oh, Vincent, how brave she must be! I don't think I ever could have done that, with a pistol pointing straight at you, and all those dreadful men round, and no hope of a rescue; it's awful even to think of."

"It was an awful moment, as you may imagine," Vincent replied. "I shall never forget the scene, or Lucy's steadfast face as she faced that man; and you see at that time I was a perfect stranger to her-- only a fugitive Confederate officer whom she shielded from his pursuers."

"Go on, Vincent; please go on," Annie said. "Tell us what happened next."

Vincent continued his narrative to the end, with, however, many interruptions and questions on the part of the girls. His mother said little, but sat holding his hand in hers.

"It has been a wonderful escape, Vincent," she said when he had finished. "Bring your Lucy here when you like, and I shall be ready to receive her as my daughter, and to love her for her own sake as well as yours. She must be not only a brave but a noble girl, and you did perfectly right to lose not a single day after you had taken her safely home in asking her to be your wife. I am glad to think that some day the Orangery will have so worthy a mistress. I will write to her at once. You have not yet told us what she is like, Vincent."

"I am not good at descriptions, but you shall see her photograph when I get it."

"What, haven't you got one now?"

"She had not one to give me. You see, when the troubles began she was little more than a child, and since that time she has scarcely left home, but she promised to have one taken at once and send it me, and then, if it is a good likeness, you will know all about it."

"Mother, when you write to-night," Rosie said, "please send her your photograph and ours, and say we all want one of our new relative that is to be."

"I think, my dear, you can leave that until we have exchanged a letter or two. You will see Vincent's copy, and can then wait patiently for your own."

"And now, mother, I have told you all of my news; let us hear about every one here. How are all the old house hands, and how is Dinah? Tony is at Washington, I know, because I saw in the paper that he had made a sudden attack upon Jackson."

Mrs. Wingfield's face fell.

"That is my one piece of bad news, Vincent. I wish you hadn't asked the question until to-morrow, for I am sorry that anything should disturb the pleasure of this first meeting; still as you have asked the question I must answer it. About ten days ago a negro came, as I afterward heard from Chloe, to the back entrance and asked for Dinah. He said he had a message for her. She went and spoke to him, and then ran back and caught up her child. She said to Chloe, 'I have news of my husband. I think he is here. I will soon be back again.' Then she ran out, and has never returned. We have made every inquiry we could, but we have not liked to advertise for her, for it may be that she has met her husband, and that he persuaded her to make off at once with him to Yorktown or Fortress Monroe."

"This is bad news indeed, mother," Vincent said. "No, I do not think for a moment that she has gone off with Tony. There could be no reason why she should have left so suddenly without telling any one, for she knew well enough that you would let her go if she wished it; and I feel sure that neither she nor Tony would act so ungratefully as to leave us in this manner. No, mother, I feel sure that this has been done by Jackson. You know I told you I felt uneasy about her before I went. No doubt the old rascal has seen in some Northern paper an account of his son having been attacked in the streets of Washington, and recaptured by Tony, and he has had Dinah carried off from a pure spirit of revenge. Well, mother," he went on in answer to an appealing look from her, "I will not put myself out this first evening of my return, and will say no more about it. There will be plenty of time to take the matter up to-morrow. And now about all our friends and acquaintances. How are they getting on? Have you heard of any more of my old chums being killed since I was taken prisoner at Antietam?"

It was late in the evening before Vincent heard all the news. Fortunately, the list of casualties in the army of Virginia had been slight since Antietam; but that battle had made many gaps among the circle of their friends, and of these Vincent now heard for the first time, and he learned too, that although no battle had been fought since Antietam, on the 17th of September, there had been a sharp skirmish near Fredericksburg, and that the Federal army, now under General Burnside, who had succeeded McClellan, was facing that of Lee, near that town, and that it was believed that they would attempt to cross the Rappahannock in a few days.

It was not until he retired for the night that Vincent allowed his thoughts to turn again to the missing woman. Her loss annoyed and vexed him much more than he permitted his mother to see. In the first place, the poor girl's eagerness to show her gratitude to him upon all occasions, and her untiring watchfulness and care during his illness from his wound, had touched him, and the thought that she was now probably in the hands of brutal taskmasters was a real pain to him. In the next place, he had, as it were, given his pledge to Tony that she should be well cared for until she could be sent to join him. And what should he say now when the negro wrote to claim her? Then, too, he felt a personal injury that the woman should be carried off when under his mother's protection, and he was full of indignation and fury at the dastardly revenge taken by Jackson. Upon hearing the news he had at once mentally determined to devote himself for some time to a search for Dinah; but the news that a great battle was expected at the front interfered with his plan. Now that he was back, capable of returning to duty, his place was clearly with his regiment; but he determined that while he would rejoin at once, he would as soon as the battle was over, if he were unhurt, take up the search. His mother and sisters were greatly distressed when at breakfast he told them that he must at once report himself as fit for duty, and ready to join his regiment.

"I was afraid you would think so," Mrs. Wingfield said, while the girls wept silently; "and much as I grieve at losing you again directly you have returned, I can say nothing against it. You have gone through many dangers, Vincent, and have been preserved to us through them all. We will pray that you may be so to the end. Still, whether or not, I as a Virginian woman cannot grudge my son to the service of my country, when all other mothers are making the same sacrifice; but it is hard to give you up when but yesterday you returned to us."

## CHAPTER XV. FREDERICKSBURG.

AS soon as breakfast was over Vincent mounted Wildfire--which had been sent back after he had been taken prisoner, and rode into Richmond. There he reported himself at headquarters as having returned after escaping from a Federal prison, and making his way through the lines of the enemy.

"I had my shoulder-bone smashed in a fight with some Yankees," he said, "and was laid up in hiding for six weeks; but have now fairly recovered. My shoulder, at times, gives me considerable pain, and although I am desirous of returning to duty and rejoining my regiment until the battle at Fredericksburg has taken place, I must request that three months' leave be granted to me after that to return home and complete my cure, promising of course to rejoin my regiment at once should hostilities break out before the spring."

"We saw the news that you had escaped," the general said, "but feared, as so long a time elapsed without hearing from you, that you had been shot in attempting to cross the lines. Your request for leave is of course granted, and a note will be made of your zeal in thus rejoining on the very day after your return. The vacancy in the regiment has been filled up, but I will appoint you temporarily to General Stuart's staff, and I shall have great pleasure in to-day filling up your commission as captain. Now let me hear how you made your escape. By the accounts published in the Northern papers it seemed that you must have had a confederate outside the walls."

Vincent gave a full account of his escape from prison and a brief sketch of his subsequent proceedings, saying only that he was in the house of some loyal people in Tennessee, when it was attacked by a party of Yankee bushwhackers, that these were beaten off in the fight, but that he himself had a pistol bullet in his shoulder. He then made his way on until compelled by his wound to lay up for six weeks in a lonely farmhouse near Mount Pleasant; that afterward in the disguise of a young farmer he had made a long detour across the Tennessee river and reached Georgia.

"When do you leave for the front, Captain Wingfield?"

"I shall be ready to start to-night, sir."

"In that case I will trouble you to come round here this evening. There will be a fast train going through with ammunition for Lee at ten o'clock, and I shall have a bag of despatches for him, which I will trouble you to deliver. You will find me here up to the last moment. I will give orders that a horse-box be put on to the train."

After expressing his thanks Vincent took his leave. As he left the general's quarters, a young man, just alighting from his horse, gave a shout of greeting.

"Why, Wingfield, it is good to see you! I thought you were pining again in a Yankee dungeon, or had got knocked on the head crossing the lines. Where have you sprung from, and when did you arrive?"

"I only got in yesterday after sundry adventures which I will tell you about presently. When did you arrive from the front?"

"I came down a few days ago on a week's leave on urgent family business," the young man laughed, "and I am going back again this afternoon by the four o'clock train."

"Stay till ten," Vincent said, "and we will go back together. There is a special train going through with ammunition, and as everything will make way for that it will not be long behind the four o'clock, and likely enough may pass it on the way. There is a horse-box attached to it, and as I only take one horse there will be room for yours."

"I haven't brought my horse down," Harry Furniss said; "but I will certainly go with you by the ten o'clock. Then we can have a long talk. I don't think I have seen you since the day you asked me to lend you my boat two years ago."

"Can you spare me two hours now?" Vincent asked. "You will do me a very great favor if you will."

Harry Furniss looked at his watch. "It is eleven o'clock now; we have a lot of people to lunch at half-past one, and I must be back by then."

"You can manage that easy enough," Vincent replied; "in two hours from the time we leave here you can be at home."

"I am your man, then, Vincent. Just wait five minutes. I have to see some one in here."

A few minutes later Harry Furniss came out again and mounted.

"Now which way, Vincent? and what is it you want me for?"

"The way is to Jackson's place at the Cedars, the why I will tell you about as we ride."

Vincent then recounted his feud with the Jacksons, of which, up to the date of the purchase of Dinah Morris, his friend was aware, having been present at the sale. He now heard of the attack upon young Jackson by Tony, and of the disappearance of Dinah Morris.

"I should not be at all surprised, Wingfield, if your surmises are correct, and that old scoundrel has carried off the girl to avenge himself upon Tony. Of course, if you could prove it, it would be a very serious offense; for the stealing a slave, and by force too, is a crime with a very heavy penalty, and has cost men their lives before now. But I don't see that you have anything like a positive proof, however strong a case of suspicion it may be. I don't see what you are going to say when you get there."

"I am going to tell him that if he does not say what he has done with the girl, I will have his son arrested for treachery as soon as he sets foot in the Confederacy again."

"Treachery!" Furniss said in surprise; "what treachery has he been guilty of? I saw that he was one of those who escaped with you, and I rather wondered at the time at you two being mixed up together in anything. I heard that he had been recaptured through some black fellow that had been his slave, but I did not read the account. Have you got proof of what you say?"

"Perhaps no proof that would hold in a court of law," Vincent replied, "but proof enough to make it an absolute certainty to my mind."

Vincent then gave an account of their escape, and of the anonymous denunciation of himself and Dan.

"Now," he said, "no one but Dan knew of the intended escape, no one knew what clothes he had purchased, no one could possibly have known that I was to be disguised as a preacher and Dan as my servant. Therefore the information must have been given by Jackson."

"I have not the least doubt but that the blackguard did give it, Wingfield; but there is no proof."

"I consider that there is a proof--an absolute and positive proof," Vincent asserted, "because no one else could have known it."

"Well, you see that as a matter of fact the other officer did know it, and might possibly have given the information."

"But why should he? The idea is absurd. He had never had a quarrel with me, and he owed his liberty to me."

"Just so, Wingfield. I am as certain that it was Jackson as you are, because I know the circumstances; but you see there is no more absolute proof against one man than against the other. It is true that you had had a quarrel with Jackson some two years before, but you see you had made it up and had become friends in prison--so much so that you selected him from among a score of others in the same room to be the companion of your flight. You and I, who know Jackson, can well believe him guilty of an act of gross ingratitude--of ingratitude and treachery; but people who do not know would hardly credit it as possible--that a man could be such a villain. The defense he would set up would be that in the first place there is no shadow of evidence that he more than the other turned traitor. In the second place he would be sure to say that such an accusation against a Confederate officer is too monstrous and preposterous to be entertained for a moment; and that doubtless your negro, although he denies the fact, really chattered about his doings to the negroes he was lodging with, and that it was through them that some one got to know of the disguise you would wear. We know that it wasn't so, Wingfield; but ninety-nine out of every hundred white men in the South would rather believe that a negro had chattered than that a Confederate officer had been guilty of a gross act of treachery and ingratitude."

Vincent was silent. He felt that what his companion said was the truth; and that a weapon by which he had hoped to force the elder Jackson into saying what he had done with Dinah would probably fail in its purpose. The old man was too astute not to perceive that there was no real proof against his son, and would therefore be unlikely at once to admit that he had committed a serious crime, and to forego his revenge.

"I will try at any rate," he said at last; "and if he refuses I will publish the story in the papers. When the fellow gets back from Yankee-land he may either call me out or demand a court of inquiry. I may not succeed in getting a verdict from twelve white men, but I think I can convince every one of our own class that the fellow did it; and when this battle that is expected is over I have got three months' leave, and I will move heaven and earth to find the woman; and if I do, Jackson will either have to bolt or stand a trial, with the prospect of ten years' imprisonment if he is convicted. In either case we are not likely to have his son about here again; and if he did venture back and brought an action against me, his chance of getting damages would be a small one."

Another half-hour's ride brought them to the Cedars. They dismounted at the house, and fastening their horses to the portico knocked at the door. It was opened by a negro.

"Tell your master," Vincent said, "that Mr. Wingfield wishes to speak to him."

Andrew Jackson himself came to the door.

"To what do I owe the very great pleasure of this visit, Mr. Wingfield?" he said grimly.

"I have come to ask you what you have done with Dinah Morris, whom, I have every ground for believing, you have caused to be kidnaped from my mother's house."

"This is a serious charge, young gentleman," Andrew Jackson said, "and one that I shall call upon you to justify in the law-courts. Men are not to be charged with criminal actions even by young gentlemen of good Virginian families."

"I shall be quite ready to meet you there, Mr. Jackson, whenever you choose; but my visit here is rather to give you an opportunity of escaping the consequences that will follow your detection as the author of the crime; for I warn you that I will bring the crime home to you, whatever it costs me in time and money. My offer is this: produce the woman and her child, and not only shall no prosecution take place, but I will remain silent concerning a fact which affects the honor of your son."

Andrew Jackson's face had been perfectly unmoved during this conversation until he heard the allusion to his son. Then his face changed visibly.

"I know nothing concerning which you can attack the honor of my son, Mr. Wingfield," he said, with an effort to speak as unconcernedly as before.

"My charge is as follows," Vincent said quietly: "I was imprisoned at Elmira with a number of other officers, among them your son. Thinking that it was time for the unpleasantness that had been existing between us to come to an end, I offered him my hand. This he accepted and we became friends. A short time afterward a mode of escape offered itself to me, and I proved the sincerity of my feelings toward him by offering to him and another officer the means of sharing my escape. This they accepted. Once outside the walls, I furnished them with disguises that had been prepared for them, assuming myself that of a minister. We then separated, going in different directions, I myself being accompanied by my negro servant, to whose fidelity I owed our escape. Two days afterward an anonymous writer communicated to the police the fact that I had escaped in the disguise of a minister, and was accompanied by my black servant. This fact was only known to the negro, myself, and the two officers. My negro, who had released me, was certainly not my betrayer; the other officer could certainly have had no possible motive for betraying me. There remains, therefore, only your son, whose hostility to me was notorious, and who had expressed himself with bitterness against me on many occasions, and among others in the hearing of my friend Mr. Furniss here. Such being the case, it is my intention to charge him before the military authorities with this act of treachery. But, as I have said, I am willing to forego this and to keep silence as to your conduct with reference to my slave Dinah Morris, if you will restore her and her child uninjured to the house from which you caused her to be taken."

The sallow cheeks of the old planter had grown a shade paler as he listened to Vincent's narrative, but he now burst out in angry tones:

"How dare you, sir, bring such an infamous accusation against my son--an accusation, like that against myself, wholly unsupported by a shred of evidence? Doubtless your negro had confided to some of his associates his plans for assisting you to escape from prison, and it is from one of these that the denunciation has come. Go, sir, report where you will what lies and fables you have invented; but be assured that I and my son will seek our compensation for such gross libels in the courts."

"Very well, sir," Vincent said, as he prepared to mount his horse; "if you will take the trouble to look in the papers to-morrow, you will see that your threats of action for libel have no effect whatever upon me."

"The man is as hard as a rock, Wingfield," Furniss said, as they rode off together. "He wilted a little when you were telling your story, but the moment he saw you had no definite proofs he was, as I expected he would be, ready to defy you. What shall you do now?"

"I shall ride back into Richmond again and give a full account of my escape from the jail, and state that I firmly believe that the information as to my disguise was given by Jackson, and that it was the result of a personal hostility which, as many young men in Richmond are well aware, has existed for some time between us."

"Well, you must do as you like, Wingfield, but I think it will be a risky business."

"It may be so," Vincent said; "but I have little doubt that long before Jackson is exchanged I shall have discovered Dinah, and shall prosecute Jackson for theft and kidnaping, in which case the young man will hardly venture to prosecute me or indeed to show his face in this part of the country."

That evening the two young officers started for the front, and the next morning the Richmond papers came out with a sensational heading, "Alleged Gross Act of Treachery and Ingratitude by a Confederate Officer."

It was the 10th of December when Vincent joined the army at Fredericksburg. He reported himself to General Stuart, who received him with great cordiality.

"You are just in time, Wingfield," he said. "I believe that in another twenty-four hours the battle will be fought. They have for the last two days been moving about in front, and apparently want us to believe that they intend to cross somewhere below the town; but all the news we get from our spies is to the effect that these are only feints and that they intend to throw a bridge across here. We know, anyhow, they have got two trains concealed opposite, near the river. Burnside is likely to find it a hard nut to crack. Of course they are superior in number to us, as they always are; but as we have always beat them well on level ground I do not think their chances of getting up these heights are by any means hopeful. Then, too, their change of commanders is against them. McClellan fought a drawn battle against us at Antietam and showed himself a really able general in the operations in front of Richmond. The army have confidence in him, and he is by far the best man they have got so far, but the fools at Washington have now for the second time displaced him because they are jealous of him. Burnside has shown himself a good man in minor commands, but I don't think he is equal to command such a vast army as this; and besides, we know from our friends at Washington that he has protested against this advance across the river, but has been overruled. You will see Fredericksburg will add another to the long list of our victories."

Vincent shared a tent with another officer of the same rank in General Stuart's staff. They sat chatting till late, and it was still dark when they were suddenly aroused by an outbreak of musketry down at the river.

"The general was right," Captain Longmore, Vincent's companion, exclaimed. "They are evidently throwing a bridge across the river, and the fire we hear comes from two regiments of Mississippians who are posted down in the town under Barksdale."

It was but the work of a minute to throw on their clothes and hurry out. The night was dark and a heavy fog hung over the river. A perfect roar of musketry came up from the valley. Drums and bugles were sounding all along the crest. At the same moment they issued out General Stuart came out from his tent, which was close by.

"Is that you, Longmore? Jump on your horse and ride down to the town. Bring back news of what is going on."

A few minutes later an officer rode up. Some wood had been thrown on the fire, and by its light Vincent recognized Stonewall Jackson.

"Have you any news for us?" he asked.

"Not yet, I have sent an officer down to inquire. The enemy have been trying to bridge the river.

"I suppose so," Jackson replied. "I have ordered one of my brigades to come to the head of the bank as soon as they can be formed up, to help Barksdale if need be, but I don't want to take them down into the town. It is commanded by all the hills on the opposite side, and we know they have brought up also all their artillery there."

In a few minutes Captain Longmore returned.

"The enemy have thrown two pontoon bridges across, one above and one below the old railway bridge. The Mississippians have driven them back once, but they are pushing on the work and will soon get it finished; but General Barksdale bids me report that with the force at his command he can repulse any attempt to cross."

The light was now breaking in the east, but the roar of musketry continued under the canopy of fog. General Lee, Longstreet, and others had now arrived upon the spot, and Vincent was surprised that no orders were issued for troops to reinforce those under General Barksdale. Presently the sun rose, and as it gained in power the fog slowly lifted, and it was seen that the two pontoon bridges were complete; but the fire of the Mississippians was so heavy that although the enemy several times attempted to cross they recoiled before it. Suddenly a gun was fired from the opposite height, and at the signal more than a hundred pieces of artillery opened fire upon the town. Many of the inhabitants had left as soon as the musketry fire began, but the slopes behind it soon presented a sad spectacle. Men, women, and children poured out from the town, bewildered with the din and terrified by the storm of shot and shell that crashed into it. Higher and higher the crowd of fugitives made their way until they reached the crest; among them were weeping women and crying children, many of them in the scantiest attire and carrying such articles of dress and valuables as they had caught up when startled by the terrible rain of missiles. In a very few minutes smoke began to rise over the town, followed by tongues of flame, and in half an hour the place was on fire in a score of places.

All day the bombardment went on without cessation and Fredericksburg crumbled into ruins. Still, in spite of this terrible fire the Mississippians clung to the burning town amid crashing walls, falling chimneys, and shells exploding in every direction. As night fell the enemy poured across the bridges, and Barksdale, contesting every foot of ground, fell back through the burning city and took up a position behind a stone wall in its rear.

Throughout the day not a single shot had been fired by the Confederate artillery, which was very inferior in power to that of the enemy. General Lee had no wish finally to hinder the passage of the Federals, the stubborn resistance of Barksdale's force being only intended to give him time to concentrate all his army as soon as he knew for certain the point at which the enemy was going to cross; and he did not wish, therefore, to risk the destruction of any of his batteries by calling down the Federal fire upon them.

During the day the troops were all brought up into position. Longstreet was on the left and Jackson on the right, while the guns, forty-seven in number, were in readiness to take up their post in the morning on the slopes in front of them. On the extreme right General Stuart was posted with his cavalry and horse artillery. The night passed quietly and by daybreak the troops were all drawn up in their positions.

As soon as the sun rose it was seen that during the night the enemy had thrown more bridges across and that the greater portion of the army was already over. They were, indeed, already in movement against the Confederate position, their attack being directed toward the portion of the line held by Jackson's division. General Stuart gave orders to Major Pelham, who commanded his horse artillery, and who immediately brought up the guns and began the battle by opening fire on the flank of the enemy. The guns of the Northern batteries at once replied, and for some hours the artillery duel continued, the Federal guns doing heavy execution. For a time attacks were threatened from various points, but about ten o'clock, when the fog lifted, a mass of some 55,000 troops advanced against Jackson. They were suffered to come within 800 yards before a gun was fired, and then fourteen guns opened upon them with such effect that they fell back in confusion.

At one o'clock another attempt was made, covered by a tremendous fire of artillery. For a time the columns of attack were kept at bay by the fire of the Confederate batteries, but they advanced with great resolution, pushed their way through Jackson's first line, and forced them to fall back. Jackson brought up his second line and drove the enemy back with great slaughter until his advance was checked by the fire of the Northern artillery.

All day the fight went on, the Federals attempting to crush the Confederate artillery by the weight of their fire in order that their infantry columns might again advance. But although outnumbered by more than two to one the Confederate guns were worked with great resolution, and the day passed and darkness begun to fall without their retiring from the positions they had taken up. Just at sunset General Stuart ordered all the batteries on the right to advance. This they did and opened their fire on the Northern infantry with such effect that these fell back to the position near the town that they had occupied in the morning.

On the left an equally terrible battle had raged all day, but here the Northern troops were compelled to cross open ground between the town and the base of the hill, and suffered so terribly from the fire that they never succeeded in reaching the Confederate front. Throughout the day the Confederates held their position with such ease that General Lee considered the affair as nothing more than a demonstration of force to feel his position, and expected an even sterner battle on the following day. Jackson's first and second lines, composed of less than 15,000 men, had repulsed without difficulty the divisions of Franklin and Hooker, 55,000 strong; while Longstreet with about the same force had never been really pressed by the enemy, although on that side they had a force of over 50,000 men.

In the morning the Northern army was seen drawn up in battle array as if to advance for fresh assault, but no movement was made. General Burnside was in favor of a fresh attack, but the generals commanding the various divisions felt that their troops, after the repulse the day before, were not equal to the work, and were unanimously of opinion that a second assault should not be attempted. After remaining for some hours in order of battle they fell back into the town and two days later the whole army recrossed the Rappahannock River. The loss of the Confederates was 1,800 men, who were for the most part killed or wounded by the enemy's artillery, while the Federal loss was no less than 13,771. General Burnside soon afterward resigned his command, and General Hooker, an officer of the same politics as the president and his advisers, was appointed to succeed him.

The cavalry had not been called upon to act during the day, and Vincent's duties were confined to carrying orders to the commanders of the various batteries of artillery posted in that part of the field, as these had all been placed under General Stuart's orders. He had many narrow escapes by shot and fragments of shells, but passed through the day uninjured.

General Lee has been blamed for not taking advantage of his victory and falling upon the Federals on the morning after the battle; but although such an assault might possibly have been successful he was conscious of his immense inferiority in force, and his troops would have been compelled to have advanced to the attack across ground completely swept by the fire of the magnificently served Northern artillery posted upon their commanding heights. He was moreover ignorant of the full extent of the loss he had inflicted upon the enemy, and expected a renewed attack by them. He was therefore, doubtless, unwilling to risk the results of the victory he had gained and of the victory he expected to gain should the enemy renew their attack, by a movement which might not be successful, and which would at any rate have cost him a tremendous loss of men, and men were already becoming scarce in the Confederacy.

As soon as the enemy had gone back across the river and it was certain that there was little chance of another forward movement on their part for a considerable time, Vincent showed to General Stuart the permit he had received to return home until the spring on leave, and at once received the general's permission to retire from the staff for a time.

He had not been accompanied by Dan on his railway journey to the front, having left him behind with instructions to endeavor by every means to find some clew as to the direction in which Dinah had been carried off. He telegraphed on his way home the news of his coming, and found Dan at the station waiting for him.

"Well, Dan, have you obtained any news?" he asked as soon as his horse had been removed from its box, and he had mounted and at a foot-pace left the station, with Dan walking beside him.

"No, sah; I hab done my best, but I cannot find out anyting. The niggers at Jackson's all say dat no strangers hab been there wid de old man for a long time before de day dat Dinah was carried off. I have been over dar, massa, and hab talked wid the hands at de house. Dey all say dat no one been dere for a month. Me sure dat dey no tell a lie about it, because dey all hate Massa Jackson like pison. Den de lawyer, he am put de advertisement you told him in the papers: Five hundred dollars to whoever would give information about de carrying off of a female slave from Missy Wingfield, or dat would lead to de discovery of her hiding-place. But no answer come. Me heard Missy Wingfield say so last night."

"That's bad, Dan; but I hardly expected anything better. I felt sure the old fox would have taken every precaution, knowing what a serious business it would be for him if it were found out. Now I am back I will take the matter up myself, and we will see what we can do. I wish I could have set about it the day after she was carried away. It is more than a fortnight ago now, and that will make it much more difficult than it would have been had it been begun at once."

"Well, Vincent, so you have come back to us undamaged this time," his mother said after the first greeting. "We were very anxious when the news came that a great battle had been fought last Friday; but when we heard the next morning the enemy had been repulsed so easily we were not so anxious, although it was not until this morning that the list of killed and wounded was published, and our minds set at rest."

"No, mother; it was a tremendous artillery battle, but it was a little more than that--at least on our side. But I have never heard anything at all like it from sunrise to sunset. But, after all, an artillery fire is more frightening than dangerous, except at comparatively close quarters. The enemy must have fired at least fifty shots for every man that was hit. I counted several times, and there were fully a hundred shots a minute, and I don't think it lessened much the whole day. I should think they must have fired two or three hundred rounds at least from each gun. The roar was incessant, and what with the din they made, and the replies of our own artillery, and the bursting of shells, and the rattle of musketry, the din at times was almost bewildering. Wildfire was hit with a piece of shell, but fortunately it was not a very large one, and he is not much the worse for it, but the shock knocked him off his legs; of course I went down with him, and thought for a moment I had been hit myself No; it was by far the most hollow affair we have had. The enemy fought obstinately enough, but without the slightest spirit or dash, and only once did they get up anywhere near our line, and then they went back a good deal quicker than they came."

"And now you are going to be with us for three months, Vincent?"

"I hope so, mother; at least if they do not advance again. I shall be here off and on. I mean to find Dinah Morris if it is possible, and if I can obtain the slightest clew I shall follow it up and go wherever it may lead me."

"Well, we will spare you for that, Vincent. As you know, I did not like your mixing yourself up in that business two years ago, but it is altogether different now. The woman was very willing and well conducted, and I had got to be really fond of her. But putting that aside, it is intolerable that such a piece of insolence as the stealing of one of our slaves should go unpunished. Therefore if you do find any clew to the affair we will not grumble at your following it up, even if it does take you away from home for a short time. By the by, we had letters this morning from a certain young lady in Georgia inclosing her photograph, and I rather fancy there is one for you somewhere."

"Where is it, mother?" Vincent asked, jumping from his seat.

"Let me think," Mrs. Wingfield replied. "Did either of you girls put it away, or where can it have been stowed?" The girls both laughed.

"Now, Vincent, what offer do you make for the letter? Well, we won't tease you," Annie went on as Vincent gave an impatient exclamation. "Another time we might do so, but as you have just come safely back to us I don't think it will be fair, especially as this is the very first letter. Here it is"--and she took out of the workbox before her the missive Vincent was so eager to receive.

## CHAPTER XVI. THE SEARCH FOR DINAH.

"By the by, Vincent," Mrs. Wingfield remarked next morning at breakfast, "I have parted with Pearson."

"I am glad to hear it, mother. What! did you discover at last that he was a scamp?"

"Several things that occurred shook my confidence in him, Vincent. The accounts were not at all satisfactory, and it happened quite accidentally that when I was talking one day with Mr. Robertson, who, as you know, is a great speculator in tobacco, I said that I should grow no more tobacco, as it really fetched nothing. He replied that it would be a pity to give it up, for so little was now cultivated that the price was rising, and the Orangery tobacco always fetched top prices. 'I think the price I paid for your crop this year must at any rate have paid for the labor that is to say, paid for the keep of the slaves and something over.' He then mentioned the price he had given, which was certainly a good deal higher than I had imagined. I looked to my accounts next morning, and found that Pearson had only credited me with one-third of the amount he must have received, so I at once dismissed him. Indeed, I had been thinking of doing so some little time before, for money is so scarce and the price of produce so low that I felt I could not afford to pay as much as I have been giving him."

"I am afraid I have been drawing rather heavily, mother," Vincent put in.

"I have plenty of money, Vincent. Since your father's death we have had much less company than before, and I have not spent my income. Besides, I have a considerable sum invested in house property and other securities. But I have, of course, since the war began been subscribing toward the expenses of the war--for the support of hospitals and so on. I thought at a time like this I ought to keep my expenses down at the lowest point, and to give the balance of my income to the State."

"How did Jonas take his dismissal, mother?"

"Not very pleasantly," Mrs. Wingfield replied; "especially when I told him that I had discovered he was robbing me. However, he knew better than to say much, for he has not been in good odor about here for some time. After the fighting near here there were reports that he had been in communication with the Yankees. He spoke to me about it at the time, but as it was a mere matter of rumor, originating, no doubt, from the fact that he was a Northern man by birth, I paid no attention to them."

"It is likely enough to be true," Vincent said. "I always distrusted the vehemence with which he took the Confederate side. How long ago did this happen?"

"It is about a month since I dismissed him."

"So lately as that! Then I should not be at all surprised if he had some hand in carrying off Dinah. I know he was in communication with Jackson, for I once saw them together in the street, and I fancied at the time that it was through him that Jackson learned that Dinah was here. It is an additional clew to inquire into, anyhow. Do you know what has become of him since he left you?"

"No; I have heard nothing at all about him, Vincent, from the day I gave him a check for his pay in this room. Farrell, who was under him, is now in charge of the Orangery. He may possibly know something of his movements."

"I think Farrell is an honest fellow," Vincent said "He was always about doing his work quietly never bullying or shouting at the hands, and yet seeing that they did their work properly. I will ride out and see him at once."

As soon as breakfast was over Vincent started, and found Farrell in the fields with the hands.

"I am glad to see you back, sir," the man said heartily.

"Thank you, Farrell. I am glad to be back, and I am glad to find you in Pearson's place. I never liked the fellow, and never trusted him."

"I did not like him myself, sir, though we always got on well enough together. He knew his work, and got as much out of the hands as any one could do; but I did not like his way with them. They hated him."

"Have you any idea where he went when he left here?"

"No, sir; he did not come back after he got his dismissal. He sent a man in a buggy with a note to me, asking me to send all his things over to Richmond. I expect he was afraid the news might get here as soon as he did, and that the hands would give him an unpleasant reception, as indeed I expect they would have done."

"You don't know whether he has any friends anywhere in the Confederacy to whom he would be likely to go?"

"I don't know about friends, sir; but I know he has told me he was overseer, or partner, or something of that sort, in a small station down in the swamps of South Carolina. I should think, from things he has let drop, that the slaves must have had a bad time of it. I rather fancy he made the place too hot for him, and had to leave; but that was only my impression."

"In that case he may possibly have made his way back there," Vincent said. "I have particular reasons for wishing to find out. You don't know anything about the name of the place?" The man shook his head.

"He never mentioned the name in my hearing."

"Well, I must try to find out, but I don't quite see how to set about it," Vincent said. "By the way, de you know where his clothes were sent to?"

"Yes; the man said that he was to take them to Harker's Hotel. It's a second-rate hotel not far from the railway station."

"Thank you. That will help me. I know the house. It was formerly used by Northern drummers and people of that sort."

After riding back to Richmond and putting up his horse, Vincent went to the hotel there. Although but a secondary hotel it was well filled, for people from all parts of the Confederacy resorted to Richmond, and however much trade suffered, the hotels of the town did a good business. He first went up to the clerk in a little office at the entrance.

"You had a man named Pearson," he said, "staying here about a month ago. Will you be good enough to tell me on what day he left?"

The clerk turned to the register, and said after a minute's examination:

"He came on the 14th of November, and he left on the 20th."

This was two days after the date on which Dinah had been carried off.

In American hotels the halls are large and provided with seats, and are generally used as smoking and reading-rooms by the male visitors to the hotel. At Harker's Hotel there was a small bar at the end of the hall, and a black waiter supplied the wants of the guests seated at the various little tables. Vincent seated himself at one of these and ordered something to drink. As the negro placed it on the table he said:

"I will give you a dollar if you will answer a few questions."

"Very good, sah. Dat am a mighty easy way to earn a dollar."

"Do you remember, about a month ago, a man named Pearson being here?"

The negro shook his head.

"Me not know de names of de gentlemen, sah. What was de man like?"

"He was tall and thin, with short hair and a gray goatee--a regular Yankee."

"Me remember him, sah. Dar used to be plenty ob dat sort here. Don't see dem much now. Me remember de man, sah, quite well. Used to pass most of de day here. Didn't seem to have nuffin to do."

"Was he always alone, or did he have many people here to see him?"

"Once dar war two men here wid him, sah, sitting at dat table ober in de corner. Rough-looking fellows dey war. In old times people like dat wouldn't come to a 'spectable hotel, but now most ebery one got rough clothes, can't get no others, so one don't tink nuffin about it; but dose fellows was rough-looking besides dar clothes. Didn't like dar looks nohow. Dey only came here once. Dey was de only strangers that came to see him. But once Massa Jackson--me know him by sight--he came here and talk wid him for a long time. Earnest sort of talk dat seemed to be. Dey talk in low voice, and I noticed dey stopped talking when any one sat down near dem."

"You don't know where he went to from here, I suppose?"

"No, sah, dat not my compartment. Perhaps de outside porter will know. Like enough he take his tings in hand-truck to station. You like to see him, sah?"

"Yes, I should like to have a minute's talk with him. Here is your dollar."

The waiter rang a bell, and a minute later the outdoor porter presented himself.

"You remember taking some tings to station for a tall man wid gray goatee, Pomp?" the waiter asked. "It was more dan tree weeks ago. I tink he went before it was light in de morning. Me seem to remember dat."

The negro nodded.

"Me remember him bery well, sah. Tree heavy boxes and one bag, and he only give me quarter dollar for taking dem to de station. Mighty mean man dat."

"Do you know what train he went by?"

"Yes, sah, it was de six o'clock train for de souf."

"You can't find out wher his luggage was checked for?"

"I can go down to station, sah, and see if I can find out. Some of de men dar may remember."

"Here is a dollar for yourself," Vincent said, "and another to give to any of the men who can give you the news. When you have found out come and tell me. Here is my card and address."

"Bery well, sah. Next time me go up to station me find about it, for sure, if any one remember dat fellow."

In the evening the negro called at the house and told Vincent that he had ascertained that a man answering to his description and having luggage similar to that of Pearson had had it checked to Florence in South Carolina.

Vincent now called Dan into his counsel and told him what he had discovered. The young negro had already given proof of such intelligence that he felt sure his opinion would be of value.

"Dat all bery plain, sah," Dan said when Vincent finished his story. "Me no doubt dat old rascal Jackson give money to Pearson to carry off de gal. Ob course he did it just to take revenge upon Tony. Pearson he go into de plot, because, in de fust place, it vex Missy Wingfield and you bery much; in de second place, because Jackson gib him money; in de third place, because he get hold of negro slave worf a thousand dollar. Dat all quite clear. He not do it himself, but arrange wid oder fellows, and he stop quiet at de hotel for two days after she gone so dat no one can 'spect his having hand in de affair."

"That is just how I make it out, Dan; and now he has gone off to join them."

Dan thought for some time.

"Perhaps dey join him dar, sah, perhaps not; perhaps him send him baggage on there and get out somewhere on de road and meet them."

"That is likely enough, Dan. No doubt Dinah was taken away in a cart or buggy. As she left two days before he did, they may have gone from forty to sixty miles along the road, to some place where he may have joined them. The men who carried her off may either have come back or gone on with him. If they wanted to go south they would go on; if they did not, he would probably have only hired them to carry her off and hand her over to him when he overtook them. I will look at the timetable and see where that train stops. It is a fast train, I see," he said, after consulting it; it stops at Petersburg, fifteen miles on, and at Hicks Ford, which is about fifty miles. I should think the second place was most likely, as the cart could easily have got there in two days. Now, Dan, you had better start to-morrow morning, and spend two days there if necessary; find out if you can if on the twentieth of last month any one noticed a vehicle of any kind, with two rough men in it, and with, perhaps, a negro woman. She might not have been noticed, for she may have been lying tied up in the bottom of the cart, although it is more likely they frightened her by threats into sitting up quiet with them. They are sure not to have stopped at any decent hotel, but will have gone to some small place, probably just outside the town.

"I will go with you to Mr. Renfrew the first thing in the morning and get him to draw up a paper testifying that you are engaged in lawful business, and are making inquiries with a view to discovering a crime which has been committed, and recommending you to the assistance of the police in any town you may go to. Then if you go with that to the head constable at Hicks Ford he will tell you which are the places at which such fellows as these would have been likely to put up for the night, and perhaps send a policeman with you to make inquiries. If you get any news telegraph to me at once. I will start by the six o'clock train on the following morning. Do you be on the platform to meet me, and we can then either go straight on to Florence, or, should there be any occasion, I will get out there; but I don't think that is likely. Pearson himself will, to a certainty, sooner or later, go to Florence to get his luggage, and the only real advantage we shall get if your inquiries are successful will be to find out for certain whether he is concerned in the affair. We shall then only have to follow his traces from Florence."

Two days later Mr. Renfrew received a telegram from the head constable at Hicks Ford: "The two men with cart spent day here, 20th ult. Were joined that morning by another man--negro says Pearson. One man returned afternoon, Richmond. Pearson and the other drove off in buggy. A young negress and child were with them. Is there anything I can do?"

Mr. Renfrew telegraphed back to request that the men, who were kidnaping the female slave, should if possible be traced and the direction they took ascertained. He then sent the message across to Vincent, who at once went to his office.

"Now," the lawyer said, "you must do nothing rashly in this business, Vincent. They are at the best of time a pretty rough lot at the edge of these Carolina swamps, and at present things are likely to be worse than usual. If you were to go alone on such an errand you would almost certainly be shot. In the first place, these fellows would not give up a valuable slave without a struggle; and in the next place, they have committed a very serious crime. Therefore it is absolutely necessary that you should go armed with legal powers and backed by the force of the law. In the first place, I will draw up an affidavit and sign it myself, to the effect that a female slave, the property of Vincent Wingfield, has, with her male child, been kidnaped and stolen by Jonas Pearson and others acting in association with him, and that we have reason to know that she has been conveyed into South Carolina. This I will get witnessed by a justice of the peace, and will then take it up to Government House. There I will get the usual official request to the governor of South Carolina to issue orders that the aid of the law shall be given to you in recovering the said Dinah Morris and her child and arresting her abductors. You will obtain an order to this effect from the governor, and armed with it you will, as soon as you have discovered where the woman is, call upon the sheriff of the county to aid you in recovering her, and in arresting Pearson and his associates."

"Thank you, sir. That will certainly be the best way. I run plenty of risk in doing my duty as an officer of the state, and I have no desire whatever to throw my life away at the hands of ruffians such as Pearson and his allies."

Two hours later Vincent received from Mr. Renfrew the official letter to the governor of South Carolina, and at six o'clock next morning started for Florence. On the platform of the station at Hicks Ford Dan was waiting for him.

"Jump into the car at the end, Dan; I will come to you there, and you can tell me all the news. We are going straight on to Columbia. Now, Dan," Vincent went on when he joined him--for in no part of the United States were negroes allowed to travel in any but the cars set apart for them--"what is your news? The chief constable telegraphed that they had, as we expected, been joined by Pearson here."

"Yes, sah, dey war here for sure. When I get here I go straight to de constable and tell him dat I was in search of two men who had kidnaped Captain Wingfield's slave. De head constable he Richmond man, and ob course knew all about de family; so he take de matter up at once and send constable wid me to seberal places where it likely dat the fellows had put up, but we couldn't find nuffin about dem. Den next morning we go out again to village four mile out of de town on de norf road, and dere we found sure 'nough dat two men, wid negro wench and chile, had stopped dere. She seem bery unhappy and cry all de time. De men say dey bought her at Richmond, and show de constable of de village de paper dat dey had bought a female slave Sally Moore and her chile. De constable speak to woman, but she seem frightened out of her life and no say anything. Dey drive off wid her early in de morning. Den we make inquiries again at de town and at de station. We find dat a man like Pearson get out. He had only little hand-bag with him. He ask one of de men at de station which was de way to de norf road. Den we find dat one of de constables hab seen a horse and cart wid two men in it, with negro woman and child. One of de men look like Yankee--dat what make him take notice of it. We s'pose dat oder man went back to Richmond again."

"That is all right, Dan, and you have done capitally. Now at Florence we will take up the hunt. It is a long way down there; and if they drive all the way, as I hope they will, it will take them a fortnight, so that we shall have gained a good deal of time on them. The people at the station are sure to remember the three boxes that lay there for so long without being claimed. Of course they may have driven only till they got fairly out of reach. Then they may either have sold the horse and trap, or the fellow Pearson has with him may have driven it back. But I should think they would most likely sell it. In that case they would not be more than a week from the time they left Richmond to the time they took train again for the south. However, whether they have got a fortnight or three weeks' start of us will not make much difference. With the description we can give of Pearson, and the fact that there was a negress and child, and those three boxes, we ought to be able to trace him."

It was twelve at night when the train arrived at Florence. As nothing could be done until next morning Vincent went to an hotel. As soon as the railway officials were likely to be at their offices he was at the station again. The tip of a dollar secured the attention of the man in the baggage-room.

"Three boxes and a black bag came on here a month ago, you say, and lay here certainly four or five days--perhaps a good deal longer. Of course I remember them. Stood up in that corner there. They had been checked right through. I will look at the books and see what day they went. I don't remember what sort of men fetched them away. Maybe I was busy at the time, and my mate gave them out. However, I will look first and see when they went. What day do you say they got here?"

"They came by the train that left Richmond at six o'clock on the morning of the 20th."

"Then they got in late that night or early next morning. Ah, the train was on time that day, and got in at half-past nine at night. Here they are--three boxes and a bag, numbers 15020, went out on the 28th. Yes, that's right enough. Now I will just ask my mate if he remembers about their going out."

The other man was called. Oh, yes, he remembered quite well the three boxes standing in the corner. They went out some time in the afternoon. It was just after the train came in from Richmond. He noticed the man that asked for them. He got him to help carry out the boxes and put them into a cart. Yes, he remembered there was another man with him, and a negress with a child. He wondered at the time what they were up to, but supposed it was all right. Yes, he didn't mind trying to find out who had hired out a cart for the job. Dessay he could find out by to-morrow--at any rate he would try. Five dollars are worth earning anyway.

Having put this matter in train, Vincent, leaving Dan at Florence, went down at once to Charleston. Here, after twenty-four hours' delay, he obtained a warrant for the arrest of Jonas Pearson and others on the charge of kidnaping, and then returned to Florence. He found that the railway man had failed in obtaining any information as to the cart, and concluded it must have come in from the country on purpose to meet the train.

"At any rate," Vincent said, "it must be within a pretty limited range of country. The railway makes a bend from Wilmington to this place and then down to Charleston, so this is really the nearest station to only a small extent of country."

"That's so," the railway man said. He had heard from Dan a good deal about the case, and had got thoroughly interested in it. "Either Marion or Kingstree would be nearer, one way or the other, to most of the swamp country. So it can't be as far as Conwayborough on the north or Georgetown on the south, and it must lie somewhere between Jeffries' Creek and Lynch's Creek; anyhow it would be in Marion County--that's pretty nigh sure. So if I were you I would take rail back to Marion Court house, and see the sheriff there and have a talk over the matter with him. You haven't got much to go upon, because this man you are after has been away from here a good many years and won't be known; besides, likely enough he went by some other name down here. Anyhow, the sheriff can put you up to the roads, and the best way of going about the job."

"I think that would be the best way," Vincent said. "We shall be able to see the county map too and to learn all the geography of the place."

"You have got your six-shooters with you, I suppose, because you are as likely as not to have to use them?"

"Yes, we have each got a Colt; and as I have had a good deal of practice, it would be awkward for Pearson if he gives me occasion to use it."

"After what I hear of the matter," the man said, "I should say your best plan is just to shoot him at sight. It's what would serve him right. You bet there will be no fuss over it. It will save you a lot of trouble anyway."

Vincent laughed.

"My advice is good," the man went on earnestly. "They are a rough lot down there, and hang together. You will have to do it sudden, whatever you do, or you will get the hull neighborhood up agin you."

On reaching Marion Courthouse they sought out the sheriff, produced the warrant signed by the States' authority, and explained the whole circumstances.

"I am ready to aid you in any way I can," the sheriff said when he concluded; "but the question is, where has the fellow got to? You see he may be anywhere in this tract;" and he pointed out a circle on the map of the county that hung against the wall. "That is about fifty mile across, and a pretty nasty spot, I can tell you. There are wide swamps on both sides of the creek, and rice grounds and all sorts. There ain't above three or four villages altogether, but there may be two or three hundred little plantations scattered about, some big and some little. We haven't got anything to guide us in the slightest, not a thing, as I can see."

"The man who was working under Pearson, when he was with us, told me he had got the notion that he had had to leave on account of some trouble here. Possibly that might afford a clew."

"It might do so," the sheriff said. "When did he come to you?"

"I think it was when I was six or seven years old. That would be about twelve or thirteen years ago; but, of course, he may not have come direct to us after leaving here."

"We can look anyway," the sheriff said, and, opening a chest, he took out a number of volumes containing the records of his predecessors. "Twelve years ago! Well, this is the volume. Now, Captain Wingfield, I have got some other business in hand that will take me a couple of hours. I will leave you out this volume and the one before it and the one after it, and if you like to go through them you may come across the description of some man wanted that agrees with that of the man you are in search of."

It took Vincent two hours and a half to go through the volume, but he met with no description answering to that of Pearson.

"I will go through the first six months of the next year," he said to himself, taking up that volume, "and the last six months of the year before."

The second volume yielded no better result, and he then turned back to the first of the three books. Beginning in July, he read steadily on until he came to December. Scarcely had he begun the record of that month than he uttered an exclamation of satisfaction.

"December 2nd.--Information laid against gang at Porter's Station, near Lynch's Creek. Charged with several robberies and murders in different parts of the county. Long been suspected of having stills in the swamps. Gang consists of four besides Porter himself. Names of gang, Jack Haverley, Jim Corben, and John and James Porter. Ordered out posse to start to-morrow.

"December 5th.--Returned from Porter's Station. Surprised the gang. They resisted. Haverley, Corben, and James Porter shot. John Porter escaped, and took to swamp. Four of posse wounded; one, William Hannay, killed. Circulated description of John Porter through the county. Tall and lean; when fifteen years old shot a man in a brawl, and went north. Has been absent thirteen years. Assumed the appearance of a northern man and speaks with Yankee twang. Father was absent at the time of attack. Captured three hours after. Declares he knows nothing about doings of the gang. Haverley and Corben were friends of his sons. Came and went when they liked. Will be tried on the 15th."

On the 16th there was another entry:

"William Porter sentenced to three years' imprisonment for giving shelter to gang of robbers. Evidence wanting to show he took any actual part in their crimes."

The sheriff had been in and out several times during the five hours that Vincent's search had taken up. When he returned again Vincent pointed out the entry he had found.

"I should not be at all surprised if that's our man," the sheriff said. "I know old Porter well, for he is still alive and bears a pretty bad reputation still, though we have never been able to bring him to book. I remember all the circumstances of that affair, for I served upon the posse. While Porter was in prison his house was kept for him by a married daughter and her husband. There was a strong suspicion that the man was one of the gang too, but we couldn't prove it. They have lived there ever since. They have got five or six field hands, and are said to be well off. We have no doubt they have got a still somewhere in the swamps, but we have never been able to find it. I will send a man off to-morrow to make inquiries whether any stranger has arrived there lately. Of course, Pearson will not have kept that name, and he will not have appeared as John Porter, for he would be arrested on a fresh warrant at once for his share in that former business. I think, Captain Wingfield, you had better register at the hotel here under some other name. I don't suppose that he has any fear of being tracked here; still it is just possible his father may have got somebody here and at Florence to keep their eyes open and let him know if there are any inquiries being made by strangers about a missing negress. One cannot be too careful. If he got the least hint, his son and the woman would be hidden away in the swamps before we could get there, and there would be no saying when we could find him."

Vincent took the sheriff's advice, and entered his name in the hotel book as Mr. Vincent. Late in the evening the sheriff came round to him.

"I have just sent summonses to six men. I would rather have had two or three more, but young men are very scarce around here now; and as with you and myself that brings it up to eight that ought to be sufficient, as these fellows will have no time to summon any of their friends to their assistance. Have you a rifle, Captain Wingfield?"

"No; I have a brace of revolvers."

"They are useful enough for close work," the sheriff said, "but if they see us coming, and barricade their house and open fire upon us, you will want something that carries further than a revolver. I can lend you a rifle as well as a horse if you will accept them."

Vincent accepted the offer with thanks. The next morning at daylight he went round to the sheriff's house, where six determined-looking men, belonging to the town or neighboring farms, were assembled. Slinging the rifle that the sheriff handed him across his back, Vincent at once mounted, and the party set off at a brisk trot.

"My man came back half an hour ago," the sheriff said to Vincent as they rode along. "He found out that a man answering to your description arrived with another at Porter's about a fortnight ago, and is staying there still. Whether they brought a negress with them or not no one seems to have noticed. However, there is not a shadow of doubt that it is our man, and I shall be heartily glad to lay hold of him; for a brother of mine was badly wounded in that last affair, and though he lived some years afterward he was never the same man again. So I have a personal interest in it, you see."

"How far is it to Porter's?"

"About thirty-five miles. We shall get there about two o'clock, I reckon. We are all pretty well mounted and can keep at this pace, with a break or two, till we get there. I propose that we dismount when we get within half a mile of the place. We will try and get hold of some one who knows the country well, and get him to lead three of us round through the edge of the swamp to the back of the house. It stands within fifty yards of the swamp. I have no doubt they put it there so that they might escape if pressed, and also to prevent their being observed going backward and forward to that still of theirs."

This plan was followed out. A negro lad was found who, on the promise of a couple of dollars, agreed to act as guide. Three of the party were then told off to follow him, and the rest, after waiting for half an hour to allow them to make the detour, mounted their horses and rode down at a gallop to the house. When they were within a short distance of it they heard a shout, and a man who was lounging near the door ran inside. Almost instantly they saw the shutters swing back across the windows, and when they drew up fifty yards from the door the barrels of four rifles were pushed out through slits in the shutters.

The sheriff held up his hand. "William Porter, I want a word with you."

A shutter in an upper room opened, and an elderly man appeared with a rifle in his hand.

"William Porter," the sheriff said, "I have a warrant for the arrest of two men now in your house on the charge of kidnaping a female slave, the property of Captain Wingfield here. I have no proof that you had any share in the matter, or that you are aware that the slave was not honestly obtained. In the second place, I have a warrant for the arrest of your son John Porter, now in your house and passing recently under the name of Jonas Pearson, on the charge of resisting and killing the officers of the law on the 5th of December, 1851. I counsel you to hand over these men to me without resistance. You know what happened when your sons defied the law before, and what will happen now if you refuse compliance."

"Yah!" the old man shouted. "Do you suppose we are going to give in to five men? Not if we know it. Now, I warn you, move yourself off while I let you, else you will get a bullet in you before I count three."

"Very well, then. You must take the consequences," the sheriff replied, and at once called the party to fall back.

"We must dismount," he said in answer to Vincent's look of surprise; "they would riddle us here on horseback in the open. Besides we must dismount to break in the door."

They rode back a quarter of a mile, and then dismounted. The sheriff took two heavy axes that hung from his saddle, and handed them to two of the men.

"I reckoned we should have trouble," he said. "However, I hope we sha'n't have to use these. My idea is to crawl up through the corn-field until we are within shooting distance, and then to open fire at the loopholes. They have never taken the trouble to grub up the stumps, and each man must look out for shelter. I want to make it so hot for them that they will try to bolt to the swamp, and in that case they will be covered by the men there. I told them not to fire until they got quite close; so they ought to dispose of three of them, and as they have got pistols they will be able to master the others; besides, directly we hear firing behind, we shall jump up and make a rush round. Do you, sir, and James Wilkins here, stop in front. Two of them might make a rush out behind, and the others, when they have drawn us off, bolt in front."

Several shots were fired at the party as they made their way across to the end of the field, where the tall stalks of maize were still standing, though the corn had been gathered weeks before. As soon as they reached the shelter they separated, each crawling through the maize until they arrived within fifty yards of the house. There were, as the sheriff had said, many stumps still standing, and each ensconced himself behind one of those, and began to reply to the fire that the defenders had kept up whenever they saw a movement among the corn stalks.

At such a distance the shutters were but of slight advantage to the defenders of the house; for the assailants were all good shots, and the loopholes afforded excellent targets at such a distance. After a few shots had been fired from the house the fire of the defenders ceased, the men within not daring to protrude the rifles through the loopholes, as every such appearance was instantly followed by a couple of shots from the corn patch.

"Give me one of those axes," the sheriff said. "Now, Withers, do you make a rush with me to the door. Get your rifle loaded before you start, and have your revolver handy in your belt. Now, Captain Wingfield, do you and the other two keep a sharp lookout at the loopholes, and see that they don't get a shot at us as we run. Now, Withers," and the sheriff ran forward. Two rifles were protruded through the loopholes. Vincent and his companions fired at once. One of the rifles gave a sharp jerk and disappeared, the other was fired, and Withers dropped his axe, but still ran forward. The sheriff began an onslaught at the door, his companion's right arm being useless. A minute later the sharp crack of rifles was heard in the rear, and the sheriff and two men rushed in that direction, while Vincent and the other lay watching the door. Scarcely had the sheriff's party disappeared round the house than the door was thrown open, and Pearson ran out at full speed. Vincent leaped to his feet.

"Surrender," he said, "or you are a dead man."

Jonas paused for a moment with a loud imprecation, and then leveling a revolver, fired. Vincent felt a moment's pain in the cheek, but before he could level his rifle his companion fired, and Pearson fell forward dead. A minute later the sheriff and his party ran round.

"Have you got him?" he asked.

"He will give no more trouble, sheriff," the young man who fired said. "I fancy I had him plum between the eyes. How about the others?"

"Dick Matheson is killed; he got two bullets in his body. The other man is badly wounded. There are no signs of old Porter."

They now advanced to the door, which stood open. As the sheriff entered there was a sharp report, and he fell back shot through the heart. The rest made a rush forward. Another shot was fired, but this missed them, and before it could be repeated they had wrested the pistol from the hand of Matheson's wife. She was firmly secured, and they then entered the kitchen, where, crouched upon the floor, lay some seven or eight negro men and women in an agony of terror. Vincent's question, "Dinah, where are you?" was answered by a scream of delight; and Dinah, who had been covering her child with her body, leaped to her feet.

"It's all right, Dinah," Vincent said; "but stay here, we haven't finished this business yet."

"I fancy the old man's upstairs," one of the men said. "It was his rifle, I reckon, that disappeared when we fired."

It was as he expected. Porter was found dead behind the loophole, a bullet having passed through his brain. The deputy-sheriff, who was with the party, now took the command. A cart and horse were found in an out-building; in these the wounded man, who was one of those who had taken part in the abduction of Dinah, was placed, together with the female prisoner and the dead body of the sheriff. The negroes were told to follow; and the horses having been fetched the party mounted and rode off to the next village, five miles on their way back. Here they halted for the night, and the next day went on to Marion Courthouse, Vincent hiring a cart for the conveyance of Dinah and the other women. It was settled that Vincent's attendance at the trial of the two prisoners would not be necessary, as the man would be tried for armed resistance to the law, and the woman for murdering the sheriff. The facts could be proved by other witnesses, and as there could be no doubt about obtaining convictions, it would be unnecessary to try the charge against the man for kidnaping. Next day, accordingly, Vincent started with Dinah and Dan for Richmond. Two months afterward he saw in the paper that Jane Matheson had been sentenced to imprisonment for life, the man to fourteen years.

## CHAPTER XVII. CHANCELLORSVILLE.

THE news of the fight between the sheriff's posse and the band at Lynch's Creek was telegraphed to the Richmond papers by their local agent upon the day after it occurred. The report said that Captain Wingfield, a young officer who had frequently distinguished himself, had followed the traces of a gang, one of whom was a notorious criminal who had evaded the pursuit of the law and escaped from that section fifteen years ago, and had, under an assumed name, been acting as overseer at Mrs. Wingfield's estate of the Orangery. These men had carried off a negress belonging to Mrs. Wingfield, and had taken her down South. Captain Wingfield, having obtained the assistance of the sheriff with a posse of determined men, rode to the place which served as headquarters for the gang. Upon being summoned to surrender the men opened a fire upon the sheriff and his posse. A sharp fight ensued, in which the sheriff was killed and one of his men wounded; while the four members of the gang were either killed or taken prisoners. It was reported that a person occupying a position as a planter in the neighborhood of Richmond is connected with this gang.

The reporter had obtained his news from Vincent, who had purposely refrained from mentioning the names of those who had fallen. He had already had a conversation with the wounded prisoner. The latter had declared that he had simply acted in the affair as he had been paid to do by the man he knew in Richmond as Pearson, who told him that he wanted him to aid in carrying off a slave woman, who was really his property, but had been fraudulently taken from him. He had heard him say that there was another interested in the affair, who had his own reasons for getting the woman out of the way, and had paid handsomely for the job. Who that other was Pearson had never mentioned.

Vincent saw that he had no absolute evidence against Jackson, and therefore purposely suppressed the fact that Pearson was among the killed in hopes that the paragraph would so alarm Jackson that he would at once decamp. His anticipations were entirely justified; for upon the day of his return to Richmond he saw a notice in the paper that the Cedars, with its field hands, houses, and all belonging to it, was for sale. He proceeded at once to the estate agent, and learned from him that Jackson had come in two days before and had informed him that sudden and important business had called him away, and that he was starting at once for New York, where his presence was urgently required, and that he should attempt to get through the lines immediately. He had asked him what he thought the property and slaves would fetch. Being acquainted with the estate, he had given him a rough estimate, and had, upon Jackson's giving him full power to sell, advanced him two-thirds of the sum. Jackson had apparently started at once; indeed, he had told him that he should take the next train as far North as he could get.

Vincent received the news with great satisfaction. He had little doubt that Jackson had really made down to the South, and that he would try to cross the lines there, his statement that he intended to go direct North being merely intended to throw his pursuers off his track should a warrant be issued against him. However, it mattered little which way Jackson had gone, so that he had left the State.

There was little chance of his ever returning; for even when he learned that his confederate in the business had been killed in the fight, he could not be certain that the prisoner who had been taken was not aware of the share he had in the business.

A fortnight later Vincent went down into Georgia and brought back Lucy Kingston for a visit to his mother. She had already received a letter from her father in reply to one she had written after reaching her aunt's protection, saying how delighted he was to hear that she had crossed the lines, for that he had suffered the greatest anxiety concerning her, and had continually reproached himself for not sending her away sooner. He said that he was much pleased with her engagement to Captain Wingfield, whom he did not know personally, but of whom he heard the most favorable reports from various Virginian gentlemen to whom he had spoken since the receipt of her letter.

Lucy remained at Richmond until the beginning of March, when Vincent took her home to Georgia again, and a week after his return rejoined the army on the Rappahannock. Every effort had been made by the Confederate authorities to raise the army of General Lee to a point that would enable him to cope with the tremendous force the enemy were collecting for the ensuing campaign. The drain of men was now telling terribly, and Lee had at the utmost 40,000 to oppose the 160,000 collected under General Hooker.

The first fight of the campaign had already taken place when Vincent rejoined the army. A body of 3,000 Federal cavalry had crossed the river on the 17th of March at Kelley's Ford, but had been met by General Fitz Lee with about 800 cavalry, and after a long and stubborn conflict had been driven back with heavy loss across the river. It was not until the middle of April that the enemy began to move in earnest. Every ford was watched by Stuart's cavalry, and the frequent attempts made by the Federal horse to push across to obtain information were always defeated.

On the 27th of April General Hooker's preparations were complete. His plan of action was that 20,000 men should cross the river near the old battlefield of Fredericksburg, and thus lead the Confederates to believe that this was the point of attack. The main body were, however, to cross at Kelley's Ford, many miles higher up the river, and to march down toward Fredericksburg. The other force was then to recross, march up the river, cross at Kelley's Ford, and follow and join the main army. At the same time the Federal cavalry, which was very numerous and well-organized, was, under General Stoneman, to strike down through the country toward Richmond, and thus cut the Confederate communication with their capital, and so prevent Longstreet's division, which was lying near Richmond, from rejoining Lee.

The passage of the river was effected at the two fords without resistance on the 29th of April, and upon the same day the cavalry column marched south. General Lee directed a portion of his cavalry under General Fitz Lee to harass and delay this column as much as possible. Although he had with him but a few hundred men, he succeeded in doing good service in cutting off detached bodies of the enemy, capturing many officers and men, and so demoralizing the invaders that, after pushing on as far as the James River, Stoneman had to retreat in great haste across the Rapidan River.

Hooker having crossed the river, marched on to Chancellorsville, where he set to to entrench himself, having sent word to General Sedgwick, who commanded the force that had crossed near Fredericksburg, to recross, push round, and join as soon as possible. Chancellorsville was a large brick mansion standing in the midst of fields surrounded by extensive forests. The country was known as the Wilderness. Within a range of many miles there were only a few scattered houses, and dense thickets and pine-woods covered the whole country. Two narrow roads passed through the woods, crossing each other at Chancellorsville; two other roads led to the fords known as Ely's Ford and the United States Ford. As soon as he reached Chancellorsville Hooker set his troops to work cutting down trees and throwing up earthworks for infantry and redoubts for artillery, erecting a double line of defenses. On these he mounted upward of a hundred pieces of artillery, commanding the narrow roads by which an enemy must approach, for the thickets were in many places so dense as to render it impossible for troops to force their way through them.

When Sedgwick crossed the river, Lee drew up his army to oppose him; but finding that no more troops crossed, and that Sedgwick did not advance, he soon came to the conclusion that this was not the point at which the enemy intended to attack, and in twenty-four hours one of Stuart's horsemen brought the news that Hooker had crossed the Rappahannock at Kelley's Ford and the Rapidan at Ely's Ford. Lee at once left one division to face General Sedgwick, and ordered the three others to join General Anderson, who with 8,000 men had fallen back before Hooker's advance, and taken his post at Tabernacle Church, about halfway between Fredericksburg and Tabernacle. Lee himself rode forward at once and joined Anderson.

Jackson led the force from Fredericksburg, and pressed the enemy back toward Chancellorsville until he approached the tremendous lines of fortifications, and then fell back to communicate with Lee. That night a council of war was held, and it was agreed that an attack upon the front of the enemy's position was absolutely impossible. Hooker himself was so positive that his position was impregnable that he issued a general order of congratulation to his troops, saying that "the enemy must now ingloriously fly or give us battle on our own ground, where certain destruction awaits him."

Jackson then suggested that he should work right round the Wilderness in front of the enemy's position, march down until well on its flank, and attack it there, where they would be unprepared for an assault. The movement was one of extraordinary peril. Lee would be left with but one division in face of an immensely superior force; Jackson would have to perform an arduous march exposed to an attack by the whole force of the enemy; and both might be destroyed separately without being able to render the slightest assistance to each other. At daybreak on the 2d of May Jackson mustered his troops for the advance. He had in the course of the night caught a severe cold. In the hasty march he had left his blankets behind him. One of his staff threw a heavy cape over him as he lay on the wet ground. During the night Jackson woke, and thinking that the young officer might himself be suffering from the want of his cape, rose quietly, spread the cape over him, and lay down without it. The consequence was a severe cold, which terminated in an attack of pneumonia that, occurring at a time when he was enfeebled by his wounds, resulted in his death. If he had not thrown that cape over the officer it is probable that he would have survived his wounds.

At daybreak the column commenced its march. It had to traverse a narrow and unfrequented road through dense thickets, occasionally crossing ground in sight of the enemy, and at the end to attack a tremendous position held by immensely superior forces. Stuart with his cavalry moved on the flank of the column whenever the ground was open, so as to conceal the march of the infantry from the enemy. As the rear of the column passed a spot called the Furnace, the enemy suddenly advanced and cut off the 23d Georgia, who were in the rear of the column, and captured the whole regiment with the exception of a score of men. At this point the road turned almost directly away from Chancellorsville, and the enemy believed that the column was in full retreat, and had not the least idea of its real object.

So hour after hour the troops pressed on until they reached the turnpike road passing east and west through Chancellorsville, which now lay exactly between them and the point that they had left in the morning. Jackson's design was to advance upon this line of road, to extend his troops to the left and then to swing round, cut the enemy's retreat to the fords, and capture them all. Hooker had already been joined by two of Sedgwick's army corps, and had now six army corps at Chancellorsville, while Jackson's force consisted of 22,000 men. Lee remained with 13,000 at Tabernacle. The latter general had not been attacked, but had continued to make demonstrations against the Federal left, occupying their attention and preventing them from discovering how large a portion of his force had left him.

It was at five o'clock in the evening that Jackson's troops, having gained their position, advanced to the attack. In front of them lay Howard's division of the Federals, intrenched in strong earthworks covered by felled trees; but the enemy were altogether unsuspicious of danger, and it was not until with tumultuous cheers the Confederates dashed through the trees and attacked the entrenchment that they had any suspicion of their presence. They ran to their arms, but it was too late. The Confederates rushed through the obstacles, climbed the earthworks, and carried those in front of them, capturing 700 prisoners and five guns. The rest of the Federal troops here, throwing away muskets and guns, fled in wild confusion. Steadily the Confederates pressed on, driving the enemy before them, and capturing position after position, until the whole right wing of the Federal army was routed and disorganized. For three hours the Confederates continued their march without a check; but owing to the denseness of the wood, and the necessity of keeping the troops in line, the advance was slow, and night fell before the movement could be completed. One more hour of daylight and the whole Federal army would have been cut off and captured, but by eight o'clock the darkness in the forest was so complete that all movement had to be stopped.

Half an hour later one of the saddest incidents of the war took place. General Jackson with a few of his staff went forward to reconnoiter. As he returned toward his lines, his troops in the dark mistook them for a reconnoitering party of the enemy and fired, killing or wounding the whole of them, General Jackson receiving three balls. The enemy, who were but a hundred yards distant, at once opened a tremendous fire with grape toward the spot, and it was some time before Jackson could be carried off the field. The news that their beloved general was wounded was for some time kept from the troops; but a whisper gradually spread, and the grief of his soldiers was unbounded, for rather would they have suffered a disastrous defeat than that Stonewall Jackson should have fallen.

General Stuart assumed the command, General Hill, who was second in command, having, with many other officers, been wounded by the tremendous storm of grape and canister that the Federals poured through the wood when they anticipated an attack. At daybreak the troops again moved forward in three lines, Stuart placing his thirty guns on a slight ridge, where they could sweep the lines of the Federal defenses. Three times the position was won and lost; but the Confederates fought with such fury and resolution, shouting each time they charged the Federal ranks "Remember Jackson," that the enemy gradually gave way, and by ten o'clock Chancellorsville itself was taken, the Federals being driven back into the forest between the houses and the river.

Lee had early in the morning begun to advance from his side to the attack, but just as he was moving forward the news came that Sedgwick had recrossed at Fredericksburg, captured a portion of the Confederate force there, and was advancing to join Hooker. He at once sent two of his three little divisions to join the Confederates who were opposing Sedgwick's advance, while with the three or four thousand men remaining to him, he all day made feigned attacks upon the enemy's position, occupying their attention there, and preventing them from sending reinforcements to the troops engaged with Stuart. At night he himself hurried away, took the command of the troops opposed to Sedgwick, attacked him vigorously at daybreak, and drove him with heavy loss back across the river. The next day he marched back with his force to join in the final attack upon the Federals; but when the troops of Stuart and Lee moved forward they encountered no opposition. Hooker had begun to carry his troops across the river on the night he was hurled back out of Chancellorsville, and the rest of his troops had crossed on the two following nights.

General Hooker issued a pompous order to his troop after getting across the river, to the effect that the movement had met with the complete success he had anticipated from it; but the truth soon leaked out. General Sedgwick's force had lost 6,000 men, Hooker's own command fully 20,000 more; but splendid as the success was, it was dearly purchased by the Confederates at the price of the life of Stonewall Jackson. His arm was amputated the day after the battle; he lived for a week, and died not so much from the effect of his wounds as from the pneumonia, the result of his exposure to the heavy dew on the night preceding his march through the Wilderness.

During the two days' fighting Vincent Wingfield had discharged his duties upon General Stuart's staff. On the first day the work had been slight, for General Stuart, with the cannon, remained in the rear, while Jackson's infantry attacked and carried the Federal retrenchments. Upon the second day, however, when Stuart assumed the command, Vincent's duties had been onerous and dangerous in the extreme. He was constantly carrying orders from one part of the field to the other, amid such a shower of shot and shell that it seemed marvelous that any one could exist within it. To his great grief Wildfire was killed under him, but he himself escaped without a scratch. When he came afterward to try to describe the battle to those at home he could give no account of it.

"To me," he said, "it was simply a chaos of noise and confusion. Of what was going on I knew nothing. The din was appalling. The roar of the shells, the hum of grape and canister, the whistle of bullets, the shouts of the men, formed a mighty roar that seemed to render thinking impossible. Showers of leaves fell incessantly, great boughs of trees were shorn away, and trees themselves sometimes came crashing down as a trunk was struck full by a shell. The undergrowth had caught fire, and the thick smoke, mingled with that of the battle, rendered it difficult to see or to breathe. I had but one thought, that of making my way through the trees, of finding the corps to which I was sent, of delivering my message, and finding the general again. No, I don't think I had much thought of danger, the whole thing was somehow so tremendous that one had no thought whatever for one's self. It was a sort of terrible dream, in which one was possessed of the single idea to get to a certain place. It was not till at last we swept across the open ground down to the house, that I seemed to take any distinct notice of what was going on around me. Then, for the first time, the exulting shouts of the men, and the long lines advancing at the double, woke me up to the fact that we had gained one of the most wonderful victories in history, and had driven an army of four or five times our own strength from a position that they believed they had made impregnable."

The defeat of Hooker for a time put a stop to any further advance against Richmond from the North. The Federal troops, whose term of service was up, returned home, and it was months before all the efforts of the authorities of Washington could place the army in a condition to make a renewed advance. But the Confederates had also suffered heavily. A third of the force with which Jackson had attacked had fallen, and their loss could not be replaced, as the Confederates were forced to send every one they could raise to the assistance of the armies in the West, where Generals Banks and Grant were carrying on operations with great success against them. The important town of Vicksburg, which commanded the navigation of the Mississippi, was besieged, and after a resistance lasting for some months, surrendered, with its garrison of 25,000 men, on the 3d of July, and the Federal gunboats were thus able to penetrate by the Mississippi and its confluents into the heart of the Confederacy.

Shortly after the battle of Chancellorsville, Vincent was appointed to the command of a squadron of cavalry that was detached from Stuart's force and sent down to Richmond to guard the capital from any raids by bodies of Federal cavalry. It had been two or three times menaced by flying bodies of horsemen, and during the cavalry advance before the battle of Chancellorsville small parties had penetrated to within three miles of the city, cutting all the telegraph wires, pulling up rails, and causing the greatest terror. Vincent was not sorry for the change. It took him away from the great theater of the war, but after Chancellorsville he felt no eager desire to take part in future battles. His duties would keep him near his home, and would give ample scope for the display of watchfulness, dash, and energy. Consequently he took no part in the campaign that commenced in the first week in June.

Tired of standing always on the defensive, the Confederate authorities determined to carry out the stop that had been so warmly advocated by Jackson earlier in the war, and which might at that time have brought it to a successful termination. They decided to carry the war into the enemy's country. By the most strenuous efforts Lee's army was raised to 75,000 men, divided into three great army corps, commanded by Longstreet, Ewell, and Hill. Striking first into Western Virginia, they drove the Federals from Winchester, and chased them from the State with the loss of nearly 4,000 prisoners and 30 guns. Then they entered Maryland and Pennsylvania, and concentrating at Gettysburg they met the Northern army under Meade, who had succeeded Hooker. Although great numbers of the Confederates had seen their homes wasted and their property wantonly destroyed, they preserved the most perfect order in their march through the North, and the Federals themselves testify to the admirable behavior of the troops, and to the manner in which they abstained from plundering or inflicting annoyance upon the inhabitants.

At Gettysburg there was three days' fighting. In the first a portion only of the forces were engaged, the Federals being defeated and 5,000 of their men taken prisoners. Upon the second the Confederates attacked the Northerners, who were posted in an extremely strong position, but were repulsed with heavy loss. The following day they renewed the attack, but after tremendous fighting again failed to carry the height. Both parties were utterly exhausted. Lee drew up his troops the next day, and invited an attack from the Federals; but contented with the success they had gained they maintained their position, and the Confederates then fell back, Stuart's cavalry protecting the immense trains of wagons loaded with the stores and ammunition captured in Pennsylvania.

But little attempt was made by the Northerners to interfere with their retreat. On reaching the Potomac they found that a sudden rise had rendered the fords impassable. Intrenchments and batteries were thrown up, and for a week the Confederate army held the lines, expecting an attack from the enemy, who had approached within two miles; but the Federal generals were too well satisfied with having gained a success when acting on the defensive in a strong position to risk a defeat in attacking the position of the Confederates, and their forces remained impassive until pontoon bridges were thrown across the river, and the Confederate army, with their vast baggage train, had again crossed into Virginia. The campaign had cost the Northern army 23,000 men in killed, wounded, and prisoners, besides a considerable number of guns. The Confederates lost only two guns, left behind in the mud, and 1,500 prisoners, but their loss in killed and wounded at Gettysburg exceeded 10,000 men. Even the most sanguine among the ranks of the Confederacy were now conscious that the position was a desperate one. The Federal armies seemed to spring from the ground. Strict discipline had taken the place of the disorder and insubordination that had first prevailed in their ranks. The armies were splendidly equipped. They were able to obtain any amount of the finest guns, rifles, and ammunition of war from the workshops of Europe; while the Confederates, cut off from the world, had to rely solely upon the makeshift factories they had set up, and upon the guns and stores they captured from the enemy.

The Northerners had now, as a blow to the power of the South, abolished slavery, and were raising regiments of negroes from among the free blacks of the North, and from the slaves they took from their owners wherever their armies penetrated the Southern States. Most of the Confederate ports had been either captured or were so strictly blockaded that it was next to impossible for the blockade-runner to get in or out, while the capture of the forts on the Mississippi enabled them to use the Federal flotillas of gunboats to the greatest advantage, and to carry their armies into the center of the Confederacy.

Still, there was no talk whatever of surrender on the part of the South, and, indeed, the decree abolishing slavery, and still more the action of the North in raising black regiments, excited the bitterest feeling of animosity and hatred. The determination to fight to the last, whatever came of it, animated every white man in the Southern States, and, although deeply disappointed with the failure of Lee's invasion of the North, the only result was to incite them to greater exertions and sacrifices. In the North an act authorizing conscription was passed in 1863, but the attempt to carry it into force caused a serious riot in New York, which was only suppressed after many lives had been lost and the city placed under martial law.

While the guns of Gettysburg were still thundering, a Federal army of 18,000 men under General Gillmore, assisted by the fleet, had laid siege to Charleston. It was obstinately attacked and defended. The siege continued until the 5th of September, when Fort Wagner was captured; but all attempts to take Fort Sumter and the town of Charleston itself failed, although the city suffered greatly from the bombardment. In Tennessee there was severe fighting in the autumn, and two desperate battles were fought at Chickamauga on the 19th and 20th of September, General Bragg, who commanded the Confederate army there, being reinforced by Longstreet's veterans from the army of Virginia. After desperate fighting the Federals were defeated, and thirty-six guns and vast quantities of arms captured by the Confederates. The fruits of the victory, however, were very slight, as General Bragg refused to allow Longstreet to pursue, and so to convert the Federal retreat into a rout, and the consequence was that this victory was more than balanced by a heavy defeat inflicted upon them in November at Chattanooga by Sherman and Grant. At this battle General Longstreet's division was not present.

The army of Virginia had a long rest after their return from Gettysburg, and it was not until November that the campaign was renewed. Meade advanced, a few minor skirmishes took place, and then, when he reached the Wilderness, the scene of Hooker's defeat, where Lee was prepared to give battle, he fell back again across the Rappahannock.

The year had been an unfortunate one for the Confederates. They had lost Vicksburg, and the defeat at Chattanooga had led to the whole State of Tennessee falling into the hands of the Federals, while against these losses there was no counterbalancing success to be reckoned.

In the spring of 1864 both parties prepared to the utmost for the struggle. General Grant, an officer who had shown in the campaign in the West that he possessed considerable military ability, united with immense firmness and determination of purpose, was chosen as the new commander-in-chief of the whole military force of the North. It was a mighty army, vast in numbers, lavishly provided with all materials of war. The official documents show that on the 1st of May the total military forces of the North amounted to 662,000 men. Of these the force available for the advance against Richmond numbered 284,630 men. This included the army of the Potomac, that of the James River, and the army in the Shenandoah Valley--the whole of whom were in readiness to move forward against Richmond at the orders of Grant.

To oppose these General Lee had less than 53,000 men, including the garrison of Richmond and the troops in North Carolina. Those stationed in the seaport towns numbered in all another 20,000, so that if every available soldier had been brought up Lee could have opposed a total of but 83,000 men against the 284,000 invaders.

In the West the numbers were more equally balanced. General Sherman, who commanded the army of invasion there, had under his orders 230,000 men, but as more than half this force was required to protect the long lines of communication and to keep down the conquered States, he was able to bring into the field for offensive operations 99,000 men, who were faced by the Confederate army under Johnston of 58,000 men. Grant's scheme was, that while the armies of the North were, under his own command, to march against Richmond, the army of the West was to invade Georgia and march upon Atlanta.

His plan of action was simple, and was afterward stated by himself to be as follows: "I determined first to use the greatest number of troops practicable against the main force of the enemy, preventing him from using the same force at different seasons against first one and then another of our armies, and the possibility of repose for refitting and producing necessary supplies for carrying on resistance. Second, to hammer continuously against the armed force of the enemy and his resources until, by mere attrition if in no other way, there should be nothing left to him but submission."

This was a terrible programme, and involved an expenditure of life far beyond anything that had taken place. Grant's plan, in fact, was to fight and to keep on fighting, regardless of his own losses, until at last the Confederate army, whose losses could not be replaced, melted away. It was a strategy that few generals have dared to practice, fewer still to acknowledge.

On the 4th of May the great army of the Potomac crossed the Rapidan and advanced toward Chancellorsville. Lee moved two divisions of his army to oppose them. Next morning the battle began at daybreak on the old ground where Lee had defeated Hooker the year before. All day long the division of Ewell supported the attack of the army corps of Sedgwick and Hancock. Along a front of six miles, in the midst of the thick forest, the battle raged the whole of the day. The Confederates, in spite of the utmost efforts of the Northerners, although reinforced in the afternoon by the army corps of General Burnside, held their position, and when night put an end to the conflict the invaders had not gained a foot of ground.

As soon as the first gleam of light appeared in the morning the battle recommenced. The Federal generals, Sedgwick, Warren, and Hancock, with Burnside in reserve, fell upon Hill and Ewell. Both sides had thrown up earthworks and felled trees as a protection during the night. At first the Confederates gained the advantage; but a portion of Burnside's corps was brought up and restored the battle, while on the left flank of the Federals Hancock had attacked with such vigor that the Confederates opposed to him were driven back.

At the crisis of the battle, Longstreet, who had marched all night, appeared upon the ground, drove back Hancock's men, and was on the point of aiding the Confederates in a decisive attack upon the enemy, when, riding rapidly forward into the wood to reconnoiter, he was, like Jackson, struck down by the fire of his own men. He was carried to the rear desperately, and it was feared for a time mortally wounded, and his loss paralyzed the movement which he had prepared. Nevertheless during the whole day the fight went on with varying success, sometimes one side obtaining a slight advantage, the other then regaining the ground they had lost.

Just as evening was closing in a Georgia brigade, with two other regiments, made a detour, and fell furiously upon two brigades of the enemy, and drove them back in headlong rout for a mile and a half, capturing their two generals and many prisoners. The artillery, as on the previous day, had been little used on either side, the work being done at short range with the rifle, the loss being much heavier among the thick masses of the Northerners than in the thinner lines of the Confederates. Grant had failed in his efforts to turn Lee's right and to accomplish his direct advance; he therefore changed his base and moved his army round toward Spotsylvania.

Lee soon perceived his object, and succeeded in carrying his army to Spotsylvania before the Federals reached it.

On the afternoon of Monday, the 9th, there was heavy fighting and on the 10th another pitched battle took place. This time the ground was more open, and the artillery was employed with terrible effect on both sides. It ended, however, as the previous battles had done, by the Confederates holding their ground.

Upon the next day there was but little fighting. In the night the Federals moved quietly through the wood, and at daybreak four divisions fell upon Johnston's division of Ewell's corps, took them completely by surprise, and captured the greater part of them.

But Lee's veterans soon recovered from their surprise and maintained their position until noon. Then the whole Federal army advanced, and the battle raged till nightfall terminated the struggle, leaving Lee in possession of the whole line he had held, with the exception of the ground lost in the morning.

For the next six days the armies faced each other, worn out by incessant fighting, and prevented from moving by the heavy rain which fell incessantly. They were now able to reckon up the losses. The Federals found that they had lost, in killed, wounded, or missing, nearly 30,000 men; while Lee's army was diminished by about 12,000.

While these mighty battles had been raging the Federal cavalry under Sheridan had advanced rapidly forward, and, after several skirmishes with Stuart's cavalry, penetrated within the outer intrenchments round Richmond. Here Stuart with two regiments of cavalry charged them and drove them back, but the gallant Confederate officer received a wound that before night proved fatal. His loss was a terrible blow to the Confederacy, although his successor in the command of the cavalry, General Wade Hampton, was also an officer of the highest merit.

In the meantime General Butler, who had at Fort Monroe under his command two corps of infantry, 4,000 cavalry, and a fleet of gunboats and transports, was threatening Richmond from the east. Shipping his men on board the transports he steamed up the James River, under convoy of the fleet, and landed on a neck of land known as Bermuda Hundred. To oppose him all the troops from North Carolina had been brought up, the whole force amounting to 19,000 men, under the command of General Beauregard. Butler, after various futile movements, was driven back again to his intrenched camp at Bermuda Hundred, where he was virtually besieged by Beauregard with 10,000 men, the rest of that general's force being sent up to reinforce Lee.

In western Virginia, Breckenridge, with 3,500 men, was called upon to hold in check Sigel, with 15,000 men. Advancing to Staunton, Breckenridge was joined by the pupils of the military college at Lexington, 250 in number, lads of from 14 to 17 years of age. He came upon Sigel on the line of march, and attacked him at once. The Federal general placed a battery in a wood and opened fire with grape. The commander of the Lexington boys ordered them to charge, and, gallantly rushing in through the heavy fire, they charged in among the guns, killed the artillerymen, drove back the infantry supports, and bayoneted their colonel. The Federals now retired down the valley to Strasburg, and Breckenridge was able to send a portion of his force to aid Lee in his great struggle.

After his six days' pause in front of Lee's position at Spotsylvania, Grant abandoned his plan of forcing his way through Lee's army to Richmond, and endeavored to outflank it; but Lee again divined his object, and moved round and still faced him. After various movements the armies again stood face to face upon the old battle-grounds on the Chickahominy. On the 3d of June the battle commenced at half-past four in the morning. Hancock at first gained an advantage, but Hill's division dashed down upon him and drove him back with great slaughter; while no advantage was gained by them in other parts of the field. The Federal loss on this day was 13,000, and the troops were so dispirited that they refused to renew the battle in the afternoon.

Grant then determined to alter his plan altogether, and sending imperative orders to Butler to obtain possession of Petersburg, embarked Smith's corps in transports, and moved with the rest of his army to join that general there. Smith's corps entered the James River, landed, and marched against Petersburg. Beauregard had at Petersburg only two infantry and two cavalry regiments under General Wise, while a single brigade fronted Butler at Bermuda Hundred. With this handful of men he was called upon to defend Petersburg and to keep Butler bottled up in Bermuda Hundred until help could reach him from Lee. He telegraphed to Richmond for all the assistance that could be sent to him, and was reinforced by a brigade, which arrived just in time, for Smith had already captured a portion of the intrenchments, but was now driven out.

The next day Beauregard was attacked both by Smith's and Hancock's corps, which had now arrived. With 8,000 men he kept at bay the assaults of two whole army corps, having in the meantime sent orders to Gracie, the officer in command of the brigade before Butler, to leave a few sentries there to deceive that general, and to march with the rest of his force to his aid. It arrived at a critical moment. Overwhelmed by vastly superior numbers, many of the Confederates had left their posts, and Breckenridge was in vain trying to rally them when Gracie's brigade came up. The position was reoccupied and the battle continued.

At noon Burnside with his corps arrived and joined the assailants; while Butler, discovering at last that the troops in front of him were withdrawn, moved out and barred the road against reinforcements from Richmond. Nevertheless the Confederates held their ground all the afternoon and until eleven o'clock at night, when the assault ceased.

At midnight Beauregard withdrew his troops from the defenses that they were too few to hold, and set them to work to throw up fresh intrenchments on a shorter line behind. All night the men worked with their bayonets, canteens, and any tools that came to hand.

It was well for them that the enemy were so exhausted that it was noon before they were ready to advance again, for by this time help was at hand. Anderson, who had succeeded to the command of Longstreet's corps, and was leading the van of Lee's army, forced his way through Butler's troops and drove him back into the Bermuda Hundred, and leaving one brigade to watch him marched with another into Petersburg just as the attack was recommenced. Thus reinforced Beauregard successfully defeated all the assaults of the enemy until night fell. Another Federal army corps came up before morning, and the assault was again renewed, but the defenders, who had strengthened their defenses during the night, drove their assailants back with terrible loss. The whole of Lee's army now arrived, and the rest of Grant's army also came up, and that general found that after all his movements his way to Richmond was barred as before. He was indeed in a far worse position than when he had crossed the Rapidan, for the morale of his army was much injured by the repeated repulses and terrible losses it had sustained. The new recruits that had been sent to fill up the gaps were far inferior troops to those with which he had commenced the campaign. To send forward such men against the fortifications of Petersburg manned by Lee's veteran troops was to court defeat, and he therefore began to throw up works for a regular siege.

Fighting went on incessantly between the outposts, but only one great attempt was made during the early months of the siege to capture the Confederate position. The miners drove a gallery under the works, and then drove other galleries right and left under them. These were charged with eight thousand pounds of powder. When all was ready, masses of troops were brought up to take advantage of the confusion which would be caused by the explosion, and a division of black troops were to lead the assault. At a quarter to five in the morning of the 30th of July the great mine was exploded, blowing two guns, a battery, and its defenders into the air, and forming a huge pit two hundred feet long and sixty feet wide. Lee and Beauregard hurried to the scene, checked the panic that prevailed, brought up troops, and before the great Federal columns approached the breach the Confederates were ready to receive them. The assault was made with little vigor, the approaches to the breach were obstructed by abattis, and instead of rushing forward in a solid mass they occupied the great pit, and contented themselves with firing over the edge of the crater, where regiments and divisions were huddled together. But the Confederate batteries were now manned, and from the works on either side of the breach, and from behind, they swept the approaches, and threw shell among the crowded mass. The black division was now brought up, and entered the crater, but only added to the confusion. There was no officer of sufficient authority among the crowded mass there to assume the supreme command. No assistance could be sent to them, for the arrival of fresh troops would but have added to the confusion. All day the conflict went on, the Federals lining the edge of the crater, and exchanging a heavy musketry fire with the Confederate infantry, while the mass below suffered terribly from the artillery fire. When night closed the survivors of the great column that had marched forward in the morning, confident that victory was assured to them, and that the explosion would lay Petersburg open to capture, made their retreat, the Confederates, however, taking a considerable number of prisoners. The Federal loss in killed, wounded and captured was admitted by them to be 4,000; the

Confederate accounts put it down at 6,000.

After this terrible repulse it was a long time before Grant again renewed active operations, but during the months that ensued his troops suffered very heavily from the effects of fever, heightened by the discouragement they felt at their want of success, and at the tremendous losses they had suffered since they entered Virginia on their forward march to Richmond.

## CHAPTER XVIII. A PERILOUS UNDERTAKING.

VINCENT Wingfield had had an arduous time of it with his squadron of cavalry. He had taken part in the desperate charge that checked the advance of Sheridan's great column of cavalry which approached within three miles of Richmond, the charge that had cost the gallant Stuart his life; and the death of his beloved general had been a heavy blow for him. Jackson and Stuart, two of the bravest and noblest spirits of the Confederate army, were gone. Both had been personally dear to Vincent, and he felt how grievous was their loss to the cause for which he was fighting; but he had little time for grief. The enemy, after the tremendous battles of the Wilderness, swung their army round to Cold Harbor, and Vincent's squadron was called up to aid Lee in his struggle there. Then they were engaged night and day in harassing the enemy as they marched down to take up their new base at Petersburg, and finally received orders to ride round at full speed to aid in the defense of that place.

They had arrived in the middle of the second day's fighting, and dismounting his men Vincent had aided the hard-pressed Confederates in holding their lines till Longstreet's division arrived to their assistance. A short time before the terrible disaster that befell the Federals in the mine they exploded under the Confederate works, he was with General Wade Hampton, who had succeeded General Stuart in the command of the cavalry, when General Lee rode up.

"They are erecting siege works in earnest," General Lee said. "I do not think that we shall have any more attacks for the present. I wish I knew exactly where they are intending to place their heavy batteries. If I did we should know where to strengthen our defenses, and plant our counter batteries. It is very important to find this out; but now that their whole army has settled down in front of us, and Sheridan's cavalry are scouring the woods, we shall get no news, for the farmers will no longer be able to get through to tell us what is going on.

"I will try and ride round, if you like, general," Vincent said. "By making a long detour one could get into the rear of their lines and pass as a farmer going into camp to sell his goods."

"It would be a very dangerous service, sir," General Lee said. "You know what the consequence would be if you were caught?"

"I know the consequence," Vincent said; "but I do not think, sir, that the risk is greater than one runs every time one goes into battle."

"Perhaps not," General Lee replied; "but in one case one dies fighting for one's country by an honorable death, in the other--" and he stopped.

"In the other one is shot in cold blood," Vincent said quietly. "One dies for one's country in either case, sir; and it does not much matter, so far as I can see, whether one is killed in battle or shot in cold blood. As long as one is doing one's duty, one death is surely as honorable as the other."

"That is true enough," General Lee said, "although it is not the way men generally view the matter. Still, sir, if you volunteer for the work, I do not feel justified in refusing the opportunity of acquiring information that may be of vital consequence to us. When will you start?"

"In half an hour, sir. I shall ride back to Richmond, obtain a disguise there, and then go round by train to Burksville Junction and then ride again until I get round behind their lines. Will you give me an order for my horse and myself to be taken?"

"Very well, sir," General Lee said. "So be it. May God be with you on your way and bring you safely back."

Vincent rode off to his quarters.

"Dan," he said, "I am going away on special duty for at least three days. I have got a couple of letters to write, and shall be ready to start in half an hour. Give the horse a good feed and have him at the door again by that time."

"Am I to go with you, sah?"

"No, Dan; I must go by myself this time."

Dan felt anxious as he went out, for it was seldom that his master ever went away without telling him where he was going, and he felt sure that the service was one of unusual danger; nor was his anxiety lessened when at the appointed time Vincent came out and handed him two letters.

"You are to keep these letters, Dan, until I return, or till you hear that something has happened to me. If you hear that, you are to take one of these letters to my mother, and take the other yourself to Miss Kingston. Tell her before you give it her what has happened as gently as you can. As for yourself, Dan, you had your letters of freedom long ago, and I have left you five hundred dollars; so that you can get a cabin and patch of your own, and settle down when these troubles are over."

"Let me go with you, master," Dan said, with the tears streaming down his cheeks. "I would rather be killed with you a hundred times than get on without you."

"I would take you if I could, Dan; but this is a service that I must do alone. Good-by, my boy; let us hope that in three or four days at the outside I shall be back here again safe and sound."

He wrung Dan's hand, and then started at a canter and kept on at that pace until he reached Richmond. A train with stores was starting for the south in a few minutes; General Lee's order enabled Vincent to have a horse-box attached at once, and he was soon speeding on his way. He alighted at Burksville Junction, and there purchased some rough clothes for himself and some country-fashioned saddlery for his horse. Then, after changing his clothes at an inn and putting the fresh saddlery on his horse, he started.

It was getting late in the afternoon, but he rode on by unfrequented roads, stopping occasionally to inquire if any of the Federal cavalry had been seen in the neighborhood, and at last stopped for the night at a little village inn. As soon as it was daybreak he resumed his journey. He had purchased at Burksville some colored calico and articles of female clothing, and fastened the parcel to the back of his saddle. As he rode forward now he heard constant tales of the passing of parties of the enemy's cavalry, but he was fortunate enough to get well round to the rear of the Federal lines before he encountered any of them. Then he came suddenly upon a troop.

"Where are you going to, and where have you come from?"

"Our farm is a mile away from Union Grove," he said, "and I have been over to Sussex Courthouse to buy some things for my mother."

"Let me see what you have got there," the officer said. "You are rebels to a man here, and there's no trusting any of you."

Vincent unfastened the parcel and opened it. The officer laughed.

"Well, we won't confiscate them as contraband of war."

So saying he set spurs to his horse and galloped on with his troop. Vincent rode on to Union Grove, and then taking a road at random kept on till he reached a small farmhouse. He knocked at the door, and a woman came out.

"Mother," he said, "can you put me up for a couple of days? I am a stranger here, and all the villages are full of soldiers."

The woman looked at him doubtfully.

"What are you doing here?" she asked at last. "This ain't a time for strangers; besides a young fellow like you ought to be ashamed to show yourself when you ought to be over there with Lee. My boys are both there and my husband. You ought to be ashamed of yourself, a strong-looking young fellow like you, to be riding about instead of fighting the Yankees. Go along! you will get no shelter here. I would scorn to have such as you inside my doors."

"Perhaps I have been fighting there," Vincent said significantly. "But one can't be always fighting, and there are other things to do sometimes. For instance, to find out what the Yankees are doing and what are their plans."

"Is that so?" the woman asked doubtfully.

"That is so," he answered earnestly. "I am an officer in Wade Hampton's cavalry, and, now Sheridan's troopers have cut off all communication, I have come out to find for General Lee where the Yankees are building their batteries before Petersburg."

"In that case you are welcome," the woman said. "Come straight in. I will lead your horse out and fasten him up in the bush, and give him a feed there. It will never do to put him in the stable; the Yankees come in and out and they'd take him off sharp enough if their eyes fell on him. I think you will be safe enough even if they do come. They will take you for a son of mine, and if they ask any questions I will answer them sharp enough."

"I wonder they have left you a feed of corn," Vincent said, when the woman returned after taking away his horse.

"It's no thanks to them," she answered; "they have cleared out everything that they could lay their hands on. But I have been expecting it for months, and, as I have had nothing to do since my man and boys went away, I have been digging a great pit in the wood over there, and have buried most all my corn, and have salted my pigs down and buried them in barrels; so they didn't find much. They took the old horse and two cows; but I hope the old horse will fall down the first time they uses him, and the cow meat will choke them as eats it. Now, is there anything as I can do to help you?"

"I want a basket with some eggs and chickens or vegetables to take into their camp to sell, but I am afraid I have not much chance of getting them."

"I can help you there too," the woman said. "I turned all my chickens into the wood the day I heard the Yankees had landed. They have got rather wild like; but I go out and give them some corn every evening. I expect if we look about we shall find some nests; indeed I know there are one or two of them sitting. So if you will come out with me we can soon knock down five or six of the creatures, and maybe get a score or two of eggs. As for vegetables, a horde of locusts couldn't have stripped the country cleaner than they have done."

They went out into the wood. Six hens were soon killed, and hunting about they discovered several nests and gathered about three dozen eggs. Vincent aided in plucking the chickens and they then returned to the house.

"You had best take a bite before you go," she said. "It's noon now, and you said you started at daybreak. Always get a meal when you can, say I."

She produced a loaf and some bacon from a little cupboard hidden by her bed, and Vincent, who, now he thought of it, was feeling hungry, made a hearty meal.

"I will pay you for these chickens and eggs at once," he said. "There is no saying whether I shall come back again."

"I will not say no to your paying for the chickens and eggs," she said, "because money is scarce enough, and I may have long to wait before my man and the boys come back; but as to lodging and food I would not touch a cent. You are welcome to all I have when it's for the good cause." Vincent started with the basket on his arm, and after walking three miles came upon the Federal camps.

Some of the regiments were already under canvas, others were still bivouacked in the open air, as the store-ships carrying the heavy baggage had not yet arrived. The generals and their staffs had taken up their quarters in the villages. Vincent had received accurate instructions from his hostess as to the position of the various villages, and avoided them carefully, for he did not want to sell out his stock immediately. He had indeed stowed two of the fowls away in his pocket so that in case any one insisted upon buying up all his stock he could place these in his basket and still push on.

He avoided the camps as much as he could. He could see the smoke rising in front of him, and the roar of guns was now close at hand. He saw on his right an elevated piece of ground, from which a good view could be obtained of the fortifications upon which the Federals were working. A camp had been pitched there, and a large tent near the summit showed that some officer of superior rank had his quarters there. He made a detour so as to come up at the back of the hill and when he reached the top he stood looking down upon the line of works.

They were nearly half a mile distant. The intervening ground had already been stripped of its hedges, and the trees cut down to form gabions, fascines, and platforms for the cannon. Thousands of men were at work; but in some parts they were clustered much more thickly than in others, and Vincent had no difficulty in determining where the principal batteries were in course of construction along this portion of the position. He was still gazing intently when two horsemen rode up from behind.

"Hallo you, sir! What are you looking at?" one of them asked sharply. "What are you spying about here?"

Vincent turned slowly round with a silly smile on his lips.

"I am spying all them chaps at work," he said. "It reminds me for all the world of an ant-hill. Never did see so many chaps before. What be they a-doing? Digging a big drain or making a roadway, I guess."

"Who are you, sir?" the officer asked angrily.

"Seth Jones I be, and mother's sent me to sell some fowls and eggs. Do you want to buy any? Fine birds they be."

"Why, Sheridan," laughed the other officer, "this is a feather out of your cap. I thought your fellows had cleared out every hen-roost within twenty miles of Petersburg already."

"I fancy they have emptied most of them," the general said grimly. "Where do you come from, lad?"

"I comes from over there," Vincent said, jerking his thumb back. "I lives there with mother. Father and the other boys they have gone fighting Yanks; but they wouldn't take me with them 'cause I ain't sharp in my wits, though I tells them I could shoot a Yank as well as they could if they showed me."

"And who do you suppose all those men are?" General Sheridan asked, pointing toward the trenches.

"I dunno," Vincent replied. "I guess they be niggers. There be too many of them for whites; besides whites ain't such fools to work like that. Doesn't ye want any fowl?" and he drew back the cloth and showed the contents of the basket.

"Take them as a matter of curiosity, general," the other officer laughed. "It will be downright novelty to you to buy chickens."

"What do you want for them, boy?"

"Mother said as I wasn't to take less nor a dollar apiece."

"Greenbacks, I suppose?" the officer asked.

"I suppose so. She didn't say nothing about it; but I has not seen aught but greenbacks for a long time since."

"Come along, then," the officer said; "we will take them."

They rode up to the large tent, and the officers alighted, and gave their horses to two of the soldiers.

"Give your basket to this soldier."

"I want the basket back again. Mother would whop me if I came back without the basket again."

"All right," the officer said; "you shall have it back in a minute."

Vincent stood looking anxiously after the orderly.

"Do you think that boy is as foolish as he seems?" General Sheridan asked his companion. "He admits that he comes of a rebel family."

"I don't think he would have admitted that if he hadn't been a fool. I fancy he is a half-witted chap. They never would have left a fellow of his age behind."

"No, I think it's safe," Sheridan said; "but one can't be too particular just at present. See, the trees in front hide our work altogether from the rebels, and it would be a serious thing if they were to find out what we are doing."

"That boy could not tell them much even if he got there," the other said; "and from this distance it would need a sharp eye and some military knowledge to make out anything of what is going on. Where does your mother live, boy?"

"I ain't going to tell you," Vincent said doggedly "Mother said I wasn't to tell no one where I lived, else the Yankee thieves would be a-coming down and stealing the rest of our chickens."

The officers laughed.

"Well, go along, boy; and I should advise you not to say anything about Yankee thieves another time, for likely enough you will get a broken head for your pains."

Vincent went off grumbling, and with a slow and stumbling step made his way over the brow of the hill and down through the camps behind. Here he sold his last two fowls and his eggs, and then walked briskly on until he reached the cottage from which he had started.

"I am glad to see you back," the woman said as he entered. "How have you got on?"

"Capitally," he said. "I pretended to be half an idiot, and so got safely out, though I fell into Sheridan's hands. He suspected me at first, but at last he thought I was what I looked--a fool. He wanted to know where you lived, but I wouldn't tell him. I told him you told me not to tell any one, 'cause if I did the Yankee thieves would be clearing out the rest of the chickens."

"Did you tell him that, now?" the woman said in delight; "he must have thought you was a fool. Well, it's a good thing the Yanks should hear the truth sometimes. Well, have you done now?"

"No, I have only seen one side of their works yet; I must try round the other flank to-morrow. I wish I could get something to sell that wouldn't get bought up by the first people I came to, something I could peddle among the soldiers."

"What sort of thing?"

"Something in the way of drinks, I should say," Vincent said. "I saw a woman going among the camps. She had two tin cans and a little mug. I think she had lemonade or something of that sort."

"It wouldn't be lemonade," the woman said "I haven't seen a lemon for the last two years; but they do get some oranges from Florida. Maybe it was that, or perhaps it was spirits and water."

"Perhaps it was," Vincent agreed; "though I don't think they would let any one sell spirits in the camp."

"I can't get you any lemons or oranges neither," the woman said; "but I might make you a drink out of molasses and herbs, with some spirits in it. I have got a keg of old rye buried away ever since my man went off, six months ago; I am out of molasses, but I dare say I can borrow some from a neighbor, and as for herbs they are about the only thing the Yankees haven't stole. I think I could fix you up something that would do. As long as it has got spirits in it, it don't much matter what you put in besides, only it wouldn't do to take spirits up alone. You can call it plantation drink, and I don't suppose any one would ask too closely what it's made of."

"Thank you, that will do capitally."

The next morning Vincent again set out, turning his steps this time toward the right flank of the Federal position. He had in the course of the evening made a sketch of the ground he had seen, marking in all the principal batteries, with notes as to the number of guns for which they seemed to be intended.

"Look here," he said to the woman before leaving. "I may not be as lucky to-day as I was yesterday. If I do not come back to-night, can you find any one you can trust to take this piece of paper round to Richmond? Of course he would have to make his way first up to Burksville junction, and then take train to Richmond. When he gets there he must go down to Petersburg, and ask for General Lee. I have written a line to go with it, saying what I have done this for, and asking the general to give the bearer a hundred dollars."

"I will take it myself," the woman said; "not for the sake of the hundred dollars, though I ain't saying as it wouldn't please the old man when he comes back to find I had a hundred dollars stored away; but for the cause. My men are all doing their duty, and I will do mine. So trust me, and if you don't come back by daybreak to-morrow morning, I will start right away with these letters. I will go out at once and hide them somewhere in case the Yanks should come and make a search. If you are caught they might, like enough, trace you here, and then they would search the place all over and maybe set it alight. If you ain't here by nightfall I shall sleep out in the wood, so if they come they won't find me here. If anything detains you, and you ain't back till after dark, you will find me somewhere near the tree where your horse is tied up."

Provided with a large can full of a liquor that the woman compounded, and which Vincent, on tasting, found to be by no means bad, he started from the cottage. Again he made his way safely through the camps, and without hindrance lounged up to a spot where a large number of men belonging to one of the negro regiments were at work.

"Plantation liquor?" he said, again assuming a stupid air, to a black sergeant who was with them. "First-rate stuff; and only fifteen cents a glass."

"What plantation liquor like?" the negro asked. "Me not know him."

"First-rate stuff," Vincent repeated. "Mother makes it of spirit and molasses and all sorts. Fifteen cents a glass."

"Well, I will take a glass," the sergeant said. "Mighty hot work dis in de sun; but don't you say nuffin about the spirit. Ef dey ask you, just you say molasses and all sorts, dat's quite enough. De white officer won't let spirits be sold in de camp.

"Dat bery good stuff," he said, smacking his lips as he handed back the little tin measure. "You sell him all in no time." Several of the negroes now came round, and Vincent disposed of a considerable quantity of his plantation liquor. Then he turned to go away, for he did not want to empty his can at one place. He had not gone many paces when a party of three or four officers came along.

"Hallo, you sir, what the deuce are you doing here?" one asked angrily. "Don't you know nobody is allowed to pass through the lines?"

"I didn't see no lines. What sort of lines are they? No one told me nothing about lines. My mother sent me out to sell plantation liquor, fifteen cents a glass."

"What's it like?" one of the officers said laughing. "Spirits, I will bet a dollar, in some shape or other. Pour me out a glass. I will try it, anyhow."

Vincent filled the little tin mug, and handed it to the officer. As he lifted his face to do so there was a sudden exclamation.

"Vincent Wingfield!" and another officer drawing his sword attacked him furiously, shouting, "A spy! Seize him! A Confederate spy!"

Vincent recognized with astonishment in the Federal officer rushing at him with uplifted sword his old antagonist, Jackson. Almost instinctively he whirled the can, which was still half full of liquor, round his head and dashed it full in the face of his antagonist, who was knocked off his feet by the blow. With a yell of rage he started up again and rushed at Vincent. The latter snatched up a shovel that was lying close by and stood his ground. The officers were so surprised at the suddenness of the incident and the overthrow of their companion, and for the moment so amused at the latter's appearance, covered as he was from head to foot with the sticky liquor and bleeding from a cut inflicted by the edge of the can, that they were incapable of interference.

Blinded with rage, and with the liquid streaming into his eyes, Jackson rushed at Vincent. The latter caught the blow aimed at him on the edge of the shovel, and then swinging his weapon round smote his antagonist with all his strength, the edge of the shovel falling fairly upon his head. Without a cry the traitor fell dead in his tracks. The other officers now drew their swords and rushed forward. Vincent, seeing the futility of resistance, threw down his shovel. He was instantly seized.

"Halloo there!" the senior officer called to the men, who had stopped in their work and were gazing at the sudden fray that had arisen, "a sergeant and four men." Four of the negro soldiers and a sergeant at once stepped forward. "Take this man and conduct him to the village. Put him in a room, and stay there with him. Do you, sergeant, station yourself at the door, so that I shall know where to find you. Put on your uniforms and take your guns." The men put on their coats, which they had removed while at work, shouldered their muskets, and took their places, two on each side of the prisoner. The officers then turned to examine their prostrate comrade.

"It's all over with him," one said, stooping down; "the shovel has cut his skull nearly in half. Well, I fancy he was a bad lot. I don't believe in Southerners who come over to fight in our ranks; besides he was at one time in the rebel army."

"Yes, he was taken prisoner," another said. "Then his father, who had to bolt from the South, because, he said, of his Northern sympathies, but likely enough for something else, came round, made interest somehow and got his son released, and then some one else got him a commission with us. He always said he had been obliged to fight on the other side, but that he had always been heart and soul for the North; anyhow, he was always blackguarding his old friends. I always doubted the fellow. Well, there's an end of him; and anyhow he has done useful service at last by recognizing this spy. Fine-looking young fellow that. He called him Vincent Wingfield. I seem to remember the name; perhaps I have read it in some of the rebel newspapers we got hold of; likely enough some one will know it. Well, I suppose we had better have Jackson carried into camp."

Four more of the negroes were called out, and these carried the body into the camp of his regiment. An officer was also sent from the working party to report the capture of a spy to his colonel.

"I will report it to the general," the latter said; "he rode along here about a quarter of an hour ago, and may not be back again for some hours. As we have got the spy fast it cannot make any difference."

As he was marched back to the village Vincent felt that there was no hope for him whatever. He had been denounced as a spy, and although the lips that had denounced him had been silenced forever, the mischief had been done. He could give no satisfactory account of himself. He thought for a moment of declaring that a mistake had been made, but he felt that no denial would counterbalance the effect of Jackson's words. The fury, too, with which the latter had attacked him would show plainly enough that his assailant was absolutely certain as to his identity, and even that there had been a personal feud between them. Then he thought that if he said that he was the son of the woman in the line she would hear him out in the assertion. But it was not likely that this would be accepted as against Jackson's testimony; besides, inquiry among her neighbors would certainly lead to the discovery that she was speaking an untruth, and might even involve her in his fate as his abettor. But most of all he decided against this course because it would involve the telling of a lie.

Vincent considered that while in disguise, and doing important service for his country, he was justified in using deceit; but merely for the purpose of saving his own life, and that perhaps uselessly, he would not lie. His fate, of course, was certain. He was a spy, and would be shot for it. Vincent had so often been in the battlefield, so often under a fire from which it seemed that no one could come alive, that the thought that death was at hand had not for him the terrors that possess those differently circumstanced. He was going to die for the Confederacy as tens of thousands of brave men had died before, and he rejoiced over the precaution he had taken as to the transmission of his discoveries on the previous day, and felt sure that General Lee would do full justice to his memory, and announce that he had died in doing noble service to the country.

He sighed as he thought of his mother and sisters; but Rose had been married in the spring, and Annie was engaged to an officer in General Beauregard's staff. Then he thought of Lucy away in Georgia and for the first time his lip quivered and his cheek paled.

The negro guards, who had been enlisted but a few weeks, were wholly ignorant of their duties, and having once conveyed their prisoner into the room, evidently considered that all further necessity for military strictness was at an end. They had been ordered to stay in the room with the prisoner, but no instructions had been given as to their conduct there. They accordingly placed their muskets in one corner of the room, and proceeded to chatter and laugh without further regarding him.

Under other circumstances this carelessness would have inspired Vincent with the thought of escape, but he knew that it was out of the question here. There were Federal camps all round and a shout from the negroes would send a hundred men in instant pursuit of him. There was nothing for him to do but to wait for the end, and that end would assuredly come in the morning. From time to time the door opened, and the negro sergeant looked in. Apparently his ideas on the subject of discipline were no stricter than those of his men, for he made no remark as to their carelessness. Presently, when he looked in, the four soldiers were standing at the window watching a regiment passing by on its way to take its share of the work in the trenches. Vincent, who was sitting at a table, happened to look up, and was astonished at seeing the sergeant first put his finger on his lips, then take off his cap, put one hand on his heart, and gesticulate with the other.

Vincent gazed at him in blank surprise, then he started and almost sprang to his feet, for in the Yankee sergeant he recognized Tony Morris; but the uplifted hand of the negro warned him of the necessity of silence. The negro nodded several times, again put his hand on his heart, and then disappeared. A thrill of hope stirred every vein in Vincent's body. He felt his cheeks flush and had difficulty in maintaining his passive attitude. He was not, then, utterly deserted; he had a friend who would, he was sure, do all in his power to aid him.

It was extraordinary indeed that it should be Tony who was now his jailer; and yet, when he thought it over, it was not difficult to understand. It was natural enough that he should have enlisted when the black regiments were raised. He had doubtless heard his name shouted out by Jackson, and had, as Vincent now remembered, stepped forward as a sort of volunteer when the officer called for a sergeant and four men.

Yes, Tony would doubtless do all in his power to save him. Whether it would be possible that he could do so was doubtful; but at least there was a hope, and with it the feeling of quiet resignation with which Vincent had faced what appeared to be inevitable at once disappeared, and was succeeded by a restless longing for action. His brain was busy at once in calculating the chances of his being ordered for instant execution or of the sentence being postponed till the following morning, and, in the latter case, with the question of what guard would be probably placed over him, and how Tony would set about the attempt to aid him to escape.

Had the general been in camp when he was brought in he would probably have been shot at sunset, but if he did not return until the afternoon he would most likely order the sentence to be carried out at daybreak. In any case, as he was an officer, some time might be granted to him to prepare for death. Then there was the question whether he would be handed over to a white regiment for safekeeping or left in the hands of the black regiment that had captured him. No doubt after the sentence was passed the white officers of that regiment would see that a much stricter watch than that now put over him was set.

It was not probable that he would still be in charge of Tony, for as the latter would be on duty all day he would doubtless be relieved. In that case how would he manage to approach him, and what means would he use to direct the attention of the sentries in another direction? He thought over the plans that he himself would adopt were he in Tony's place. The first thing would be, of course, to make the sentries drunk if possible. This should not be a difficult task with men whose notions of discipline were so lax as those of the negroes; but it would be no easy matter for Tony to obtain spirits, for these were strictly prohibited in the Federal camp. Perhaps he might help Tony in this way. He fortunately had a small notebook with a pencil in his pocket, and as his guards were still at the window he wrote as follows:

"I am captured by the Yankees. So far as I can see, my only chance of escape is to make the sentries drunk. The bearer is absolutely to be trusted. Give him his canteen full of spirits, and tell him what I have written here."

He tore this page out, folded it up, and directed it to Mrs. Grossmith, Worley Farm, near Union. Presently Tony looked in again and Vincent held up the note. The sergeant stepped quickly forward and took it, and then said sharply to the men:

"Now den, dis not keeping guard. Suppose door open and dis fellow run away. What dey say to you? Two of you keep your eye on dis man. Suppose Captain

Pearce come in and find you all staring out window. He kick up nice bobbery."

Thus admonished as to their duty, two of the negroes took up their muskets and stood with their backs to the door, with their eyes fixed on the prisoner with such earnestness that Vincent could not suppress a smile. The negroes grinned responsively.

"Dis bad affair, young sah," one said; "bery bad affair. Ob course we soldiers ob de Union, and got to fight if dey tell us; but no like dis job ob keeping guard like dis."

"It can't be helped," Vincent said; "and of course you must do your duty. I am not going to jump up the chimney or fly through the window, and as there are four of you, to say nothing of the sergeant outside, you needn't be afraid of my trying to escape."

"No sah, dat not possible nohow; we know dat bery well. Dat's why we no trouble to look after you. But as de sargent say watch, ob course we must watch. We bery pleased to see you kill dat white officer. Dat officer bery hard man and all de men hate him, and when you knock him down we should like to hab given cheer. We all sorry for you; still you see, sah, we must keep watch. If you were to get away, dar no saying what dey do to us."

"That's all right," Vincent said; "I don't blame you at all. As you say, that was a very bad fellow. I had quarreled with him before, because he treated his slaves so badly."

## CHAPTER XIX. FREE.

IT was not until late in the afternoon that a white officer entered, and ordered the soldiers to conduct the prisoner to the general's tent.

"What is your name, sir, and who are you?" the general asked as he was brought in. "I hear that you were denounced by Lieutenant Jackson as being a spy, and that he addressed you as Vincent Wingfield. What have you got to say to the charge?"

"My name is Vincent Wingfield, sir," Vincent replied quietly. "I am upon the staff of General Wade Hampton, and in pursuance of my duty I came here to learn what I could of your movements and intentions."

The general was silent for a moment.

"Then, sir, as you are an officer, you must be well aware of the consequence of being discovered in disguise here. I regret that there is no course open to me but to order you to be shot as a spy to-morrow morning."

One of the officers who was standing by the general here whispered to him.

"Ah, yes, I remember," he said. "Are you the same officer, sir, who escaped from Elmira?"

"I am, sir," Vincent replied; "and at the same time aided in the escape of the man who denounced me to-day, and who then did his best to have me arrested by sending an anonymous letter stating the disguise in which I was making my way through the country. I was not surprised to find that he had carried his treachery further, and was now fighting against the men with whom he had formerly served."

"He deserved the fate that has befallen him," the general said. "Still this does not alter your position. I regret that I must order my sentence to be carried out."

"I do not blame you, sir. I knew the risks I ran when I accepted the mission. My only regret is that I failed in supplying my general with the information they required."

The general then turned to the officer who had brought Vincent up.

"This officer will remain in charge of your men for to-night, Captain Pearce. You will see that the sentence is carried into effect at daybreak. I need not tell you that a vigilant guard must be placed over him."

Vincent was again marched back to the village, but the officer halted the party when he arrived there.

"Stop here a few minutes, sergeant," he said. "That room is required for an officer's quarters. I will look round and find another place."

In a few minutes he returned, and Vincent was conducted to a shed standing in the garden of one of the houses.

"Place one man on guard at the door and another behind," he said to the sergeant. "Let the other two relieve them, and change the watch once an hour."

The sergeant saluted.

"De men hab been on duty since daylight, sah, and none of us hab had anything to eat."

"Oh, I forgot that," the officer replied. "Very well, I will send another party to relieve you at once."

In ten minutes another sergeant and four men arrived at the spot, and Tony and his companions returned to the camp.

As soon as Tony had devoured a piece of bread he left the camp, walked with careless gait through the camps behind, and went on until he reached a village in which were comparatively few soldiers. He went up to a woman who was standing at a door.

"Missus," he said, "I hab got a letter to take, and I ain't bery sure as to de name. Will you kindly tell me what is de address writ on dis paper?"

The woman looked at it.

"Mrs. Grossmith, Worley Farm, near Union. That's about two miles along the road. If you go on any one will tell you which is Mrs. Grossmith's."

Tony hurried on, for he wanted to get back to the camp before it was dark. He had no difficulty in finding Worley Farm.

"Now, then, what do you want?" its owner said sharply, as she opened the door in reply to his knock. "There's nothing for you here. You can look round if you like.

It's been all stripped clean days ago, so I tell you."

"Me no want anything, ma'am. Me hab a letter for you." The woman in surprise took the note and opened it. She read it through and looked earnestly at Tony.

"He says you are to be trusted," she said. "Is that so?"

"I would gib my life for him twenty times over," Tony replied. "He got me away from a brutal master and bought my wife out ob slavery for me. What does he say, ma'am? For de Lord sake tell me. Perhaps he tell me how to get him clar."

The woman read out the contents of the note.

"Dat's it, missus, sure enough; dat's the way," he exclaimed in delight. "Me tink and tink all day, and no manage to tink of anything except to shoot de sentry and fight wid de oders and get him out; but den all de oder sojers come running down, and no chance to escape. If me can get de spirits dat's easy enough. Me make dem all drunk as hogs."

"I can give you that," the woman said. "Is there anything else you will want? What are you going to do with him if you get him free? They will hunt you down like vermin."

"I tought we might get down to de river and get ober somehow. Dere will be no getting trou der cavalry. Dey will hab dem on every road."

"Well, you want some clothes, anyhow; you can't go about in these soldier clothes. The first Yank you came across would shoot you for a deserter, and the first of our men as a traitor. Well, by the time you get back to-night, that is if you do come back, I will get up a chest I've get buried with my men's clothes in it. They didn't want to take them away to the war with them, so I hid them up."

She had by this time dug up the keg from its hiding-place, and now filled Tony's canteen.

"Tank you, missus; de Lord bress you for what you've done, wheder I get Massa Wingfield off or wheder we bofe get killed ober de job. But I must get back as fast as I can. Ef it was dark before I got to camp dey would wonder whar I had been."

"Oh, you have plenty of time," the woman said; "it won't be dark till eight o'clock, and it's not seven yet. I will set to and boil a good chunk of pork and bake some cakes. It's no use getting out of the hands of the Yanks and then going and getting starved in the swamps."

Directly Tony got back to his regiment he strolled over to the shed where

Vincent was confined. Two sentinels were on duty, the sergeant and the two other men were lying at full length en the ground some twenty yards away. Their muskets were beside them, and it was evident to Tony by the vigilant watch that they kept upon the shed that their responsibility weighed heavily upon them and that Captain Pearce had impressed upon them that if the prisoner escaped they would certainly be shot.

"Well, Sergeant John Newson," Tony began, "I hab just walked ober to see how you getting on. It am a mighty 'sponsible business dis. I had six hours of him, and it make de perspiration run down my back to tink what a job it would be for me if dat fellow was to run away."

"Dat's just what dis chile feel, Sergeant Tony Morris; I am zactly like dat, and dat's what dese men feel too. We am all on guard. De captain say, put two on guard at de shed and let de oders relieb dem ebery hour. So dey shall; but dose off duty must watch just the same. When it gets dark we get close up, so as to be ready to jump in directly we hear a stir. Dis fellow no fool us."

"Dat's the way, Sergeant Newson, dat am de way. Neber close your eye, but keep a sharp look on dem. It's a pity dat you not in camp to-night."

"How am dat, how am dat?" the sergeant asked.

"To tell you de truf, sergeant, tree or four ob us hab smuggled in some spirits, and you are one of dose who would hab come in for a share of it if you had been dere."

"Golly!" the sergeant exclaimed; "but dat is bery unfortunate. Can't you manage to bring me a little here?"

"Well, you know, it's difficult to get out ob camp."

"Oh, you could get through. Dere is no fear about you being caught."

"I don't know," Tony replied with an air of reluctance. "Well, I will see about it. Ef I can crawl troo de sentries, and bring some for you and de oders, I will. It will help keep you awake and keep out de damp.

"Dat's right down good ob you," the other said cordially. "You good man, Tony Morris; and if I can do as much for you anoder time, I do it."

Having settled this, Tony went round to the hospital tent in rear of the regiment, having tied up his face with a handkerchief.

"Well, what is it, sergeant?" the negro, who acted as an orderly and sometimes helped the surgeon mix his drugs, asked. "De doctor am gone away, and I don't 'spect he come back again to-night."

"Dat am bery bad ting," Tony said dolefully. "Can't you do something for me, Sam Smith? I tink you know quite as much about de medicines as de doctor himself."

"Not quite so much, sergeant, not quite so much; but I'se no fool, and my old mother she 'used to make medicine for de plantation and knew a heap about herbs, so it am natural dat I should take to it. What can I gib you?"

"Well, Sam, you see sometimes I'se 'flicted dre'fful wid de faceache him just go jump, jump, jump, as ef he bust right up. Mose times I find de best ting am to put a little laudabun in my mouf, and a little on bit of rag and put him outside. De best ting would be for you to gib me little bottle of him; den when de pain come on I could jess take him, and not be troubling you ebery day. And Sam, jus you whisper--I got hold of a little good stuff. You gib me tin mug; me share what I hab got wid you."

The negro grinned with delight, and going into the tent brought out a tin mug.

"Dat's all right, Sam; but you hab no brought de bottle of laudabun too. You just fetch dat, and I gib you de spirit."

The negro went in again, and in two minutes returned with a small bottle of laudanum.

"Dat's a fair exchange," Tony said, taking it, and handing to the man his mug half full of spirit.

"Dat am someting like," the black said, looking with delight at the liberal allowance. "Me drink him de last ting at night, den me go to sleep and no one 'spect nuffin'. Whereber you get dat spirit?"

"Never you mind, Sam," Tony said with a grin. "Dar's more where dat comes from, and maybe you will get anoder taste ob it."

Then after leaving the hospital tent he poured half the spirits away, for he had not now to depend upon the effect of that alone; and it were better not to give it too strong, for that might arouse the suspicion of the guard. Then he uncorked the bottle of laudanum.

"I don't know how much to gib," he said to himself. "No good to kill dem. Me don't 'spect de stuff bery strong. Dese rogues sell all sorts of stuff to de government. Anyting good enough for de soldier. Dey gib him rotten boots, and rotten cloth, and bad powder, and all sorts of tings. I spect dey gib him bad drugs too. However, me must risk it. Dis bottle not bery big, anyhow--won't hold more dan two or three teaspoon. Must risk him."

So saying he poured the contents of the vial into the canteen, and then going to a water-cart filled it up. He waited until the camp was quiet, and then, taking off his boots and fastening in his belt his own bayonet and that of one of the men sleeping near, he quietly and cautiously made his way out of camp. There were no sentries placed here, for there was no fear whatever of an attack, and he had little difficulty in making his way round to the back of the village to the spot where Vincent was confined. He moved so quietly that he was not perceived until he was within a few yards of the shed.

"Sergeant Newson, am you dere?"

"Bress me, what a start you hab given me, for suah!" the sergeant said. "I did not hear you coming.

"You didn't s'pose I was coming along shouting and whistling, Sergeant Newson? Don't you talk so loud. Dar am no saying who's about."

"Hab you brought de stuff?"

"You don't suppose I should hab come all dis way to tell you I hab not got it. How am de prisoner?"

"Oh, he's dere all right. My orders was to look in at dat little winder ebery five minutes, and dat when it began to get dark me was to tie him quite tight, and me hab done so. And one of de sentries goes in every five minutes and feels to see if de ropes are tight. He am dar, sure enough."

"Dat's quite right, Sergeant Newson. I knew when you came to have me as de captain knew what he was doing when he choose you for dis job. He just pick out de man he considers de very best in de regiment. Now, here is de spirit; and fuss-rate stuff it am, too."

"Golly, but it am strong!" the sergeant said, taking a long gulp at the canteen. "Dat warm de cockles ob de heart in no time. Yes, it am good stuff--just de ting for dis damp air. I hear as a lot of de white soldiers are down wid de fever already, and dere will be lots and lots more if we stop here long. Here, you two men, take a drink of dis; but mind, you mustn't tell no one 'bout it. Dis a secret affair."

The two negroes each took a long drink, and returned the canteen with warm expressions of approval.

"De oder men are on duty," the sergeant said with the air of a man who knew his business; "dey mustn't hab none of it, not until dey comes off. As we are de relief, it am proper and right dat we drink a drop out of a canteen ef we want it."

"Quite so, Sergeant Newson," Tony said in a tone of admiration. "Dat's de way to manage dese tings--duty first and pleasure afterward."

"It am nearly time to relieve guard," the other said; "and den dey can have a drink."

In five minutes the two soldiers relieved those on guard, and they also took a long drink at the canteen, to which the sergeant also again applied his lips.

"Now I must be going," Tony said. "I will leave the canteen with you, sergeant. I have got some more of the stuff over there, and I dare say you will like another drink before morning."

So saying he stole away, but halted and lay down twenty yards distant. In ten minutes he heard the sergeant say:

"I feel as if I could do just five minutes' sleep. You keep your eyes on de shed, and ef you hear any officer coming his rounds you wake me up."

Tony waited another half-hour and then crawled up. The sergeant was lying on his back sound asleep; the two men with him were on their faces, with their rifles pointing toward the shed, as if they had dropped off to sleep while they were staring at it. Then he crawled on to the shed. The soldier on sentry at the back had grounded his musket and was leaning against the shed fast asleep, while the one at the door had apparently slid down in a sitting position and was snoring.

"I hope I haben't given it to dem too strong," Tony said to himself; "but it can't be helped anyhow."

He opened the door and entered the shed.

"Are you awake, Marse Wingfield?"

"Yes, I am awake, Tony. Thank God you have come! How did you manage it?"

"I hab managed it, sah, and dey are all fast asleep," Tony said, as he cut the ropes which bound Vincent.

"Now, sah, let's be going quick. Dar am no saying when dey may come round to look after de guards. Dat's what I hab been worrying about de last quarter ob an hour."

Vincent sprang to his feet as the ropes fell from him, and grasped Tony's hand.

"Here am a bayonet, sah. I hope we sha'n't want to use dem, but dar am no saying."

They made their way cautiously across the fields till they approached another camp. A few sentries were walking up and down in front of it, but they crawled round these and passed through the space between the regiment and that next to it. Several other camps were passed; and then, when Vincent knew that they were well in rear of the whole of them, they rose to their feet and started forward at a run. Suddenly Tony touched Vincent, and they both stood still. A distant shout came through the air, followed by another and another.

"I 'spect dey hab found out we have gone, sah. Dey go round two or tree times in de night to see dat de sentries are awake. Now, sah, come along."

They were on the road now, and ran at full speed until they approached Union. They left the track as they neared the village, and as they did so they heard the sound of a horse at full gallop behind them.

"That's an orderly taking the news of our escape. Sheridan's cavalry are scattered all over the country, and there are two squadrons at Union Grove. The whole country will be alive at daybreak."

Making their way through the fields they soon struck the track leading to Worley Farm, and in a few minutes were at the door. The woman opened it at once.

"I have been watching for you," she said, "and I am real glad you have got safe away. Wait a minute and I will strike a light."

"You had better not do that," Vincent said. "They have got the alarm at Union Grove already, and if any one caught sight of a light appearing in your window, it would bring them down here at once."

"They can't see the house from Union," the woman said. "Still, perhaps it will be best. Now, sir, I can't do anything for you, because my men's clothes are the same sort of cut as yours; but here's a suit for this man."

Thanking her warmly Vincent handed the things to Tony.

"Make haste and slip them on. Tony; and make your other things up into a bundle and bring them with you for a bit. We must leave nothing here, for they will search the whole country to-morrow. We will take the horse away too; not that we want it, but it would never do for it to be found here."

"Will you take your letter again?" the woman asked.

"No, I will leave it with you. It will be no use now if I get through, but if you hear to-morrow or next day that I am caught, please carry it as we arranged. What is this?" he asked as the woman handed him a bundle.

"Here are eight or ten pounds of pork," she said, "and some corn-cakes. If you are hiding away you will want something, and I reckon anyhow you won't be able to make your way to our people for a bit. Now, if you are ready I will start with you."

"You will start with us!" Vincent repeated in surprise.

"Certainly I will start with you," the woman said. "How do you think you would be able to find your way a dark night like this? No, sir; I will put you on your way till morning. But, in the first place, which line do you mean to take?"

"I do not think there is much chance of getting back the way we came," Vincent said. "By morning Sheridan's cavalry will have got a description of me, and they will be scouring the whole country. The only chance will be to go north and cross the river somewhere near Norfolk."

"I think, sah, you better go on wid your horse at once. No use wait for me. I come along on foot, find my own way."

"No, Tony, I shall certainly not do that. We will either get off or be taken together. Well, I think the best plan will be to go straight down to the river. How far is it away?"

"About fifteen miles," the woman said.

"If we got there we can get hold of a boat somehow, and either cross and then make straight for Richmond on foot, or go up the river in the boat and land in the rear of our lines. That we can settle about afterward. The first thing is to get to the river bank. We are not likely to meet with any interruption in that direction. Of course the cavalry are all on the other flank, and it will be supposed that I shall try either to work round that way or to make straight through the lines. They would hardly suspect that I shall take to the river, which is covered with their transports and store-ships."

"I think that is the best plan," the woman said. "There are scarce any villages between this and the river. It's only just when you cross the road between Petersburg and Williamsburg that you would be likely to meet a soul, even in the daytime. There is scarce even a farmhouse across this section. I know the country pretty well. Just stop a minute and I will run up to the wood and fetch down the horse. There's a big wood about a mile away, and you can turn him in there."

A few minutes later they started, Vincent leading the horse and Tony carrying the bundle of food and his castoff uniform. The woman led them by farm roads, sometimes turning off to the right or left, but keeping her way with a certainty which showed how well she was acquainted with the country. Several times they could hear the dull sound of bodies of cavalry galloping along the roads; but this died away as they got further into the country. The horse had been turned loose a mile from their starting place. Vincent removed the bridle and saddle, saying: "He will pick up enough to feed on here for some time. When he gets tired of the wood he can work his way out into a clearing."

Here Tony hid away his uniform among some thick bushes, and the three walked steadily along until the first tinge of daylight appeared on the sky. Then the woman stopped.

"The river is not more than half a mile in front of you," she said; "so I will say good-by."

"What will you do?" Vincent asked. "You might be questioned as you get near home."

"I am going to put up at the last house we passed," she said, "about three miles back. I know the people there, and they will take me in. I will stop there for a day or two, maybe, then walk back, so I shall have a true story to tell. That's all right."

Vincent said good-by to her, with many hearty thanks for the services she had rendered him, and had almost to force her to take notes for two hundred dollars from the bundle he had sewn up in the lining of his coat.

"You have saved my life," he said, "and some day I hope to be able to do more to show my gratitude; but you must take this anyhow to tide you over the hard times, and find food for your husband and sons when they come back from the war."

As soon as the woman had turned back Vincent and Tony continued on their way. The former had, as soon as they were fairly out from the Federal camp, told

Tony in a few words that his wife was safe at home and their boy flourishing, and he now gave him further details of them.

"And how came you to enter the army, Tony?"

"Well, sah, dere wasn't much choice about it. De Northern people, dey talk mighty high about der love for de negro, but I don't see much of it in der ways. Why, sah, dey is twice as scornful ob a black man as de gentleman is in de Souf. I list in de army, sah, because dey say dey go to Richmond, and den I find Dinah and de boy."

"Well, Tony, I little thought when I did you a service that it would be the means of you being able to save my life some day."

"Not much in dat, sah. You sabe my life, because dey would, for suah, hab caught me and killed me. Den you save my wife for me, den you pay out dat Jackson, and now you hab killed him. I could hab shouted for joy, sah, when I saw you hit him ober de head wid de shovel, and I saw dat dis time he gib no more trouble to no one. I should hab done for him bery soon, sah. I had my eye upon him, and the fust time we go into battle he get a ball in his back. Lucky he didn't see me. He not officer ob my company, and me look quite different in de uniform to what me was when I work on de plantation; but I know him, and wheneber I see him pass I hung down my head and I say to myself, 'My time come soon, Massa Jackson; my time come bery soon, and den we get quits.'"

"It is wrong to nourish revenge, Tony; but I really can't blame you very much as to that fellow. Still, I should have blamed you if you had killed him--blamed you very much. He was a bad man, and he treated you brutally, but you see he has been already punished a good deal."

"Yes, you knock him down, sah. Dat bery good, but not enough for Tony."

"But that wasn't all, Tony. You see, the affair set all my friends against him, and his position became a very unpleasant one. Then, you see, if it hadn't been for you he would probably have got through to our lines again after he had escaped with me. Then, you see, his father, out of revenge, stole Dinah away."

"Stole Dinah!" Tony exclaimed, stopping in his work. "Why, sah, you hab been telling me dat she is safe and well wid Mrs. Wingfield."

"So she is, Tony. But he stole her for all that, and had her carried down into Carolina; but I managed to bring her back. It's a long story, but I will tell you about it presently. Then the knowledge that I had found Dinah, and the fear of punishment for his share of taking her away, caused old Jackson to fly from the country, getting less than a quarter of the sum his estate would have fetched two or three years ago. That was what made him and his son turn Unionists. So, you see, Jackson was heavily punished for his conduct to you, and it did not need for you to revenge yourself."

"So he was, sah, so he was," Tony said thoughtfully. "Yes, it does seem as if all dese tings came on kinder one after de oder just out ob dat flogging he gabe me; and now he has got killed for just de same cause, for if he hadn't been obliged to turn Unionist he wouldn't have been in dat dar battery at de time you came dere. Yes, I sees dat is so, sah; and I'se glad now I didn't hab a chance ob shooting him down, for I should have done so for suah ef I had."

They had now reached the river. The sun was just showing above the horizon, and the broad sheet of water was already astir. Steamers were making their way up from the mouth of the river laden with stores for the army. Little tugs were hurrying to and fro. Vessels that had discharged their cargo were dropping down with the tide, while many sailing-vessels lay at anchor waiting for the turn of tide to make their way higher up. Norfolk was, however, the base from which the Federal army drew the larger portion of its stores; as there were great conveniences for landing here, and a railway thence ran up to the rear of their lines. But temporary wharfs and stages had been erected at the point of the river nearest to their camps in front of Petersburg, and here the cattle and much of the stores required for the army were landed. At the point at which Vincent and Tony had struck the river the banks were somewhat low. Here and there were snug farms, with the ground cultivated down to the river. The whole country was open and free from trees, except where small patches had been left. It was in front of one of these that Vincent and Tony were now standing.

"I do not think there is any risk of pursuit now, Tony. This is not the line on which they will be hunting us. The question is--how are we to get across?"

"It's too far to swim, sah."

"I should think it was," Vincent said with a laugh. "It's three or four miles, I should say, if it's a foot. The first question is--where are we to get a boat? I should think that some of these farmhouses are sure to have boats, but the chances are they have been seized by the Yankees long ago. Still they may have some laid up. The Yanks would not have made much search for those, though they would no doubt take all the larger boats for the use of the troops or for getting stores ashore. Anyhow, I will go to the next farmhouse and ask."

"Shall I go, sah?"

"No, Tony, they would probably take you for a runaway. No, I will go. There can be no danger. The men are all away, and the women are sure to be loyal. I fancy the few who were the other way before will have changed their minds since the Yanks landed."

They followed the bank of the river for a quarter of a mile, and then Vincent walked on to a small farmhouse standing on the slope fifty yards from the water. Two or three children who were playing about outside at once ran in upon seeing a stranger, and a moment later two women came out. They were somewhat reassured when they saw Vincent approaching alone.

"What is it, stranger?" one of them asked. "Do you want a meal? We have got little enough to offer you, but what there is you are welcome to; the Yanks have driven off our cows and pigs and the two horses, and have emptied the barns, and pulled up all the garden stuff, and stole the fowls, and carried off the bacon from the beams, so we have got but an empty larder. But as far as bread and molasses go, you are welcome."

"Thank you," Vincent said; "I am not in want of food. What I am in want of is a boat."

"Boat!" the women repeated in surprise.

"Yes, I want to got across to the other side, or else to get up the river and land between Petersburg and Bermuda."

"Sakes alive!" the woman exclaimed; "what do you want to do that for?"

"I will tell you," Vincent replied. "I know I can trust my life to any woman in the Confederacy. I am one of General Wade Hampton's officers, and I have come through their lines to find out what they are doing. I have been caught once, but managed to slip through their hands, but there is no possibility of making my way back across the country, for the Yankee cavalry are patrolling every road, and the only chance I have is of getting away by boat."

"Step right in, sir," the woman said. "It's a real pleasure to us to have one of our officers under our roof."

"I have a friend with me," Vincent said; "a faithful negro, who has helped me to escape, and who would be hung like a dog if they could lay hands on him."

"Bring him in, sir," the woman said hospitably. "I had four or five niggers till the Yanks came, but they all ran away 'cause they knew they would either be set to work or made to fight; so they went. They said they would come back again when the trouble is over; maybe they will and maybe they won't. At first the niggers about here used to look for the Yanks coming, but as the news got about of what happened to those they took from their masters, they concluded they were better off where they were. Call your boy in, sir; call him in."

Vincent gave a shout, and Tony at once came up.

"Thank you, we don't want anything to eat," Vincent went on as the woman began to put some plates on the table. "We have just had a hearty meal, and have got enough food for three or four days in that bundle. But we want a boat, or, if we can't find that, some sailors' clothes. If I had them I would keep along the river down to Norfolk. The place will be full of sailors. We should not be likely to be noticed there."

"I can't help you in that," the woman said; "but there are certainly some boats laid up along the shore. Now, Maria, who has got boats that haven't been taken?"

"I expect the Johnsons have got one," the other woman replied. "They had a small boat the boys and girls used to go out fishing in. I don't think the Yanks have got that. I expect they hid it away somewhere; but I don't know as they would let you have it. She is a close-fisted woman is Sarah Johnson."

"I could pay her for its value," Vincent said.

"Oh, well, if you could pay her she would let you have it. I don't say she wouldn't, anyhow, seeing as you are an officer, and the Yanks are after you. Still, she is close is Sarah Johnson, and I don't know as she is so set on the Confederacy as most people. I tell you what I will do, sir. I will go down and say as a stranger wants to buy her boat, and no questions asked. She is just to show where the boat is hidden, and you are to pay for it and take it away when you want it."

"That would be a very good plan," Vincent said, "if you wouldn't mind the trouble."

"The trouble is nothing," she said. "Johnson's place ain't above a mile along the shore."

"I will go with you until you get close to the house," Vincent said; "then, when you hear what she wants for the boat, I will give you the money for it, and you can show me where it is hidden."

This was accordingly done. Mrs. Johnson, after a considerable amount of bargaining with Vincent's guide, agreed to take twenty dollars for the boat, and upon receiving the money sent down one of her boys with her to show her where it was hidden. It was in a hole that had been scooped out in the steep bank some ten foot above the water's edge, and was completely hidden from the sight of any one rowing past by a small clump of bushes. When the boys had returned to the farmhouse the woman took Vincent to the spot, and they then went back together.

Here he and Tony had a long talk as to whether it would be better to put out at once or to wait till nightfall. It was finally determined that it was best to make an immediate start. A boat rowed by two men would attract little attention. It might belong to any of the ships at anchor in the river, and might be supposed to have gone on shore to fetch eggs or chickens, or with a letter or a message.

"You see, both shores are in the hands of the Yankees," Vincent said, "and there will not be any suspicion of a boat in the daytime. At night we might be hailed, and if we gave no answer fired upon, and that night bring a gunboat along to see what was the matter. No, I think it will be far best to go on boldly. There are not likely to be any bodies of Federal troops on the opposite shore except at Fortress Monroe, and perhaps opposite the point where they have got their landing below Petersburg. Once ashore we shall be safe. The peninsula opposite is covered with forest and swamp, and we shall have no difficulty in getting through however many troops they may have across it. You know the place pretty well, don't you, Tony?"

Tony nodded. "Once across, sah, all de Yank army wouldn't catch us. Me know ob lots ob hiding-places."

"Them broad hats will never do," the woman said; "but I have got some blue nightcaps I knitted for my husband. They are something like the caps I have seen some sailors wear; anyhow, they will pass at a distance, and when you take your coats and vests off, them colored flannel shirts will be just the right thing."

"That will do capitally, and the sooner we are off the better," Vincent said, and after heartily thanking the two women, and bestowing a present upon each of the children, they started along the shore.

The boat was soon got into the water, the oars put out, and they started. The tide was just low now, and they agreed to pull along at a short distance from the shore until it turned. As soon as it did so the vessels at anchor would be getting up sail to make up to the landing-place, and even had any one on board noticed the boat put out, and had been watching it, they would have other things to think about.

"It is some time since we last rowed in a boat together, Tony."

"About three years, sah; dat time when you got me safe away. I had a bad fright dat day you left me, sah. It came on to blow bery hard, and some ob de men told me dat dey did not tink you would ever get back to shore. Dat made me awful bad, sah; and me wish ober and ober again dat me hab died in de forest instead ob your taking me off in a boat and trowing away your life. I neber felt happy again, sah, till I got your letter up in Canady, and knew you had got back safe dat day."

"We had a narrow squeak of it, Tony, and were blown some distance up. We were nearly swamped a score of times, and Dan quite made up his mind that it was all up with us. However, we got through safe, and I don't think a soul, except perhaps Jackson and that rascally overseer of ours, who afterward had a hand in carrying off your wife, and lost his life in consequence, ever had a suspicion we had been doing more than a long fishing expedition. I will tell you all about it when we are going through the woods. Now I think it's pretty nearly dead water, and we will begin to edge across."

## CHAPTER XX. THE END OF THE STRUGGLE.

VINCENT directed his course so that while the boat's head was still pointing up the stream, and she was apparently moving in the same direction as the ships, she was gradually getting out to the middle of the river. Had he tried to row straight across suspicion might at once have been excited. In half an hour they were in the middle of the stream. A vessel passing under full sail swept along at a distance of a hundred yards, and they were hailed. Vincent merely waved his hand and continued his course.

"I dare say those fellows wonder what we are up to, Tony; but they are not likely to stop to inquire. In another quarter of an hour we shall be pretty safe. Ah! there's a fellow who might interfere with us," he added looking round. "Do you see that little black thing two miles ahead of us? that's a steam launch. If she sees us making over she's likely enough to come and ask us some questions. We had better head a little more toward the shore now. If it comes to a race every foot is of importance."

Up to now they had been rowing in an easy and leisurely manner, avoiding all appearance of haste. They now bent to their oars, and the boat began to travel a good deal faster through the water. Vincent glanced over his shoulder frequently at the steam launch.

"She is keeping straight on in the middle of the channel, Tony; evidently she hasn't noticed us yet."

Ten minutes after passing the ship he exclaimed sharply:

"Row, Tony, as hard as you can; the launch has just passed that ship, and has changed her course. I expect the captain has called their attention to us. It's a race now."

The boat, at the moment the launch changed her course, was rather more than halfway between the center of the channel and the shore. The launch was in the center of the channel, and three-quarters of a mile higher up. She had evidently put on steam as she started to cut off the boat, for there was now a white wave at her bow.

"I think we shall do it, Tony," Vincent said. "I don't suppose she can go above eight miles an hour and we are certainly going four, and she has more than twice as far to travel as we have."

Those on board the launch were evidently conscious that they were likely to lose the race, for in a few minutes they began to open fire with their rifles.

"Fire away," Vincent said. "You ain't likely to hit us a thousand yards off, and we haven't another three hundred to row."

The bullets whistled overhead, but none of them struck the water within many yards of the boat, and the launch was still four or five hundred yards away when the bow of the boat touched the shore. Several muskets were discharged as Vincent and Tony leaped out and plunged into the bushes that came down to the water's edge. The launch sent up a sharp series of whistles, and random shots were for some time fired into the bushes.

"It is lucky she didn't carry a small gun in her bow," Vincent said; "for though seven or eight hundred yards is a long range for a rifle, they might likely enough have hit us if they had had a gun. Now, Tony, we shall have to be careful, for those whistles are no doubt meant as an alarm; and although she cannot tell who we are, she will probably steam up, and if they have any force opposite Bermuda will give them news that two suspicious characters have landed, and they will have parties out to look for us."

"Dey can look as long as dey like, sah. Ef dose slave-hunters can't find people in de swamps what chance you tink dose soldiers have? None at all. Dey haven't got no reward before dere eyes, and dey won't want to be going in ober dere shoes into de mud and dirtying dere uniforms. No fear ob dem, sah. Dey make as much noise when dey march in de wood as a drove ob pigs. You can hear dem a quarter ob a mile away."

They tramped on through the woods through which McClellan's force had so painfully made their way during their first advance against Richmond. From time to time they could hear noises in the forest--shouts, and once or twice the discharge of firearms.

"Dey call dat hunting, I s'pose," Tony said scornfully.

They kept steadily on until it began to grow dark in the forest. They were now in the White Oak Swamp and not eight miles from Richmond, and they thought it better to pause until it became quite dark, for they might be picked up by any raiding party of cavalry. Vincent was in high spirits. Now, that he had succeeded in his enterprise, and had escaped almost by a miracle, he was eager to get back to Richmond and carry his news down to General Lee. Tony was even more anxious to push on. At last, after three years' absence, he was to see his wife and child again, and he reluctantly agreed to Vincent's proposal for a halt.

"We sha'n't stop very long, Tony; and I own I am waiting quite as much because I am hungry and want to eat, and because I am desperately tired, as from any fear of the enemy. We walked twenty miles last night from Union Grove to the river, then I walked to the boat, back to the farm and then back to the boat again-- that's three more miles--and we have gone another twenty now. I am pretty nearly dead beat, I can tell you."

"I'se tired too, sah; but I feel I could go on walking all night if I was to see Dinah in de morning."

"Well, I couldn't, Tony; not to see any one. I might be willing enough, but my legs wouldn't take me."

They ate a hearty meal, and almost as soon as they had finished Vincent stood up again.

"Well, Tony, I can feel for your impatience, and so we will struggle on. I have just been thinking that when I last left my mother a week since she said she was thinking of going out to the Orangery for a month before the leaves fell, so it is probable that she may be there now. It is only about the same distance as it is to Richmond, so we will go straight there. I shall lose a little time, of course; but I can be driven over to Richmond, so it won't be too much. Besides, I can put on a pair of slippers. That will be a comfort, for my feet feel as if they were in vises. A cup of tea won't be a bad thing, too."

During their walk through the wood Vincent had related the circumstances of the carrying away of Dinah and of her rescue. When he had finished Tony had said:

"Well, Massa Wingfield, I don't know what to say to you. I tought I owed you enuff before, but it war nothing to dis. Just to tink dat you should take all dat pains to fetch Dinah back for me. I dunno how it came to you to do it. It seems to me like as if you been sent special from heben to do dis poor nigger good. Words ain't no good, sah; but of I could give my life away a hundred times for you I would do it."

It took them nearly three hours' walking before they came in sight of the Orangery.

"There are lights in the windows," Vincent said. "Thank goodness they are there."

Vincent limped slowly along until he reached the house.

"You stay out here, Tony. I will send Dinah out to you directly. It will be better for her to meet you here alone."

Vincent walked straight into the drawing-room, where his mother and Annie were sitting.

"Why, Vincent!" Mrs. Wingfield exclaimed, starting up, "what has happened to you? What are you dressed up like that for? Is anything the matter?"

"Nothing is the matter, mother, except that I am as tired as a dog. Yes, my dress is not quite fit for a drawing-room," he laughed, looking down at the rough trousers splashed with mud to the waist, and his flannel shirt, for they had not waited to pick up their coats as they left the boat; "but nothing is the matter, I can assure you. I will tell you about it directly, but first please send for Dinah here."

Mrs. Wingfield rang the bell on the table beside her.

"Tell Dinah I want to speak to her at once," she said to the girl that answered it. Dinah appeared in a minute.

"Dinah," Vincent said, "has your boy gone to bed?"

"Yes, sah; been gone an hour ago."

"Well, just go to him, and put a shawl round him, and go out through the front door. There is some one standing there you will be glad to see."

Dinah stood with open eyes, then her hands began to tremble.

"Is it Tony, sah; for de Lord's sake, is it Tony?"

Vincent nodded, and with a little scream of joy she turned and ran straight to the front door. She could not wait now even to fetch her boy, and in another moment she was clasped in her husband's arms.

"Now, Vincent, tell us all about it," his mother said. "Don't you see we are dying of curiosity?"

"And I am dying of fatigue," Vincent said; "which is a much more painful sort of death, and I can think of nothing else until I have got these boots off. Annie, do run and tell them to bring me a pair of slippers and a cup of tea, and I shall want the buggy at the door in half an hour."

"You are not going away again to-night, Vincent, surely?" his mother said anxiously. "You do look completely exhausted."

"I am exhausted, mother. I have walked seven or eight-and-forty miles, and this cavalry work spoils one for walking altogether."

"Walked forty-eight miles, Vincent! What on earth have you done that for?"

"Not from choice, I can assure you, mother; but you know the old saying, 'Needs must when the devil drives,' and in the present case you must read 'Yankee' instead of 'the gentleman in black.'"

"But has Petersburg fallen?" Mrs. Wingfield asked in alarm.

"No; Petersburg is safe, and is likely to continue so. But you must really be patient, mother, until I have had some tea, then you can hear the story in full."

When the servant came in with the tea Vincent told her that she was to tell Dinah, whom she would find on the veranda, to bring her husband into the kitchen, and to give him everything he wanted. Then, as soon as he had finished tea, he told his mother and sister the adventures he had gone through. Both were crying when he had finished.

"I am proud of you, Vincent," his mother said. "It is hard on us that you should run such risks; still I do not blame you, my boy, for if I had ten sons I would give them all for my country."

Vincent had but just finished his story when the servant came in and said that the buggy was at the door.

"I will go in my slippers, mother, but I will run up and change my other things. It's lucky I have got a spare suit here. Any of our fellows who happened to be going down to-night in the train would think that I was mad were I to go like this."

It was one o'clock in the morning when Vincent reached Petersburg. He went straight to his quarters, as it would be no use waking General Lee at that hour. A light was burning in his room, and Dan was asleep at the table with his head on his arms. He leaped up with a cry of joy as his master entered.

"Well, Dan, here I am safe again," Vincent said cheerily. "I hope you had not begun to give me up."

"I began to be terribly frightened, sir--terribly frightened. I went dis afternoon and asked Captain Burley if he had any news ob you. He said 'No;' and asked me ef I knew where you were. I said 'No, sah;' that I knew nuffin about it except that you had gone on some dangerous job. He said he hoped that you would be back soon; and certainly, as far as dey had heard, nuffin had happened to you. Still I was bery anxious, and tought I would sit up till de last train came in from Richmond. Den I tink I dropped off to sleep."

"I think you did, Dan. Well, I am too tired to tell you anything about it now, but I have one piece of news for you; Tony has come back to his wife."

"Dat's good news, sah; bery good news. I had begun to be afraid dat Tony had been shot or hung or someting. I know Dinah hab been fretting about him though she never said much, but when I am at home she allus asks me all sorts of questions 'bout him. She bery glad woman now."

The next morning Vincent went to General Lee's quarters.

"I am heartily glad to see you back," the general said warmly as he entered. "I have blamed myself for letting you go. Well, what success have you had?"

"Here is a rough plan of the works, general. I have not had time to do it out fairly, but it shows the positions of all their principal batteries, with a rough estimate as to the number of guns that each is intended to carry."

"Excellent!" the general said, glancing over the plan. "This will give us exactly the information we want. We must set to with our counter-works at once. The country is indeed indebted to you, sir. So you managed to cheat the Yankees altogether?"

"I should have cheated them, sir; but unfortunately I came across an old acquaintance who denounced me, and I had a narrow escape of being shot."

"Well, Captain Wingfield, I must see about this business, and give orders at once. Will you come and breakfast with me at half-past eight? Then you can give me an account of your adventures."

Vincent returned to his quarters, and spent the next two hours in making a detailed drawing of the enemy's positions and batteries, and then at half-past eight walked over to General Lee's quarters. The general returned in a few minutes with

General Wade Hampton and several other officers, and they at once sat down to breakfast. As the meal was proceeding an orderly entered with a telegram for the general. General Lee glanced through it.

"This, gentlemen, is from the minister of war. I acquainted him by telegraph this morning that Captain Wingfield, who had volunteered for the dangerous service, had just returned from the Federal lines with a plan of the positions and strength of all the works that they are erecting. I said that I trusted that such distinguished service as he had rendered would be at once rewarded with promotion, and the minister telegraphs to me now that he has this morning signed this young officer's commission as major. I heartily congratulate you, sir, on your well-earned step. And now, as I see you have finished your breakfast, perhaps, you will give us an account of your proceedings."

Vincent gave a detailed account of his adventures, which were heard with surprise and interest.

"That was a narrow escape, indeed," the general said, as he finished. "It was a marvelous thing your lighting upon this negro, whom you say you had once had an opportunity of serving, just at that moment; and although you do not tell us what was the nature of the service you had rendered him, it must have been a very considerable service or he would never have risked his life in that way to save yours. When these negroes do feel attachment for their masters there are no more faithful and devoted fellows. Well, in your case certainly a good action has met with its reward; if it had not been for him there could be no question that your doom was sealed. It is a strange thing too your meeting that traitor. I remember reading about that escape of yours from the Yankee prison. He must have been an ungrateful villain, after your taking him with you."

"He was a bad fellow altogether, I am afraid," Vincent said; "and the quarrel between us was a long-standing one."

"Whatever your quarrel was," the general said hotly, "a man who would betray even an enemy to death in that way is a villain. However, he has gone to his account, and the country can forgive his treachery to her, as I have no doubt you have already done his conduct toward yourself."

A short time afterward Vincent had leave for a week, as things were quiet at Petersburg.

"Mother," he said on the morning after he got home, "I fear that there is no doubt whatever now how this struggle will end. I think we might keep Grant at bay here, but Sherman is too strong for us down in Georgia. We are already cut off from most of the Southern States, and in time Sherman will sweep round here, and then it will be all over. You see it yourself, don't you, mother?"

"Yes, I am afraid it cannot continue much longer, Vincent. Well, of course, we shall fight to the end."

"I am not talking of giving up, mother; I am looking forward to the future. The first step will be that all the slaves will be freed. Now, it seems to me that however attached they may be to their masters and mistresses they will lose their heads over this, flock into the towns, and nearly starve there; or else take up little patches of land and cultivate them, and live from hand to mouth, which will be ruin to the present owners as well as to them. Anyhow for a time all will be confusion and disorder. Now, my idea is this, if you give all your slaves their freedom at once, offer them patches of land for their own cultivation and employ them at wages, you will find that a great many of them will stop with you. There is nowhere for them to go at present and nothing to excite them, so before the general crash comes they will have settled down quietly to work here in their new positions, and will not be likely to go away."

"It is a serious step to take, Vincent," Mrs. Wingfield said, after thinking the matter over in silence for some time. "You do not think there is any probability of the ultimate success of our cause?"

"None, mother; I do not think there is even a possibility. One by one the Southern States have been wrested from the Confederacy. Sherman's march will completely isolate us. We have put our last available man in the field, and tremendous as are the losses of the enemy they are able to fill up the gaps as fast as they are made. No, mother, do not let us deceive ourselves on that head. The end must come, and that before long. The slaves will unquestionably be freed, and the only question for us is how to soften the blow. There is no doubt that our slaves, both at the Orangery and at the other plantations, are contented and happy; but you know how fickle and easily led the negroes are, and in the excitement of finding themselves free and able to go where they please, you may be sure that the greater number will wander away. My proposal is, that we should at once mark out a plot of land for each family and tell them that as long as they stay here it is theirs rent-free; they will be paid for their work upon the estate, three, four, or five days a week, as they can spare time from their own plots. In this way they will be settled down, and have crops upon their plots of land, before the whole black population is upset by the sudden abolition of slavery."

"But supposing they won't work at all, even for wages, Vincent?"

"I should not give them the option, mother; it will be a condition of their having their plots of land free that they shall work at least three days a week for wages."

"I will think over what you say, Vincent, and tell you my decision in the morning. I certainly think your plan is a good one."

The next morning Mrs. Wingfield told Vincent that she had decided to adopt his plan. He at once held a long consultation with the overseer, and decided which fields should be set aside for the allotments, choosing land close to the negroes' quarters and suitable for the raising of vegetables for sale in the town.

In the afternoon Mrs. Wingfield went down with him. The bell was rung and the whole of the slaves assembled. Vincent then made them a speech. He began by reminding them of the kind treatment they had always received, and of the good feeling that had existed between the owners of the Orangery and their slaves. He praised them for their good conduct since the beginning of the troubles, and said that his mother and himself had agreed that they would now take steps to reward them, and to strengthen the tie between them. They would all be granted their freedom at once, and a large plot of land would be given to each man, as much as he and his family could cultivate with an average of two days a week steady labor.

Those who liked would, of course, be at liberty to leave; but he hoped that none of them would avail themselves of this freedom, for nowhere would they do so well as by accepting the offer he made them. All who accepted the offer of a plot of land rent-free must understand that it was granted them upon the condition that they would labor upon the estate for at least three days a week, receiving a rate of pay similar to that earned by other freed negroes. Of course they would be at liberty to work four or five days a week if they chose; but at least they must work three days and any one failing to do this would forfeit his plot of land. "Three days' work," he said, "will be sufficient to provide all necessaries for yourselves and families and the produce of your land you can sell, and will so be able to lay by an ample sum to keep yourselves in old age. I have already plotted out the land and you shall cast lots for choice of the plots. There will be a little delay before all your papers of freedom can be made out, but the arrangement will begin from to-day, and henceforth you will be paid for all labor done on the estate."

Scarcely a word was spoken when Vincent concluded. The news was too surprising to the negroes for them to be able to understand it all at once. Dan and Tony, to whom Vincent had already explained the matter, went among them, and they gradually took in the whole of Vincent's meaning. A few received the news with great joy, but many others were depressed rather than rejoiced at the responsibilities of their new positions. Hitherto they had been clothed and fed, the doctor attended them in sickness, their master would care for them in old age. They had been literally without a care for the morrow, and the thought that in future they would have to think of all these things for themselves almost frightened them. Several of the older men went up to Mrs. Wingfield and positively declined to accept their freedom. They were quite contented and happy, and wanted nothing more. They had worked on the plantation since they had been children, and freedom offered them no temptations whatever.

"What had we better do, Vincent?" Mrs. Wingfield asked.

"I think, mother, it will be best to tell them that all who wish can remain upon the old footing, but that their papers will be made out and if at any time they wish to have their freedom they will only have to say so. No doubt they will soon become accustomed to the idea, and seeing how comfortable the others are with their pay and the produce of their gardens they will soon fall in with the rest. Of course it will decrease the income from the estate, but not so much as you would think. They will be paid for their labor, but we shall have neither to feed nor clothe them; and I think we shall get better labor than we do now, for the knowledge that those who do not work steadily will lose their plots of land, and have to go out in the world to work, their places being filled by others, will keep them steady."

"It's an experiment, Vincent, and we shall see how it works."

"It's an experiment I have often thought I should like to make, mother, and now you see it is almost forced upon us. To-morrow I will ride over to the other plantations and make the same arrangements."

During the month of August many battles took place round Petersburg. On the 12th the Federals attacked, but were repulsed with heavy loss, and 2,500 prisoners were taken. On the 21st the Confederates attacked, and obtained a certain amount of success, killing, wounding, and capturing 2,400 men. Petersburg was shelled day and night, and almost continuous fighting went on. Nevertheless, up to the middle of October the positions of the armies remained unaltered. On the 27th of that month the Federals made another general attack, but were repulsed with a loss of 1,500 men. During the next three months there was little fighting, the Confederates having now so strengthened their lines by incessant toil that even General Grant, reckless of the lives of his troops as he was, hesitated to renew the assault.

But in the South General Sherman was carrying all before him. Generals Hood and Johnston, who commanded the Confederate armies there, had fought several desperate battles, but the forces opposed to them were too strong to be driven back. They had marched through Georgia to Atlanta and captured that important town on the 1st of September, and obtained command of the network of railways, and thus cut off a large portion of the Confederacy from Richmond. Then Sherman marched south, wasting the country through which he marched, and capturing Savannah on the 21st of September.

While he was so doing, General Hood had marched into Tennessee, and after various petty successes was defeated, after two days' hard fighting, near Nashville. In the third week in January, 1865, Sherman set out with 60,000 infantry and 10,000 cavalry from Savannah, laying waste the whole country--burning, pillaging, and destroying. The town of Columbia was occupied, sacked, and burned, the white men and women and even the negroes being horribly ill-treated.

The Confederates evacuated Charleston at the approach of the enemy, setting it in flames rather than allow it to fall into Sherman's hands. The Federal army then continued its devastating route through South Carolina, and at the end of March had established itself at Goldsboro, in North Carolina, and was in readiness to aid Grant in his final attack on Richmond.

Lee, seeing the imminence of the danger, made an attack upon the enemy in front of Petersburg, but was repulsed. He had now but 37,000 men with which to oppose an enemy of nearly four times that strength in front of him, while Sheridan's cavalry, 10,000 strong, threatened his flank, and Sherman with his army was but a few days' march distant. There was fierce fighting on the 29th, 30th, and 31st of March, and on the 2d of April the whole Federal army assaulted the positions at Petersburg, and after desperate fighting succeeded in carrying them. The Confederate troops, outnumbered and exhausted as they were by the previous week's marching and fighting, yet retained their discipline, and Lee drew off with 20,000 men and marched to endeavor to effect a junction with Johnston, who was still facing Sherman. But his men had but one day's provision with them. The stores that he had ordered to await them at the point to which he directed his march had not arrived there when they reached it, and, harassed at every foot of their march by Sheridan's cavalry and Ord's infantry, the force fought its way on. The horses and mules were so weak from want of food that they were unable to drag the guns, and the men dropped in numbers from fatigue and famine. Sheridan and Ord cut off two corps, but General Lee, with but 8,000 infantry and 2,000 cavalry, still pressed forward toward Lynchburg. But Sheridan threw himself in the way, and, finding that no more could be done, General Lee and the infantry surrendered, and a few days later Generals Lee and Grant met and signed terms of peace. General Johnston's army surrendered to General Sherman, and the long and desperate struggle was at an end.

It was a dreadful day in Richmond when the news came that the lines of Petersburg were forced, and that General Lee no longer stood between the city and the invaders. The president and ministers left at once, and were followed by all the better class of inhabitants who could find means of conveyance. The negroes, Irish, and some of the lower classes at once set to work to pillage and burn, and the whole city would have been destroyed had not a Federal force arrived and at once suppressed the rioting.

Whatever had been the conduct of the Federal troops during the last year of the war, however great the suffering they had inflicted upon the unarmed and innocent population of the country through which they marched, the terms of peace that General Grant agreed upon, and which were, although with some reluctance, ratified by the government, were in the highest degree liberal and generous. No one was to be injured or molested for the share he had taken in the war. A general amnesty was granted to all, and the States were simply to return to the position in the Union that they occupied previous to the commencement of the struggle.

More liberal terms were never granted by a conqueror to the vanquished.

Vincent was with the cavalry who escaped prior to Lee's surrender, but as soon as the terms of peace were ratified the force was disbanded and he returned home. He was received with the deepest joy by his mother and sister.

"Thank God, my dear boy, that all is over, and you have been preserved to us. We are beaten, but no one can say that we have been disgraced. Had every State done its duty as Virginia has we should never have been overpowered. It has been a terrible four years, and there are few families indeed that have no losses to mourn."

"It was well you were not in Richmond, mother, the day of the riots."

"Yes; but we had our trouble here too, Vincent. A number of the slaves from some of the plantations came along this way, and wanted our hands to join them to burn down their quarters and the house, and to march to Richmond. Tony and Dan, hearing of their approach, armed themselves with your double-barreled guns, went down and called out the hands and armed them with hoes and other implements. When the negroes came up there was a desperate quarrel, but our hands stood firm, and Tony and Dan declared that they would shoot the first four men that advanced, and at last they drew off and made their way to Richmond.

"Your plan has succeeded admirably. One or two of the hands went to Richmond next day, but returned a day or two afterward and begged so hard to be taken on again that I forgave them. Since then everything has been going on as quietly and regularly as usual, while there is scarcely a man left on any of the estates near."

"And now, mother, that I find things are quiet and settled here, I shall go down to Georgia and fetch Lucy home. I shall be of age in a few months, and the house on the estate that comes to me then can be enlarged a bit, and will do very well."

"Not at all, Vincent. Annie will be married next month. Herbert Rowsell was here two days ago, and it's all settled. So I shall be alone here. It will be very lonely and dull for me, Vincent, and I would rather give up the reins of government to Lucy and live here with you, if you like the plan."

"Certainly, I should like it, mother, and so, I am sure, would Lucy."

"Well, at any rate, Vincent, we will try the experiment, and if it does not work well I will take possession of the other house."

"There is no fear of that, mother, none whatever."

"And when are you thinking of getting married, Vincent?"

"At once, mother. I wrote to her the day we were disbanded saying that I should come in a week, and would allow another week and no longer for her to get ready."

"Then, in that case, Vincent, Annie and I will go down with you. Annie will not have much to do to get ready for her own wedding. It must, of course, be a very quiet one, and there will be no array of dresses to get; for I suppose it will be some time yet before the railways are open again and things begin to come down from the North."

Happily Antioch had escaped the ravages of war, and there was nothing to mar the happiness of the wedding. Lucy's father had returned, having lost a leg in one of the battles of the Wilderness a year before, and her brother had also escaped. After the wedding they returned to their farm in Tennessee, and Mrs. Wingfield, Annie, Vincent, and Lucy went back to the Orangery.

For the next three or four years times were very hard in Virginia, and Mrs. Wingfield had to draw upon her savings to keep up the house in its former state; while the great majority of the planters were utterly ruined.

The negroes, however, for the most part remained steadily working on the estate. A few wandered away, but their places were easily filled; for the majority of the freed slaves very soon discovered that their lot was a far harder one than it had been before, and that freedom so suddenly given was a curse rather than a blessing to them.

Thus, while so many went down, the Wingfields weathered the storm, and the step that had been taken in preparing their hands for the general abolition of slavery was a complete success.

With the gradual return of prosperity to the South the prices of produce improved, and ten years after the conclusion of the rebellion the income of the Orangery was nearly as large as it had been previous to its outbreak. Vincent, two years after the conclusion of the struggle, took his wife over to visit his relations in England, and, since the death of his mother in 1879, has every year spent three or four months at home, and will not improbably ere long sell his estates in Virginia and settle in England altogether.

www.bookjungle.com *email: sales@bookjungle.com fax: 630-214-0564 mail: Book Jungle  PO Box 2226  Champaign, IL 61825*

### The Codes Of Hammurabi And Moses
### W. W. Davies

The discovery of the Hammurabi Code is one of the greatest achievements of archaeology, and is of paramount interest, not only to the student of the Bible, but also to all those interested in ancient history...

**Religion**   **ISBN:** *1-59462-338-4*   **Pages:** 132   *MSRP $12.95*   QTY

### The Theory of Moral Sentiments
### Adam Smith

This work from 1749. contains original theories of conscience amd moral judgment and it is the foundation for systemof morals.

**Philosophy**   **ISBN:** *1-59462-777-0*   **Pages:** 536   *MSRP $19.95*   QTY

### Jessica's First Prayer
### Hesba Stretton

In a screened and secluded corner of one of the many railway-bridges which span the streets of London there could be seen a few years ago, from five o'clock every morning until half past eight, a tidily set-out coffee-stall, consisting of a trestle and board, upon which stood two large tin cans, with a small fire of charcoal burning under each so as to keep the coffee boiling during the early hours of the morning when the work-people were thronging into the city on their way to their daily toil...

**Childrens**   **ISBN:** *1-59462-373-2*   **Pages:** 84   *MSRP $9.95*   QTY

### My Life and Work
### Henry Ford

Henry Ford revolutionized the world with his implementation of mass production for the Model T automobile. Gain valuable business insight into his life and work with his own auto-biography... "We have only started on our development of our country we have not as yet, with all our talk of wonderful progress, done more than scratch the surface. The progress has been wonderful enough but..."

**Biographies/**   **ISBN:** *1-59462-198-5*   **Pages:** 300   *MSRP $21.95*   QTY

www.bookjungle.com *email: sales@bookjungle.com fax: 630-214-0564 mail: Book Jungle PO Box 2226 Champaign, IL 61825*

### The Art of Cross-Examination
### Francis Wellman

QTY

I presume it is the experience of every author, after his first book is published upon an important subject, to be almost overwhelmed with a wealth of ideas and illustrations which could readily have been included in his book, and which to his own mind, at least, seem to make a second edition inevitable. Such certainly was the case with me; and when the first edition had reached its sixth impression in five months, I rejoiced to learn that it seemed to my publishers that the book had met with a sufficiently favorable reception to justify a second and considerably enlarged edition. ..

Reference     ISBN: *1-59462-647-2*     Pages:412     *MSRP $19.95*

### On the Duty of Civil Disobedience
### Henry David Thoreau

QTY

Thoreau wrote his famous essay, On the Duty of Civil Disobedience, as a protest against an unjust but popular war and the immoral but popular institution of slave-owning. He did more than write—he declined to pay his taxes, and was hauled off to gaol in consequence. Who can say how much this refusal of his hastened the end of the war and of slavery ?

Law     ISBN: *1-59462-747-9*     Pages:48     *MSRP $7.45*

### Dream Psychology Psychoanalysis for Beginners
### Sigmund Freud

QTY

Sigmund Freud, born Sigismund Schlomo Freud (May 6, 1856 - September 23, 1939), was a Jewish-Austrian neurologist and psychiatrist who co-founded the psychoanalytic school of psychology. Freud is best known for his theories of the unconscious mind, especially involving the mechanism of repression; his redefinition of sexual desire as mobile and directed towards a wide variety of objects; and his therapeutic techniques, especially his understanding of transference in the therapeutic relationship and the presumed value of dreams as sources of insight into unconscious desires.

Psychology     ISBN: *1-59462-905-6*     Pages:196     *MSRP $15.45*

### The Miracle of Right Thought
### Orison Swett Marden

QTY

Believe with all of your heart that you will do what you were made to do. When the mind has once formed the habit of holding cheerful, happy, prosperous pictures, it will not be easy to form the opposite habit. It does not matter how improbable or how far away this realization may see, or how dark the prospects may be, if we visualize them as best we can, as vividly as possible, hold tenaciously to them and vigorously struggle to attain them, they will gradually become actualized, realized in the life. But a desire, a longing without endeavor, a yearning abandoned or held indifferently will vanish without realization.

Self Help     ISBN: *1-59462-644-8*     Pages:360     *MSRP $25.45*

www.bookjungle.com email: sales@bookjungle.com fax: 630-214-0564 mail: Book Jungle PO Box 2226 Champaign, IL 61825

QTY

| | Title | ISBN | Price |
|---|---|---|---|
| ☐ | **The Rosicrucian Cosmo-Conception Mystic Christianity** by *Max Heindel*<br>The Rosicrucian Cosmo-conception is not dogmatic, neither does it appeal to any other authority than the reason of the student. It is not controversial, but is: sent forth in the hope that it may help to clear... | ISBN: *1-59462-188-8*<br>New Age/Religion Pages 646 | $38.95 |
| ☐ | **Abandonment To Divine Providence** by *Jean-Pierre de Caussade*<br>"The Rev. Jean Pierre de Caussade was one of the most remarkable spiritual writers of the Society of Jesus in France in the 18th Century. His death took place at Toulouse in 1751. His works have gone through many editions and have been republished... | ISBN: *1-59462-228-0*<br>Inspirational/Religion Pages 400 | $25.95 |
| ☐ | **Mental Chemistry** by *Charles Haanel*<br>Mental Chemistry allows the change of material conditions by combining and appropriately utilizing the power of the mind. Much like applied chemistry creates something new and unique out of careful combinations of chemicals the mastery of mental chemistry... | ISBN: *1-59462-192-6*<br>New Age Pages 354 | $23.95 |
| ☐ | **The Letters of Robert Browning and Elizabeth Barret Barrett 1845-1846 vol II**<br>by *Robert Browning* and *Elizabeth Barrett* | ISBN: *1-59462-193-4*<br>Biographies Pages 596 | $35.95 |
| ☐ | **Gleanings In Genesis (volume I)** by *Arthur W. Pink*<br>Appropriately has Genesis been termed "the seed plot of the Bible" for in it we have, in germ form, almost all of the great doctrines which are afterwards fully developed in the books of Scripture which follow... | ISBN: *1-59462-130-6*<br>Religion/Inspirational Pages 420 | $27.45 |
| ☐ | **The Master Key** by *L. W. de Laurence*<br>In no branch of human knowledge has there been a more lively increase of the spirit of research during the past few years than in the study of Psychology, Concentration and Mental Discipline. The requests for authentic lessons in Thought Control, Mental Discipline and... | ISBN: *1-59462-001-6*<br>New Age/Business Pages 422 | $30.95 |
| ☐ | **The Lesser Key Of Solomon Goetia** by *L. W. de Laurence*<br>This translation of the first book of the "Lernegton" which is now for the first time made accessible to students of Talismanic Magic was done, after careful collation and edition, from numerous Ancient Manuscripts in Hebrew, Latin, and French... | ISBN: *1-59462-092-X*<br>New Age/Occult Pages 92 | $9.95 |
| ☐ | **Rubaiyat Of Omar Khayyam** by *Edward Fitzgerald*<br>Edward Fitzgerald, whom the world has already learned, in spite of his own efforts to remain within the shadow of anonymity, to look upon as one of the rarest poets of the century, was born at Bredfield, in Suffolk, on the 31st of March, 1809. He was the third son of John Purcell... | ISBN: *1-59462-332-5*<br>Music Pages 172 | $13.95 |
| ☐ | **Ancient Law** by *Henry Maine*<br>The chief object of the following pages is to indicate some of the earliest ideas of mankind, as they are reflected in Ancient Law, and to point out the relation of those ideas to modern thought. | ISBN: *1-59462-128-4*<br>Religion/History Pages 452 | $29.95 |
| ☐ | **Far-Away Stories** by *William J. Locke*<br>"Good wine needs no bush, but a collection of mixed vintages does. And this book is just such a collection. Some of the stories I do not want to remain buried for ever in the museum files of dead magazine-numbers an author's not unpardonable vanity..." | ISBN: *1-59462-129-2*<br>Fiction Pages 272 | $19.45 |
| ☐ | **Life of David Crockett** by *David Crockett*<br>"Colonel David Crockett was one of the most remarkable men of the times in which he lived. Born in humble life, but gifted with a strong will, an indomitable courage, and unremitting perseverance... | ISBN: *1-59462-250-7*<br>Biographies/New Age Pages 424 | $27.45 |
| ☐ | **Lip-Reading** by *Edward Nitchie*<br>Edward B. Nitchie, founder of the New York School for the Hard of Hearing, now the Nitchie School of Lip-Reading, Inc, wrote "LIP-READING Principles and Practice". The development and perfecting of this meritorious work on lip-reading was an undertaking... | ISBN: *1-59462-206-X*<br>How-to Pages 400 | $25.95 |
| ☐ | **A Handbook of Suggestive Therapeutics, Applied Hypnotism, Psychic Science** by *Henry Munro* | ISBN: *1-59462-214-0*<br>Health/New Age/Health/Self-help Pages 376 | $24.95 |
| ☐ | **A Doll's House: and Two Other Plays** by *Henrik Ibsen*<br>Henrik Ibsen created this classic when in revolutionary 1848 Rome. Introducing some striking concepts in playwriting for the realist genre, this play has been studied the world over. | ISBN: *1-59462-112-8*<br>Fiction/Classics/Plays 308 | $19.95 |
| ☐ | **The Light of Asia** by *sir Edwin Arnold*<br>In this poetic masterpiece, Edwin Arnold describes the life and teachings of Buddha. The man who was to become known as Buddha to the world was born as Prince Gautama of India but he rejected the worldly riches and abandoned the reigns of power when... | ISBN: *1-59462-204-3*<br>Religion/History/Biographies Pages 170 | $13.95 |
| ☐ | **The Complete Works of Guy de Maupassant** by *Guy de Maupassant*<br>"For days and days, nights and nights, I had dreamed of that first kiss which was to consecrate our engagement, and I knew not on what spot I should put my lips..." | ISBN: *1-59462-157-8*<br>Fiction/Classics Pages 240 | $16.95 |
| ☐ | **The Art of Cross-Examination** by *Francis L. Wellman*<br>Written by a renowned trial lawyer, Wellman imparts his experience and uses case studies to explain how to use psychology to extract desired information through questioning. | ISBN: *1-59462-309-0*<br>How-to/Science/Reference Pages 408 | $26.95 |
| ☐ | **Answered or Unanswered?** by *Louisa Vaughan*<br>Miracles of Faith in China | ISBN: *1-59462-248-5*<br>Religion Pages 112 | $10.95 |
| ☐ | **The Edinburgh Lectures on Mental Science (1909)** by *Thomas*<br>This book contains the substance of a course of lectures recently given by the writer in the Queen Street Hall, Edinburgh. Its purpose is to indicate the Natural Principles governing the relation between Mental Action and Material Conditions... | ISBN: *1-59462-008-3*<br>New Age/Psychology Pages 148 | $11.95 |
| ☐ | **Ayesha** by *H. Rider Haggard*<br>Verily and indeed it is the unexpected that happens! Probably if there was one person upon the earth from whom the Editor of this, and of a certain previous history, did not expect to hear again... | ISBN: *1-59462-301-5*<br>Classics Pages 380 | $24.95 |
| ☐ | **Ayala's Angel** by *Anthony Trollope*<br>The two girls were both pretty, but Lucy who was twenty-one who supposed to be simple and comparatively unattractive, whereas Ayala was credited, as her Bombwhat romantic name might show, with poetic charm and a taste for romance. Ayala when her father died was nineteen... | ISBN: *1-59462-352-X*<br>Fiction Pages 484 | $29.95 |
| ☐ | **The American Commonwealth** by *James Bryce*<br>An interpretation of American democratic political theory. It examines political mechanics and society from the perspective of Scotsman James Bryce | ISBN: *1-59462-286-8*<br>Politics Pages 572 | $34.45 |
| ☐ | **Stories of the Pilgrims** by *Margaret P. Pumphrey*<br>This book explores pilgrims religious oppression in England as well as their escape to Holland and eventual crossing to America on the Mayflower, and their early days in New England... | ISBN: *1-59462-116-0*<br>History Pages 268 | $17.95 |

www.bookjungle.com  email: sales@bookjungle.com  fax: 630-214-0564  mail: Book Jungle  PO Box 2226  Champaign, IL 61825

QTY

**The Fasting Cure** by *Sinclair Upton*  ISBN: *1-59462-222-1*  **$13.95**
In the Cosmopolitan Magazine for May, 1910, and in the Contemporary Review (London) for April, 1910, I published an article dealing with my experiences in fasting. I have written a great many magazine articles, but never one which attracted so much attention...  New Age/Self Help/Health Pages 164

**Hebrew Astrology** by *Sepharial*  ISBN: *1-59462-308-2*  **$13.45**
In these days of advanced thinking it is a matter of common observation that we have left many of the old landmarks behind and that we are now pressing forward to greater heights and to a wider horizon than that which represented the mind-content of our progenitors...  Astrology Pages 144

**Thought Vibration or The Law of Attraction in the Thought World**  ISBN: *1-59462-127-6*  **$12.95**
by *William Walker Atkinson*  Psychology/Religion Pages 144

**Optimism** by *Helen Keller*  ISBN: *1-59462-108-X*  **$15.95**
Helen Keller was blind, deaf, and mute since 19 months old, yet famously learned how to overcome these handicaps, communicate with the world, and spread her lectures promoting optimism. An inspiring read for everyone...  Biographies/Inspirational Pages 84

**Sara Crewe** by *Frances Burnett*  ISBN: *1-59462-360-0*  **$9.45**
In the first place, Miss Minchin lived in London. Her home was a large, dull, tall one, in a large, dull square, where all the houses were alike, and all the sparrows were alike, and where all the door-knockers made the same heavy sound...  Childrens/Classic Pages 88

**The Autobiography of Benjamin Franklin** by *Benjamin Franklin*  ISBN: *1-59462-135-7*  **$24.95**
The Autobiography of Benjamin Franklin has probably been more extensively read than any other American historical work, and no other book of its kind has had such ups and downs of fortune. Franklin lived for many years in England, where he was agent...  Biographies/History Pages 332

| Name | |
|---|---|
| Email | |
| Telephone | |
| Address | |
| | |
| City, State ZIP | |

☐ Credit Card    ☐ Check / Money Order

| Credit Card Number | |
|---|---|
| Expiration Date | |
| Signature | |

Please Mail to:  Book Jungle
PO Box 2226
Champaign, IL 61825
or Fax to:  630-214-0564

## ORDERING INFORMATION

**web**: www.bookjungle.com
**email**: sales@bookjungle.com
**fax**: 630-214-0564
**mail**: Book Jungle  PO Box 2226  Champaign, IL 61825
**or PayPal** to sales@bookjungle.com

*Please contact us for bulk discounts*

## DIRECT-ORDER TERMS

**20% Discount if You Order
Two or More Books**
Free Domestic Shipping!
Accepted: Master Card, Visa,
Discover, American Express

www.ingramcontent.com/pod-product-compliance
Lightning Source LLC
Chambersburg PA
CBHW081831170426
43199CB00017B/2697